Developmental and Adapted Physical Activity Assessment

Michael Horvat, EdD
University of Georgia

Martin E. Block, PhD
University of Virginia

Luke E. Kelly, PhD
University of Virginia

Human Kinetics

Library of Congress Cataloging-in-Publication Data

Horvat, Michael A., 1947-
    Developmental and adapted physical activity assessment / Michael Horvat, Martin E.
Block, and Luke E. Kelly.
        p. cm.
    Includes bibliographical references and index.
    ISBN-13: 978-0-7360-5107-1 (hard cover)
    ISBN-10: 0-7360-5107-4 (hard cover)
    1. Physical education for children with disabilities. 2. Ability--Testing. I. Block,
Martin E., 1958- II. Kelly, Luke. III. Title.
    GV445.H665   2007
    371.91'446--dc22

                                        2006011240

ISBN-10: 0-7360-5107-4
ISBN-13: 978-0-7360-5107-1

This book is a revised edition of *Assessment in Adapted Physical Education and Therapeutic Research, Second Edition,* published in 1996 by Times Mirror Higher Education Group.

Acquisitions Editor: Bonnie Pettifor; **Developmental Editor:** Melissa Feld; **Assistant Editor:** Martha Gullo; **Copyeditor:** Patricia L. MacDonald; **Proofreader:** Julie Marx Goodreau; **Indexer:** Nancy Gerth; **Permission Manager:** Carly Breeding; **Graphic Designer:** Fred Starbird; **Graphic Artist:** Yvonne Griffith; **Photo Manager:** Laura Fitch; **Cover Designer:** Keith Blomberg; **Photographer (cover):** © Human Kinetics; **Photographer (interior):** Brenda Williams, except where otherwise noted. Photos on pages 1, 9, 23, 37, 51, 75, 107, 115, 119, 120, 127, 137, 157, and 189 © Human Kinetics. **Art Manager:** Kelly Hendren; **Illustrator:** Keri Evans; **Printer:** Edwards Brothers

Printed in the United States of America   10 9 8 7 6 5 4 3 2 1

Human Kinetics
Web site: www.HumanKinetics.com

United States: Human Kinetics
P.O. Box 5076
Champaign, IL 61825-5076
800-747-4457
e-mail: humank@hkusa.com

Canada: Human Kinetics
475 Devonshire Road Unit 100
Windsor, ON N8Y 2L5
800-465-7301 (in Canada only)
e-mail: orders@hkcanada.com

Europe: Human Kinetics
107 Bradford Road
Stanningley
Leeds LS28 6AT, United Kingdom
+44 (0) 113 255 5665
e-mail: hk@hkeurope.com

Australia: Human Kinetics
57A Price Avenue
Lower Mitcham, South Australia 5062
08 8372 0999
e-mail: liaw@hkaustralia.com

New Zealand: Human Kinetics
Division of Sports Distributors NZ Ltd.
P.O. Box 300 226 Albany
North Shore City
Auckland
0064 9 448 1207
e-mail: info@humankinetics.co.nz

I would like to dedicate this book to the memory of my mother and father, who taught me the value of hard work and doing the right thing. It is also dedicated to my wife, Glada, and children, Ian, Kala, and Michael, who make life worth living.

M.H.

This book is dedicated to my wife, Vickie, and my two daughters, Samantha and Jessica. They give me reason to run home from work and spend more time with them.

M.B.

I would like to dedicate my sections of this book in loving memory of my wife, Eileen, and to my children, Luke Andrew, Zachary, and Melissa, for being the source of my inspiration and for their ongoing support.

L.K.

Contents

Preface

Teachers and researchers in adapted physical education regularly select, administer, and interpret assessments for numerous related and discrete purposes. Characterized by enormous variability in purpose, content, difficulty, and format, assessment instruments (including their selection, administration, and interpretation) generate a vast array of questions in search of answers. Often, simply knowing the questions is the beginning of wisdom. Unfortunately, few resources that try to answer questions and clarify assessment-related issues are available to teachers of adapted physical education in professional preparation programs. We regard assessment as the cornerstone of any effort of individual instruction. Assessment is like a puzzle that requires us to fit the pieces together to present a true picture of overall functioning and capabilities. We present assessment information as a systematic, multifaceted process of gathering and interpreting information about a person. Concepts and procedures are explained, and assessment problems are presented via case studies that emphasize critical thinking and present real-life situations that teachers encounter on a daily basis. Recent test updates, including authentic assessments and rubrics; creating and validating curriculum-embedded assessment items; learning and social behavior (on-task time, attention, social interactions, behavior objectives); and the principles of assessing performance over time and correlating performance with program objectives are included.

In each chapter, students are required to discuss a case study, and formal write-ups are presented in the appendixes. Assessment information is provided that will help students and clinicians develop a written recommendation regarding placement and instructional programming. Key terms, key concepts, and review questions are included at the end of each chapter. From our perspective, assessment in adapted physical education, while always challenging, need never be confusing when sound principles are applied and understood. The teacher who masters the concepts presented in this book, unlike one who administers test items after simply reading the administration instructions, will gain credibility as a diagnostician who lights the way with carefully selected tests and thoughtful results interpretation. Students will understand what to do when tests are not available or inappropriate for their environment or population and will be able to apply assessment solutions to their problems. In this interactive text, information is presented and students generate a response to specific questions. Our continuing goal is to meet a need for clarifying assessment-related issues surrounding physical and motor assessments of persons with disabilities. Specifically, we realize that assessment is the cornerstone of the instructional process and seek to provide an updated version for professionals in adapted physical education who are developing or fine-tuning their assessment acumen. The development of this text represents a continuing effort to provide an authoritative treatise on assessment in adapted physical education. The text is intended for undergraduate and graduate programs in adapted physical education as well as all students of physical activity who are interested in assessment.

Acknowledgments

We are very excited to share this version of our textbook with our colleagues in adapted physical education and especially thank those who have continued to use this textbook in their classes. We would be remiss not to acknowledge Dr. Judy Werder and Dr. Len Kalakian. They began the process with the first treatise on physical and motor assessment of persons with disabilities more than 20 years ago, and their pioneering efforts appeared in an earlier edition with another publisher. Dr. Horvat was fortunate enough to work on a subsequent text revision with Dr. Kalakian and enjoyed the experience immensely. The authors wish to recognize and thank them for all their work as we build upon their efforts with our current edition.

Chapter 1

Whom You Are Assessing

Assessment in special education is a multifaceted process that begins by determining whether a child qualifies for special education services. Evaluation is critical in determining if a student qualifies under federal special education law and, more important, whether that disability significantly affects the child's educational performance (Gorn, 1996). The evaluation process is designed to set boundaries to determine if a child is eligible for special education services and what types of services should be provided.

Case Study 1

Josiah, a 9-year-old fourth grader at Atlantic Beach Elementary School, was diagnosed with Duchenne muscular dystrophy while in kindergarten. He was able to walk independently until the end of third grade but is currently using a manual wheelchair. Although Josiah has adapted fairly well to his wheelchair, he does have trouble in physical education, especially in tagging and fleeing games. He also has difficulty with throwing and striking patterns because he can no longer stand when doing these skills. Josiah has not qualified as a child with a disability within the Individuals with Disabilities Education Act (IDEA). However, he has qualified as a child with a disability under Section 504 of the Rehabilitation Act (he has a 504 plan rather than an individualized education plan, or IEP). Under this act he receives special transportation and physical therapy services. However, he has never received adapted physical education (APE) services. Both his parents and teachers feel it is time to assess his performance to determine if adapted physical education services are needed. Is Josiah the type of child who qualifies for assessment in APE?

Assessment in adapted physical education is similarly a complex, multifaceted process that focuses on identifying whether or not a student qualifies for services; developing appropriate goals for those children who qualify for adapted physical education services; implementing appropriate instructional activities and supports to achieve goals of the IEP; and determining the most appropriate placement for children in physical education. As is the case with special education assessments, before you can begin to assess the development of goals, instructional activities, and appropriate placement, the question of who qualifies for services must be answered. The purpose of this chapter is to review the basic legislation regarding who qualifies for adapted physical education as well as other factors related to the child that may affect assessment. The chapter begins by identifying who qualifies under IDEA, including a review of the specific conditions listed in the Individuals with Disabilities Education Act. This is followed by a review of who qualifies under Section 504 of the Rehabilitation Act, as well as the definition of *disability* in this act. Finally, the chapter concludes with a discussion of key attributes of some persons with disabilities that may influence assessment in adapted physical education.

INDIVIDUALS WITH DISABILITIES EDUCATION ACT (IDEA)

Public Law 94-142, the Education for All Handicapped Children Act (1975), was the landmark law that for the first time in the history of education in the United States provided all children aged 3 through 21 with disabilities the right to a free, appropriate education. The law has undergone several transformations and currently is in the final phases of the recent reauthorization. One of the fundamental aspects of federal legislation is the concept that only children with specific types of disabilities listed in the law can qualify for special education services. Currently, 13 conditions are considered legally recognized disabilities under the act, including the following:

Autism	Other health impairment
Deaf-blindness	Serious emotional disturbance
Deafness	Specific learning disability
Hearing impairment	Speech or language impairment
Mental retardation	Traumatic brain injury
Multiple disabilities	Visual impairment, including blindness
Orthopedic impairment	

See figure 1.1 for how these terms are defined in IDEA.

Disabilities Identified in PL 105-17 (IDEA, 1997)

I. *Autism* means a developmental disability significantly affecting verbal and nonverbal communication and social interactions, generally evident before age 3, that adversely affects a child's educational performance. Other behaviors often associated with autism are engagement in repetitive activities and stereotyped movements, resistance to environmental change or change in daily routines, and unusual responses to sensory experiences. The term does not apply if a child's educational performance is adversely affected primarily because the child has a serious emotional disturbance [34 C.F.R. § 300.7(b)(1)].

II. *Deaf-blindness* means concomitant hearing and visual impairments, the combination of which causes severe communication and other developmental educational problems that the child

(continued)

Figure 1.1 IDEA disabilities definitions.

Information from the Individuals with Disabilities Education Act (IDEA) Amendments of 1997, PL 105-17, C.F.R. § 300.7(b).

cannot accommodate in special education programs solely for deaf or blind children [34 C.F.R. § 300.7(b)(2)].

III. *Deafness* means a hearing impairment so severe that the child is hindered in processing linguistic information through hearing, with or without amplification, and educational performance is thus adversely affected [34 C.F.R. § 300.7(b)(3)].

IV. *Serious emotional disturbance* is defined as follows:

    a. The term means a condition exhibiting one or more of the following characteristics over a long period of time that adversely affects educational performance:

        i. An inability to learn that cannot be explained by intellectual, sensory, or health factors

        ii. An inability to build or maintain satisfactory interpersonal relationships with peers and teachers

        iii. Inappropriate types of behavior or feelings under normal circumstances

        iv. A general pervasive mood of unhappiness or depression

        v. A tendency to develop physical symptoms or fears associated with personal or school problems [34 C.F.R. § 300.7(b)(4)].

V. *Hearing impairment* means an impairment in hearing, whether permanent or not, and is included under the definition of deafness in this section [34 C.F.R. § 300.7(b)(5)].

VI. *Mental retardation* means significantly subaverage general intellectual functioning that exists concurrently with deficits in adaptive behavior, is manifested in the developmental period, and adversely affects the child's educational performance [34 C.F.R. § 300.7(b)(6)].

VII. *Multiple disabilities* means concomitant impairments (e.g., mentally retarded–blind, mentally retarded–orthopedically impaired), the combination of which causes such severe educational problems that the child cannot be accommodated in special education programs designed solely for children with one of the impairments. The term does not include deaf-blindness [34 C.F.R. § 300.7(b)(7)].

VIII. *Orthopedic impairment* means a severe orthopedic impairment that adversely affects the child's educational performance. The term includes impairments by congenital anomaly (e.g., club foot, absence of some member), impairments caused by some disease (e.g., poliomyelitis, bone tuberculosis), impairments from other causes (e.g., cerebral palsy, amputations), and fractures and burns that cause contractures [34 C.F.R. § 300.7(b)(8)].

IX. *Other health impairment* means limited strength, vitality, or alertness owing to chronic or acute health problems, such as a heart condition, tuberculosis, rheumatic fever, nephritis, asthma, sickle cell anemia, hemophilia, lead poisoning, leukemia, or diabetes, that adversely affect a child's educational performance [34 C.F.R. § 300.7(b)(9)].

X. *Specific learning disability* means a disorder in one or more of the basic psychological processes involved in understanding or in using language, spoken or written, that may manifest itself in an imperfect ability to listen, think, speak, write, spell, or do mathematical calculations. The term includes children who have learning problems that are primarily the result of perceptual disabilities, brain injury, minimal brain dysfunction, dyslexia, and developmental aphasia. The term does not include children who have learning problems primarily the result of visual, hearing, or motor impairments or environmental, cultural, or economic disadvantages [34 C.F.R. § 300.7(b)(10)].

XI. *Speech or language impairment* means a communication disorder such as stuttering, impaired articulation, a language impairment, or a voice impairment that inhibits the child's educational performance [34 C.F.R. § 300.7(b)(11)].

XII. *Traumatic brain injury* means an acquired injury to the brain caused by an external physical force, resulting in total or partial functional disability or psychological impairment, or both, that adversely affects a child's educational performance. The term applies to open or closed head injuries resulting in impairments of one or more areas, such as cognition; language; memory; attention; reasoning; abstract thinking; judgment; problem solving; sensory, perceptual, and motor abilities; psychological behaviors; physical functions; information processing; and speech. The term does not apply to brain injuries that are congenital or degenerative or to brain injuries induced by birth trauma [34 C.F.R. § 300.7(b)(12)].

XIII. *Visual impairment* means an impairment in vision that, even with correction, adversely affects the child's educational performance. The term includes both partially seeing and blind children [34 C.F.R. § 300.7(b)(13)].

Figure 1.1 *(continued)*

To qualify for special education services and subsequently APE services under IDEA, a child must have a condition that meets the criteria for one of the eligible disabilities. However, simply having one of these disabilities does not automatically qualify a child for special education services. To be eligible for special education services, the disability must significantly affect the child's educational performance, even with accommodations (Gorn, 1996; Horvat, Eichstaedt, Kalakian, & Croce, 2003; Wright & Wright, 2000). In other words, a label of "hearing impairment" or "other health impairment" may be a real diagnosis given by a doctor, but if students perform sufficiently, they may not qualify for special education services. Gorn (1996) calls the process a two-part test: (1) meeting one or more of the 13 categories of disabilities specified under IDEA and (2) showing need of special education and related services as a result of having one of the aforementioned disabilities. Many children adjust to their disabilities and thus perform at expected levels. Therefore, the decision of whether or not a student qualifies as a child with a disability under IDEA is based solely on educational need as determined through assessment, as opposed to a label (Gorn, 1996; Horvat, Eichstaedt, et al., 2003).

Case Study 2

Jillian is 12 years old and in seventh grade at Highland Springs Middle School. She is recovering from an automobile accident and has residual effects from a head injury. She now qualifies as a child with a disability under IDEA, and the collaborative team has asked several specialists to assess Jillian's function to determine if special services are required. Those areas that have been targeted for assessment include physical therapy, speech therapy, occupational therapy, and adapted physical education. Is Jillian the type of child who qualifies for assessment in APE?

If a child does not qualify for special education services, then he or she will not qualify for APE services (at least in the vast majority of school districts around the United States). Basically, a child must first have a qualifying disability before being considered for APE services. Once a student has qualified as a child with a disability under IDEA, the same "educational need" determination is required for APE as well. A child who qualifies for special education services does not automatically qualify for APE services. It must be determined through testing whether or not the child's disability significantly affects his or her ability to be successful in physical education.

In case study 2, Jillian has recently qualified as a child with a disability under IDEA, with the diagnosis of traumatic brain injury. Her condition must have been such that it significantly affected her educational performance. The question now is whether her condition significantly affects her ability to be successful in physical education. To make this determination, the physical educator needs to assess Jillian's physical and motor functioning. Testing might include motor abilities, physical fitness, sports skills, and behavior and social skills as they relate to her success in physical education. If it can be determined that Jillian has significant deficits in the area of physical education, then she would qualify for APE services. Conversely, Dhanya in case study 3 may perform well enough to participate in regular class activities and may not require a special class placement.

Case Study 3

Dhanya is a 14-year-old, ninth-grade rising star who attends South Woods High School. She has Down syndrome and has qualified for special education services since her preschool years. Dhanya received adapted physical education in middle school in a self-contained class with her classmates in Mr. Johnson's special education class for children with moderate and severe disabilities. However, as part of her transition assessment to high school, her collaborative team feels that Dhanya could be successful in a general physical education class with support from a teacher assistant or an APE specialist. Dhanya's IEP team is recommending an assessment to determine if her goals are still appropriate for high school, whether these goals can be implemented in general physical education with support, and what is required for her transition plan. Is Dhanya the type of child who qualifies for assessment in APE?

AMERICANS WITH DISABILITIES ACT OF 1990 (ADA)

Further assurance that persons with disabilities receive equitable services from public and private sectors comes from the Americans with Disabilities Act. Passed in 1990, this act replaced and built upon its predecessor, the Rehabilitation Act of 1973. In 1973, a full 2 years before the Education for All Handicapped Children Act, Congress passed legislation prohibiting discrimination on the basis of a disability by agencies of the federal government or agencies that receive federal money. Coined the "civil rights legislation for people with disabilities," Section 504 of the Rehabilitation Act of 1973 stated: "No otherwise qualified handicapped individual in the United States . . . shall, solely by reason of his or her handicap, be excluded from the participation in, be denied the benefits of, or be subjected to discrimination under any program or activity receiving Federal financial assistance." Public schools receive federal funding and thus are subject to the rules and regulations in the ADA. As such, schools are not allowed to discriminate against or deny access to educational programs (including physical education, recreation, and sports programs) simply because a child, teacher, or coach has a disability. More specifically, all programs and facilities need to be accessible. In addition, athletes with disabilities cannot be excluded from participation in sports or recreational activities based on the disability.

With regard to whom you assess, some children with disabilities do not qualify for special educational services under IDEA because they do not have a disability that falls under one of the 13 specified categories, or their disability is such that it does not adversely affect educational performance. However, the definition of *disability* in the ADA is much broader, including conditions that "substantially limit" at least one major life activity (Wright & Wright, 2000, p. 261). This definition accommodates individuals with disabilities who do not qualify under IDEA for special education services. IDEA eligibility requires a child to have a disability that adversely affects educational performance, while the ADA requires a child's disability to affect major life activities.

One of the major differences between the provision of special education services in IDEA and ADA is the concept of benefit from education. Under IDEA, a qualifying child with a disability must receive an individually administered program that leads to clear educational benefit. Under Section 504, a qualifying child should receive an education that is comparable to the education provided to children without disabilities. In order to make education comparable, Section 504 plans usually include such things as accessibility issues (being able to get around the school building) as well as classroom accommodations and modifications (Wright & Wright, 2000). Further, the ADA emphasizes employment via the individualized transition plan (ITP) that is required by 14 years of age. Because many employment opportunities require physical function and motor control, this necessitates the involvement of teachers in meeting the objectives of the ITP (Horvat, Eichstaedt, et al., 2003).

ATTRIBUTES AND DIMENSIONS THAT AFFECT WHOM YOU ASSESS

Many factors influence how a particular child will react to the assessment process. One child may have such limited endurance that he cannot physically complete the entire test battery in one testing period. Another child may not cognitively understand what to do, and still another child may be frightened of all the new sensory experiences in the testing environment. Anyone attempting to test a child with a disability must fully understand how the child's unique attributes affect her ability to focus on and then successfully complete the various test items in order to get a true representation of her abilities. For example, a child may demonstrate a lack of physical fitness, be overweight, or as in case study 1, be generally inefficient in movement. In addition, a lack of vision results in restrained gait and balance difficulties in unknown situations (Horvat, Ray, et al., 2003). Likewise, cognitive or behavioral difficulties may cause children to elicit a poor response, withdraw, or exert minimal effort. Each dimension may affect testing in physical education and how an examiner might accommodate children with a variety of problems or deficiencies. The examiner should be careful to avoid stereotypes concerning certain attributes, such as thinking all children with visual impairments will be overweight or not capable of achieving a certain level of fitness. The key is finding out as much as possible about each child from the teachers, parents, and other relevant persons to ensure that testing is valid and accurate.

ZERO EXCLUSION AND ZERO FAILURE

Two important concepts of IDEA are "zero exclusion" and "zero failure." Virtually every child with a disability who qualifies for special education under IDEA also qualifies for physical education services. These physical education services may need to be specially designed to meet the student's unique motor and health needs, and the services may need to be provided in restrictive settings such as at the child's home or in a hospital. But these physical education services must be provided to all children with disabilities regardless of the severity of the disability. This concept is known as zero exclusion. For example, the University of Virginia Children's Medical Center has on staff a certified adapted physical education specialist who provides services to children who need to stay in the hospital for more than 3 consecutive days. Examples of those served include children who are recovering from accidents, children receiving treatment for cancer, and children who have disabilities and need surgery or other treatment that requires an extended hospital stay.

Once a child with disabilities has qualified to receive physical education services, the program should be created and implemented in such a way as to ensure the child's success. Each child's unique abilities and needs should be addressed, and a carefully constructed, individually determined program should then be implemented. This is the concept of zero failure. Assessment is critical to ensure the success of each child with a disability in physical education. For example, a student with autism may need picture schedules and picture prompts as well as a quiet small-group setting to be successful. Another child with a physical disability may need several different types of adapted equipment plus rule modifications for various sports and games played in physical education to ensure his success. The key is to determine through assessment each child's unique abilities and strengths as well as unique concerns and needs in order to create a program that provides the best chance for the child to be successful.

What You Need to Know ▶▶▶

Key Terms

benefit from education

Individuals with Disabilities Education Act (IDEA)

zero exclusion

zero failure

Key Concepts

1. You should understand how a child qualifies for special education services under the Individuals with Disabilities Education Act. You should also understand the process for determining if a child with a disability qualifies for adapted physical education services.

2. You should be able to discuss the concepts of zero exclusion and zero failure as they relate to physical education for students with disabilities.

3. You should understand Section 504 of the Rehabilitation Act and how it applies to special education services for certain children with disabilities. You should also be able to contrast the definition of *disability* in IDEA with the definition of *disability* in Section 504.

4. You should be able to describe the key attributes and dimensions related to whom you assess in adapted physical education. You should understand how the following dimensions can influence assessment and subsequently program planning: physical and motor, perceptual, learning and cognitive, behavioral, and social.

Review Questions

1. How would you assess Josiah, the fourth grader with Duchenne muscular dystrophy? How does the fact that Josiah qualifies under Section 504 rather than IDEA affect your assessment plan?

2. Jillian, the seventh grader who was in an automobile accident and who qualifies as a child with a disability under IDEA, needs to be evaluated to determine if she qualifies

for adapted physical education services. What dimensions and attributes might you consider for inclusion in your assessment plan? Why?

3. Recall that Dhanya is a ninth-grade rising star with Down syndrome. How would you determine if Dhanya's goals are still appropriate for high school and whether these goals can be implemented in general physical education with support? Why did you choose to evaluate Dhanya this way?

Chapter 2

Why You Are Assessing

A friend comes up to you and asks if you would like to go downtown and have lunch. How do you make this decision? Do you just jump in your friend's car and go, or do you consider factors such as: Do you have any other obligations for lunch? Do you have time? Do you have enough money to buy lunch? Are you actually interested in having lunch with this friend? You probably then analyze this information to make an informed decision. Finally, you use this information to shape your response. You might respond that you would love to have lunch, but you will need to be quick because you have to be back at a certain time for your next class.

You may be saying to yourself, "What does making a decision about lunch with a friend have to do with assessment in physical education for individuals with disabilities?" It illustrates how assessment is an integral part of the decision-making process. To make an informed decision about lunch, you had to assess a number of factors, analyze the data you assessed, and then use the assessment data to make an appropriate decision. This simple example can also illustrate what can happen when you make decisions without assessing. You could have immediately said, "Sure," jumped in your friend's car, and gone downtown and had lunch. Of course it was embarrassing when you found you did not have enough money to pay for your meal and had to borrow money from your friend. Then halfway through lunch you suddenly realized that your next class started in 10 minutes, so lunch had to be cut short so your friend could drive you back to school. Finally, when you got to class late, another friend asked why you stood him up for the lunch you had planned the week before. The point here is that when you make decisions without assessing, the odds are that there will be unanticipated negative consequences. For example, you now have two friends upset with you. One is upset because you stood him up for lunch, and the other friend is upset because you stuck her with the bill and then cut lunch short because you had another obligation.

TERMINOLOGY

The focus of this chapter is to introduce assessment as an integral part of the decision-making process that underlies all teaching behavior. *Assessment* as addressed in this book is an umbrella term to describe the process used by teachers to make informed decisions. There are frequently many misconceptions regarding assessment because the term is used in different ways and may be used interchangeably with other terms such as *testing, measurement,* or *evaluation.* To avoid any confusion, the following definitions will be used for this book. *Assessing* and *testing* refer to the process of administering an instrument for the purpose of collecting performance data. Although these terms can be used interchangeably, the preferred term is *assessing. Testing* frequently has a negative connotation because it is commonly associated with summative forms of evaluation where children are graded.

Instruments, tests, assessments, items, and *tools* all describe the procedures or subsets of the procedures used to collect information on the behavior being assessed. These procedures typically define what will be assessed, the conditions under which the assessment should be performed, the equipment required, the administration instructions, and the scoring. Instruments can range in complexity from simple (e.g., one item to assess one motor skill such as catching) to complex (e.g., several items to assess each of the major components of physical fitness). Assessment instruments are commonly categorized as either norm referenced or criterion referenced. Norm-referenced instruments (NRIs) generally are standardized tests designed to collect performance data that are then compared with reference standards composed of normative data provided with the instrument. An example of a norm-referenced assessment is a softball throw for distance, where the distance thrown under standardized conditions is recorded. This score is then looked up in a normative chart to obtain a percentile score that indicates the percentage of children in the normative sample that could throw as far as this individual. Criterion-referenced instruments (CRIs) are generally less standardized and involve evaluating performance against an established set of criteria. An example of a simple CRI for skipping involves observing children and recording whether they correctly do the following:

- Move forward by stepping and then hopping
- Maintain an upright body posture
- Alternate the step–hop pattern between feet
- Move arms in opposition to the legs
- Hold arms around waist level and slightly flexed

Standardized, when used in conjunction with assessment instruments, refers to the procedures that must be followed when administering the instrument. Most NRIs tend to be highly standardized, which means explicit procedures must be adhered to. These procedures usually include how to set up the testing environ-

Peabody Developmental Motor Scales-II

Jumping Sideways

Position: Standing

Stimulus: Tape starting line (2 in. by 2 ft)

Procedure: Stand with your left side next to the line. With your hands on your hips and keeping your feet together, jump back and forth (sideways) over the line for 3 cycles without pausing between jumps (left and right equals one cycle).

Say "Jump across the line like I did."

Scoring criteria:

    2 = Child jumps back and forth for 3 cycles with hands on hips, with feet together, and without touching line or pausing between jumps.

    1 = Child jumps back and forth 1-2 cycles with hands on hips, with feet together, and without touching line or pausing between jumps.

    0 = Child lands on line or pauses between jumps.

Figure 2.1 Sample standardized instructions for an NRI item.

Adapted from M.R. Folio and R.R. Fewell, 2000, *Peabody developmental motor scales*, 2nd ed. (PRO-ED, Inc.), 27. Used with permission.

ment, what equipment to use, the administration instructions, the data recording, and how to score and interpret the results. The reason NRIs need to be so highly standardized is to ensure that any differences found in performances can be attributed to ability and not to differences in how the test was administered and scored. Figure 2.1 shows the administration instructions for the jumping sideways item from the Peabody Developmental Motor Scales (Folio & Fewell, 2000). Note that the tester must demonstrate the item exactly as described and give instructions verbatim to each student when administering this item. CRIs also have standardized procedures for administration and scoring but frequently provide the administrator a little more flexibility. For example, the administrator may be permitted to model the task or allow more trials. Since the goal of most CRIs is to get an accurate indication of the child's performance in relation to the comparison criteria, the emphasis during administration is on eliciting the best performance.

Reference standards refer to how the data collected during the assessment are interpreted. As implied in the name, NRIs are designed to allow scores to be compared with normative data collected under the same conditions on other children with similar characteristics such as age and gender. Table 2.1 shows a simple normative chart for interpreting performance on an agility test by age and gender. A 12-year-old male who ran the course in 10.3 seconds would be in the 70th percentile, meaning he ran as well as 70% of the students in the normative sample that took the test. CRIs, on the other hand, compare the students' performance against established criteria. Figure 2.2 shows a CRI for assessing the catch. In this CRI, the criteria are the five components that define the mature catching pattern. The teacher would observe the children's catching behavior and record which of the components the students could and could not perform. It should be noted that it is possible for a CRI to have norms. The Test of Gross Motor Development 2 (Ulrich, 2000) is an example of a CRI that also provides age and gender reference standards.

Table 2.1   Shuttle Run for Boys

Percentile	Age							
	9-10	11	12	13	14	15	16	17+
100th	9.2	8.7	6.8	7.0	7.0	7.0	7.3	7.0
95th	10.0	9.7	9.6	9.3	8.9	8.9	8.6	8.6
90th	10.2	9.9	9.8	9.5	9.2	9.1	8.9	8.9
85th	10.4	10.1	10.0	9.7	9.3	9.2	9.1	9.0
80th	10.5	10.2	10.0	9.8	9.5	9.3	9.2	9.1
75th	10.6	10.4	10.2	10.0	9.6	9.4	9.3	9.2
70th	10.7	10.5	10.3	10.0	9.8	9.5	9.4	9.3
65th	10.8	10.5	10.4	10.1	9.8	9.6	9.5	9.4
60th	11.0	10.6	10.5	10.2	10.0	9.7	9.6	9.5
55th	11.0	10.8	10.6	10.3	10.0	9.8	9.7	9.6
50th	11.2	10.9	10.7	10.4	10.1	9.9	9.9	9.8
45th	11.5	11.0	10.8	10.5	10.1	10.0	10.0	9.9
40th	11.5	11.1	11.0	10.6	10.2	10.0	10.0	10.0
35th	11.7	11.2	11.1	10.8	10.4	10.1	10.1	10.1
30th	11.9	11.4	11.3	11.0	10.6	10.2	10.3	10.2
25th	12.0	11.5	11.4	11.0	10.7	10.4	10.5	10.4
20th	12.2	11.8	11.6	11.3	10.9	10.5	10.6	10.5
15th	12.5	12.0	11.8	11.5	11.0	10.8	10.9	10.7
10th	13.0	12.2	12.0	11.8	11.3	11.1	11.1	11.0
5th	13.1	12.9	12.4	12.4	11.9	11.7	11.9	11.7
0	17.0	20.0	22.0	16.0	18.6	14.7	15.0	15.7

Note: Percentile scores based on age. Test scores in seconds and tenths.

Adapted, by permission, from AAHPERD, 1976, *AAHPERD youth fitness test manual* (Reston, VA: American Alliance for Health, Physical Education, Recreation and Dance).

Measurement refers to the type of data collected by the assessment instrument. Assessment of a motor skill such as throwing could involve several measures. For example, the physical educator could measure the child's knowledge of the key components of the overhand throw, how far she throws, how accurately she throws, and if she can perform the key components correctly. Each type of

Equipment and Space Requirements:

- Use an inflatable playground ball that is 6 inches in diameter.
- Catch in an outdoor field or large gymnasium at least 30 feet in length (10-foot staging area plus 20-foot catching distance).

Skill Levels	Focal Points	
1. Demonstrate the mature catch. a b c, d, e	The student demonstrates the following focal points for the mature catch, catching a playground ball (at chest height and at thigh height) thrown at slow speed from 10 feet away, on 2 of 3 trials. A playground ball thrown at slow speed will travel 10 feet in 2 seconds. a. **Stand in the path** of the approaching ball, eyes on ball, feet shoulder-width apart, knees and hips slightly flexed, weight evenly distributed on both feet, hands in front of the body at chest height. b. **Extend the arms and hands** toward the approaching ball, arms raised (chest height) or lowered (thigh height), fingers spread, fingers slightly flexed, thumbs touching (chest height) or little fingers touching (thigh height). c. **Catch the ball** between the hands with the fingers. d. **Absorb the force of the ball,** bending the elbows to retract the arms. e. **Smooth integration** (not mechanical or jerky) of the previous focal points.	
2. Demonstrate the mature catch for distance.	The student with a mature catch (skill level 1) will catch a playground ball (at chest height and at thigh height) thrown at moderate speed from a **distance** on 2 of 3 trials. A playground ball thrown at moderate speed will travel 10 feet in 1 second, 15 feet in 1½ seconds, and 20 feet in 2 seconds.	**Catching distances:** • Grades K-1 10 feet • Grades 2-3 15 feet • Grades 4-5 20 feet
3. Demonstrate the mature catch for accuracy. 20 ft 15 ft 10 ft	The student with a mature catch (skill level 1) and catch for distance (skill level 2) will move into position for **accuracy** to catch a playground ball (at chest height and at thigh height) thrown at a moderate speed on 2 of 3 trials.	**Accuracy criterion:** Catch a ball thrown to a position within 5 feet in any direction of where the student is standing. **Catching distances:** • Grades K-1 10 feet • Grades 2-3 15 feet • Grades 4-5 20 feet

Reference Data: The distance from the pitcher's mound to home plate is 35-40 feet in fastpitch softball.

Figure 2.2 Sample Everyone CAN CRI for catching.

From Kelly, Wessel, Dummer, & Sampson, forthcoming.

measurement produces a different type of data. Knowledge might be measured by a paper and pencil test composed of 10 multiple choice items. The score collected could be a percentage reflecting the number of items out of 10 the child answered correctly. Throwing distance could be measured in meters thrown, and throwing accuracy could be measured in terms of the number of times out of 10 trials the student hit a target. Finally, throwing form could be measured by a checklist that indicates which of the components of the throw were performed correctly.

What is measured by an assessment instrument has implications for both psychometrics (e.g., validity, reliability) and how the information can be used to make different types of decisions. Measurement in physical education tends to focus on either the process involved in the performance or the products produced by the performance. Process measures typically are related to CRIs, measuring motor skill performance and judging how the skill was performed. For example, when the student threw, did he start with side orientation, did he transfer his weight, and did he follow through after the ball was released? Product measures, on the other hand, focus on the outcomes or products of the performance, such as the number of repetitions, distance covered, time needed to complete a task, or number of times a target was hit out of a number of trials. As a general rule, process measures tend to be more subjective and subsequently require more skill to measure than do product measures, which tend to be more objective. Measurement issues are addressed in more detail in chapters 4 and 5.

Evaluation refers to the comparison and interpretation of multiple assessments to explain the changes that were observed. A common application of evaluation is to compare a child's entry assessment and exit assessment on an objective that was taught, with the intent of determining how much progress was made. Evaluation can be described as either formative or summative. Formative evaluation is ongoing and focuses on shaping the performance over time to reach a desired goal. Summative evaluation is performed at established intervals, with the purpose of interpreting the performance against established standards. Reassessing a child throughout an instructional unit and giving her feedback on how to improve her performance is an example of formative evaluation. Computing average percent mastery on the objectives taught during a unit or reporting a child's progress on a report card in the form of a letter grade for physical education are examples of summative evaluation.

ASSESSMENT DECISIONS

In this book, assessment is a dynamic process that precedes and informs all teaching behavior. This approach to assessment may be in marked contrast to the stereotypical view held by many teachers that assessment is a static process performed periodically to fulfill certain requirements but is not directly related to their teaching. This belief is commonly adopted when teachers do not understand the importance of collecting assessment information that matches the decision to be made.

Case Study 1

Before starting a soccer unit, Mr. Davis wants to assess kicking performance. He selects a kicking test he found in one of his college textbooks that is relatively easy to set up, administer, and score and has age and gender norms. He spends one class period administering this test and collecting his data. That night he converts the raw scores into percentiles using the age and gender norms and learns that the students' abilities range from the 10th to the 95th percentile, with most of the class performing around the 50th percentile. Based on this information, what aspect of kicking do you think he should address next class?

What is the problem with Mr. Davis' assessment? The problem is that the assessment test he selected does not match the decision he needs to make. He might be able to infer from his data that the children need work on this objective since the majority of the class performed around the 50th percentile, but he does not know what part of the skill the students specifically need to work on. For example, a child who is 5 inches (12.5 centimeters) taller and 20 pounds (9 kilograms) heavier than the other children in the class could score in the 95th percentile but have an immature kicking pattern that could benefit from instruction, regardless of his size. What Mr. Davis should use is a criterion-referenced instrument that allows him to judge which components of a mature kicking pattern his students are able to perform. This assessment data would provide him with components of the kick that children are underachieving, giving him the necessary information to develop appropriate learning activities. Since his assessment does not provide any useful information, he erroneously concludes that testing is a waste of time and that in the future he will just start teaching kicking without a prior assessment. Of course this incorrect conclusion is based on using the wrong type of assessment for the decision to be made.

Although it may appear obvious in this example that Mr. Davis did not select the appropriate assessment, it is difficult to match assessments with a wide range of abilities. For children with disabilities, teachers must make numerous decisions based on a host of factors. For example, Mary is 8 years old and is recovering from a traumatic brain injury that occurred when she was 4. To teach her to catch, several decisions need to be made, including the following:

- Is Mary developmentally ready to learn this skill?
- Does Mary possess the prerequisite skills needed to learn catching (e.g., can she visually track a moving object)?
- What are the key components of catching that Mary must be able to perform in order to successfully catch?
- Which, if any, of the key components of the catch can Mary already perform?
- What is Mary's best learning modality?
- Does Mary have any unique communication needs that must be accommodated during assessment and instruction?

- Does Mary have any behavior issues that may interfere with assessment and instruction?
- What type of ball (e.g., size, weight, texture, color) should be used when assessing and for instruction?
- What are Mary's experience and attitude toward physical education in general and toward catching specifically?
- Will Mary be able to work on this skill in the general physical education setting?
- What can be done if Mary refuses to work on catching?

The previous example highlights the wide range of instructional decisions a teacher will likely need to make when working with just one child on one motor skill. How these decisions are made is the focus of this book. The first step in the assessment process is defining what decision needs to be made. Physical educators working with children with disabilities can be called on to make decisions in three areas: identification, placement, and instruction.

Identification Decisions

Identification decisions, which may also be referred to as eligibility or classification decisions, involve determining whether a child's level of performance warrants special attention. This could involve deciding whether a student's physical fitness performance is good enough to qualify for a national physical fitness award, determining whether the deficits in children's physical and motor abilities qualify them to receive special education services, or determining what sport classification is needed for participation in a disabled sports event. In each case, there are established rules that govern how performance must be assessed as well as qualifying standards that must be met.

For example, included in figure 2.3 are the federal regulations stipulating the procedures that must be followed when evaluating children to determine if they qualify for special education services. When physical educators are called on to participate in eligibility decisions, they must be able to both select and administer appropriate assessments that meet these requirements. NRIs are typically used when making identification decisions because they provide normative interpretive data that can show the magnitude of the differences found in a student's performance compared with standards. A school could require, for example, that a child's performance be greater than two standard deviations below the mean on a standardized test to qualify for adapted physical education services. Most schools have well-defined procedures for making identification decisions. Physical educators should familiarize themselves with these procedures so that they understand their specific responsibilities as well as their roles as part of the overall assessment team.

121a.532 Evaluation Procedures

State and local educational agencies shall ensure, at a minimum, the following:

(a) Tests and other evaluation materials

    (1) are provided and administered in the child's native language or other mode of communication, unless it is clearly not feasible to do so;

    (2) have been validated for the specific purpose for which they are used; and

    (3) are administered by trained personnel in conformance with the instructions provided by their producer.

(b) Tests and other evaluation materials include those tailored to assess specific areas of educational need and not merely those designed to produce a single general intelligence quotient.

(c) Tests are selected and administered so as best to ensure that when a child with impaired sensory, manual, or speaking skills is assessed, the test results accurately reflect the child's aptitude or achievement level, or whatever other factors the test claims to measure, rather than reflect the child's impaired sensory, manual, or speaking skills (except where those skills are the factors the test claims to measure).

(d) No single procedure is used as the sole criterion for determining an appropriate educational program for a child.

(e) The evaluation is made by a multidisciplinary team or group of persons, including at least one teacher or other specialist with knowledge in the area of suspected disability.

(f) The child is assessed in all areas related to the suspected disability, including, where appropriate, health, vision, hearing, social and emotional status, general intelligence, academic performance, communicative status, and motor skills.

Figure 2.3 PL 94-142 placement procedures to follow when evaluating children for special education services. Information from *Federal Register,* August 23, 1977, PL 94-142, The Education for All Handicapped Children Act.

Placement Decisions

Placement decisions involve determining the programmatic needs of the student and the most appropriate instructional setting for addressing these needs. For students with disabilities, this means determining the most appropriate and least restrictive environment (LRE) where the physical education goals in their IEPs can be addressed and achieved. Figure 2.4 shows the federal regulations that pertain to LRE. The goal of the LRE mandate is to educate students with disabilities to the maximum extent possible in the general education environment, with the use of support services.

Placement is actually a two-part decision. First, the child's needs must be identified and a program defined to address these needs. The annual goals and short-term objectives for this program make up the IEP. Second, a decision must be made regarding where this program will be implemented. Making accurate placement decisions typically involves collecting and comparing assessment information on the content to be taught, both for the student being considered for placement and for the students in the target placement setting. For example,

Least Restrictive Environment

121a.550 General

(a) Each state educational agency shall ensure that each public agency establishes and implements procedures that meet the requirements of 121a.550-121a.556.

(b) Each public agency shall ensure that

  (1) to the maximum extent appropriate, children with disabilities, including children in public or private institutions or other care facilities, are educated with children who are not disabled; and

  (2) special classes, separate schooling, or other removal of children with disabilities from the general educational environment occurs only when the nature or severity of the disability is such that education in general classes with the use of supplementary aids and services cannot be achieved satisfactorily.

121a.551 Continuum of Alternative Placements

(a) Each public agency shall ensure that a continuum of alternative placements is available to meet the needs of children with disabilities for special education and related services.

(b) The continuum required under paragraph (a) of this section must

  (1) include the alternative placements listed in the definition of special education under 121a.13 of subpart A (instruction in general classes, special classes, special schools, and hospitals and institutions as well as home instruction) and

  (2) make provision for supplementary services (such as resource room or itinerant instruction) to be provided in conjunction with the general class placement.

121a.552 Placements

Each public agency shall ensure the following:

  (a) Each child's educational placement

    (1) is determined at least annually,

    (2) is based on his or her individualized education plan, and

    (3) is as close as possible to the child's home.

  (b) The various alternative placements included under 121a.551 are available to the extent necessary to implement the individualized education plan for each child with a disability.

  (c) Unless a child's individualized education plan requires some other arrangement, the child is educated in the school he or she would attend if the child did not have a disability.

  (d) In selecting the least restrictive environment, consideration is given to any potential harmful effect on the child or on the quality of services he or she needs.

Figure 2.4   Least restrictive environment regulations.

Information from *Federal Register,* August 23, 1977, PL 94-142, The Education for All Handicapped Children Act.

how would a physical educator determine whether a child with mild hemiplegic spastic cerebral palsy should be placed in a general seventh-grade physical education basketball unit? The teacher could review the general physical education curriculum to determine what objectives are targeted in this unit (e.g., bounce passing, dribbling with both hands, jump shots, and layups). He could then assess the child on these objectives and compare the results obtained with the target class data. Although both NRIs and CRIs can be used when making placement decisions, CRIs are more commonly administered because they provide information that can be used to inform the placement decision, formulate goals for the IEP, and plan initial instruction.

Instructional Decisions

Instructional decisions are the third and most common type of decision teachers must make. As indicated in the example of Mary, the 8-year-old recovering from traumatic brain injury, almost every action a teacher performs when teaching requires an instructional decision. These decisions can involve a wide range of assessment tools, from standardized instruments to teacher-developed checklists. The common element is that they all involve collecting data that can be used to make an informed instructional decision. An important distinction is that most assessments for instructional decisions can be built into the ongoing instruction. That is, assessment is part of the instructional process and not a separate stand-alone activity.

A stereotypical view of physical education assessment is that the teacher introduces a skill to be learned, such as the underhand serve in volleyball. The teacher typically demonstrates the underhand serve and explains how the skill is used in various games and sports. She then involves the class in select drills and activities designed to provide students an opportunity to practice and learn the underhand volleyball serve. Finally, at the end of the unit, the teacher tests the children on their underhand serving ability. A problem with this method of assessment is that it puts too much responsibility on the learner. It also communicates to children that the sole purpose of assessment is to test them. For children to learn under this method, they must be able to watch the teacher's demonstration and then determine the following:

- What are the key components of the underhand volleyball serve?
- Which of these components can they already perform correctly, and which ones do they need to work on?
- Which component should they try to correct first?
- Of the components they need to work on, what specifically are they doing wrong, and what specifically should they do differently to correct their performance?
- Finally, when given a chance to work on this skill, what should they do?

For many children who cannot automatically replicate what they see the teacher demonstrate, all these decisions are beyond their ability. Clearly, it should be the teacher's responsibility to do these tasks. The teacher should explain that in order to learn any motor skill, the students must first know the key components of the skill. The teacher should demonstrate each component and explain how the students can self-assess themselves to determine if they are performing correctly. When the children identify that they have a problem with a component, they should be encouraged to ask for assistance both from the teacher and from their peers. During instruction, the teacher should systematically observe and assess all the students and validate or correct the students' self-assessments. The teacher should also group individuals for instruction and design appropriate learning activities that focus on the specific components of the skill being taught. At the end of the unit, the teacher should systemically observe performance during game activities and record these values as the final assessment. When done correctly, children should not perceive that they are being tested but instead should view assessment as a natural part of the learning process.

IS ASSESSMENT REALLY NECESSARY?

Are you convinced now that in order to teach you must assess, or are you thinking, *I can see how assessment could be used in conjunction with teaching, but I think I can still teach without assessing?* Let's examine another case study.

Case Study 2

Mr. Brady elects not to assess his class before a soccer unit because he believes he has a pretty good idea of their soccer skills. For the first lesson, he focuses on the instep kick. He demonstrates the correct kicking pattern several times and calls particular attention to where his laces make contact with the ball. Once during his demonstration, he has to stop and prompt a child to pay attention. This child has a severe learning disability and frequently acts out in class. After Mr. Brady completes his instruction and demonstrations, he divides the class into small work groups and assigns each an activity that involves kicking. During the practice session, Mr. Brady moves around the gym, observing the class. Soon after the session begins, there is a problem with one child who has been picking up the ball and throwing it at others. Mr. Brady has to intervene, remind the child of the class rules, and warn him that not following directions will result in time-out. Mr. Brady continues to observe the class; he notices that another child is performing the skill well, so he stops the class so the other students can observe her kick. Near the end of the class, Mr. Brady runs a group activity that involves kicking. At the end of the activity, he congratulates the class for their good work on kicking and tells them to practice on their own between now and the next class. Realizing he did not have any additional behavior problems, he also mentions he is pleased that the class followed the class rules. How do you think Mr. Brady's lesson went?

If you examine Mr. Brady's class from the perspective of two children, you see a variation in the success of the lesson. Tracy had a great time, loves physical education, and plays on a local youth soccer team. She is one of the better kickers in the class and likes to show off her abilities. During the practice session, she made sure she was the one kicking when Mr. Brady came near their group. She was thrilled when Mr. Brady singled her out to demonstrate her kick. She cannot wait until the next physical education class. The other child, Ben, did not have such a great time. He does not like physical education because he cannot perform as well as other children. The other children also make fun of him. During the practice session, the kids in his group started making fun of his kicking, so he picked up the ball and threw it at them and received Mr. Brady's warning. For the rest of the class, Ben decided to just watch the other kids; he positioned himself so that he could keep an eye on Mr. Brady, and whenever the teacher came near, Ben acted as if he were working with the group. At the end of class he was disappointed to hear that they would be working on kicking again next class, but he was glad Mr. Brady didn't yell at him again. He concluded he is better off just staying out of Mr. Brady's sight during physical education rather than trying to do the skills and being laughed at by the other students.

Further, it is impossible for Mr. Brady to know what the students learned during class because he did not collect any pre- or postassessment data. If he had, he would have found that neither child learned anything about kicking. Tracy already had a mature kicking pattern before his instruction and just practiced the skill she had during class, while Ben had mastered none of the components of the kick at the start or end of the class. What Ben learned was a new coping and avoidance behavior. He practiced this new coping and avoiding skill for 20 minutes during the practice session and group activity, and Mr. Brady reinforced Ben's efforts at the end of class.

So what can you learn about assessment from Mr. Brady's lesson? First, before instruction, determine what the children need to learn and the content you plan to teach (e.g., how to kick a soccer ball), and choose an assessment instrument designed to measure how to perform that behavior. Second, use this initial assessment data to identify any learning needs, and then design appropriate learning activities and instructional groups to address these needs. Finally, continually assess during instruction to provide children with relevant feedback, to evaluate the effectiveness of your learning activities, and to ensure that children are on task and working on the appropriate component of the skill based on their assessed needs.

ASSESSMENT AND CHILDREN WITH DISABILITIES

Clearly, assessment is important when teaching all children, but it is critical when working with children with disabilities. Although some children with disabilities have excellent physical and motor skills and require no modifications in physical education, many others have multiple factors that interfere with their ability to efficiently learn in physical education. For these students, learning motor skills can be very time consuming as well as physically and emotionally draining. These children frequently start with marked developmental delays and learn at much slower rates than typical of their peers. As a result, many of these children become easily frustrated when learning motor skills and may eventually refuse to even try or will give up after only one attempt if they are not successful. In other words, these students have a low tolerance for failure. If the teacher cannot match the learning activities to their unique needs to ensure success, these children will fail and most likely give up.

Once students give up, the teacher must spend a considerable amount of time and energy redirecting and motivating them to try again. When the students do eventually agree to try again, it is imperative that they succeed. Success develops confidence both in their ability to learn and in the teacher's ability to teach them. Failure reinforces their perception that they cannot learn motor skills and also that the teacher cannot help them. The key to ensuring success and avoiding this failure cycle is assessment. For these children to learn, thrive, and enjoy physical education, the skills they are taught must be task analyzed into small, teachable components that are accurately assessed and used to design appropriate learning activities.

What You Need to Know ▶▶▶

Key Terms

assessment	instructional decisions	product measures
criterion-referenced instruments	measurement	reference standards
evaluation	norm-referenced instruments	summative evaluation
formative evaluation	placement decisions	
identification decisions	process measures	

Key Concepts

1. You should be able to explain the differences between norm-referenced instruments and criterion-referenced instruments.

2. You should be able to compare and contrast the three major types of assessment-based decisions teachers need to make in physical education when working with students with disabilities.

3. You should know the role and function of continuous assessment during instruction in physical education.

4. You should understand how student success and failure are controlled through assessment in physical education.

5. You should be able to explain the differences between formative and summative evaluation and when each is used in physical education.

Review Questions

1. Define identification decisions in physical education. When are they made? What type of assessment tools should be used when making this type of decision?

2. Define placement decisions in physical education. When are they made? What type of assessment tools should be used when making this type of decision?

3. Define instructional decisions in physical education. When are they made? What type of assessment tools should be used when making this type of decision?

4. Outline the step-by-step procedures a teacher should follow to determine what a new student in her class needs to learn for a motor skill objective targeted for instruction.

Chapter 3

Getting to Know the Child

Any proficiency demonstrated by a child today has been shaped by events that make up his or her growth and development history. When assessing performance in any domain, determining performance levels within that domain marks but one phase of the assessment process. As you develop any comprehensive assessment, you must also understand factors that may affect current performance. For example, enrichment activities, deprivation, and traumatic events as well as physical and sensory impairments are several factors that contribute to a person's present level of function. As you extend your decision-making process, you become a detective, gathering relevant background and current information from a variety of sources that can affect decision making and serve as the foundation for selecting instruction strategies. With this information, you will be better positioned to understand and plan for a child's adapted physical education future.

Knowing where a child has come from almost always provides insights into present-day performance. These insights, in turn, help lay the foundation for selecting teaching strategies that will enhance the child's potential. Getting to know a child is a process that begins not with selecting and administering tests but with a thorough knowledge of the child's background. Background information can be obtained from health and medical records, psychological workups, school files, case studies, and anecdotal reports. The purpose of this chapter is to examine the types of background information gathered before the assessment process. Key topics include the information available in the central and school files of a school district.

CENTRAL FILES

Depending on the school district, information about a child's performance may be available to the teacher from the central file. The central file is kept by the director of special education and may include such items as the following:

- Parent questionnaire and developmental history
- Results of vision and hearing screening
- Referral of concern from school support team
- IEP
- Protocol file (test protocol or history)
- Consent for evaluation
- Doctor form
- ADHD form (available in some school districts)

The central file is the primary resource for the wealth of available information and the driving force behind the treatment plan. It also contains the most up-to-date information concerning the child's progress and overall functioning. For the adapted physical education teacher, the director of special education is the link to information that may be required for physical education.

HEALTH-RELATED RECORDS

To plan an appropriate adapted physical education program, the teacher must scrutinize available health and medical records for relevant information that will aid the assessment process and subsequent program planning. Teachers must understand clearly that such records are confidential and must always be treated in an appropriate manner. In both school and agency settings, the nurse or other health personnel can assist in reviewing available records for a particular child, while parents can also be asked to share health-related information. Health and medical files should be examined for essential information:

- Chronic illnesses (e.g., diabetes, chronic heart condition, chronic asthma)
- Acute illnesses (e.g., appendicitis, chicken pox)
- Record of mild illnesses (e.g., frequency of colds, headaches, earaches) and records of absenteeism due to illness
- Sensory impairments (e.g., vision or hearing loss, speech or language difficulties)
- Physical impairments (e.g., cerebral palsy, muscular dystrophy, amputation)
- Persistence of reflexes or contraindicators to activity
- Written permission from parent or guardian to contact medical personnel in case of emergency
- Phone numbers of parents or guardians in case of emergency
- Medications, including dosages and their purposes

A quick perusal of the health file can be valuable because it often reveals vital information about the person's health history. This preliminary assessment may pinpoint areas in need of further assessment. For example, a health file may indicate that Amy receives physical therapy once per week (case study 1). It is crucial that the teacher determine reasons for and the nature of the therapy. Such information enables the teacher to work in conjunction with the therapist to provide Amy with experiences that facilitate her physical activity goals.

Case Study 1

Amy is a preschool child of 4 years of age. She has a tendency to fall while playing and has difficulty rising from a prone position. She also tilts her head to one side while reaching or stepping and has difficulty with object control skills.

After consulting with Amy's doctor, it was determined that she has a mild form of muscular dystrophy. The adapted physical education teacher should assess muscular strength (handheld dynamometer), range of motion (goniometer), and gait (gait analysis) and concurrently develop an intervention for Amy. An observational analysis can also be developed to prompt Amy for correctly throwing, reaching, and stepping as well as rising from a chair. Her intervention can then focus on specific exercises such as hand weights or surgical tubing to improve overall strength and movement.

Before obtaining health-related information from a therapist, doctor, or other allied health professional, it is essential to follow due process procedures and secure parental permission for the records to be released. In some school districts, this information may be part of the confidential file available to all school personnel. At this juncture, it may be appropriate for the teacher to contact the parent or guardian, doctor, school or agency nurse, and other therapists and allied health personnel whose names appear in the file. The file should provide an important information base and reveal the child's history, current status, and future needs. It is equally important that the teacher provide (as well as receive) relevant information (e.g., Amy has a low level of muscular strength and fatigues easily). This information will be beneficial in the instructional process to the extent that teachers understand what is required to increase or maintain physical functioning.

Teachers, along with allied professionals, the parent or guardian, and the child, must work cooperatively to plan an appropriate program based on assessment information from many sources. Because each person offers a unique perspective of the child's functioning, individual viewpoints are essential in assessing and planning an intervention. Sometimes there is the tendency for one specialist, if acting in relative isolation, to see the child only through the eyes of his or her specialty. For example, the physical therapist may think that a child with cerebral palsy should use an electric-powered wheelchair, while the classroom teacher and parent believe it is essential to promote functional strength and not rely on electronic devices. Generally, the more perspectives available, the greater the likelihood the child will be perceived and subsequently served as a whole person. This "whole person" approach reveals a wide spectrum of abilities that are often interrelated and interdependent. Finally, the more individual needs identified, the greater the likelihood that needs can be met and program objectives achieved. Included in figure 3.1 is a sample medical authorization form that can be used to gather activity-related information about

Medical Authorization Form

Developmental Adapted Physical Education
Long-Term Disability

Date sent: _____

Children should participate in physical education on a regular basis. If a permanent or long-term disability interferes with participation in the regular physical education program, an individualized physical education curriculum will be planned around the child's motor strengths and abilities. The child shall be enrolled in the *adapted program* based on completion of this form.

Child's name: _____ DOB: _____ School: _____ Grade: _____

Parent/Guardian: _____ Phone: _____

Disability: _____

Characteristics of disability: _____

Expected duration of disability: _____

Medication type (implication for physical activity): _____ Dosage: _____

Concerns: _____

The following activities will be adapted to the child's individual capabilities. Please mark any activity you would **NOT** recommend for the above child.

I. Physical fitness activities
- _____ arm–shoulder strength
- _____ abdominal strength
- _____ flexibility (range of motion)
- _____ cardiorespiratory endurance
- _____ leg strength
- _____ catching

II. Locomotor activities
- _____ creeping   _____ hopping
- _____ crawling   _____ jumping
- _____ walking   _____ skipping
- _____ running   _____ galloping
- _____ sliding

III. Nonlocomotor activities
- _____ bending   _____ lifting
- _____ twisting   _____ hanging
- _____ pushing   _____ balancing
- _____ pulling   _____ swinging

IV. Aquatics
- _____ swimming skills
- _____ water play
- _____ diving

V. Object control skills
- _____ kicking
- _____ striking
- _____ overhead throwing
- _____ underhand throwing
- _____ ball bouncing

VI. Other activities not recommended
- _____
- _____
- _____
- _____
- _____
- _____
- _____

Comments: _____

Specific activities or motor and fitness goals for child: _____

_____

Your input will assist us in determining an appropriate instructional program.

Date: _____ Signed: _____, MD

Phone number: _____

Figure 3.1 Sample medical authorization form.

a child. When seeking background information about a child, particular attention should be paid to the following:

- Medical diagnosis
- Condition's severity
- Prognosis
- Psychological evaluations
- Symptoms or characteristics with potential for impact in adapted physical education settings
- Past and current courses of treatment
- Recommended and restricted activities (source, rationale)

Teachers who attempt to secure medical information need to be aware that, for a variety of reasons, such information may not always be immediately forthcoming. Although difficulties may be encountered when communicating with doctors, a teacher has the responsibility to secure the information if possible.

The doctor may respond slowly and often cautiously for a variety of reasons. How soon or thoroughly a doctor responds may depend, in part, on how highly he prioritizes the teacher's need for information. Some doctors, concerned about medical malpractice in a society that has become excessively litigious, are hesitant to provide information that could become the basis for future litigation. For the same reason that a doctor may be hesitant to provide information, it may be equally important for the teacher to have information. Finally, a doctor is bound by confidentiality, and her willingness to respond will be better ensured when she has written permission from a parent or guardian to share patient history with the teacher. In case study 1, this is particularly important for the adapted physical education teacher because the doctor can provide valuable information concerning Amy's functional status and any contraindications for exercise.

PSYCHOLOGICAL WORKUPS

In most school settings, it is likely that the child has been referred previously for assessment by a school or agency psychologist. Such assessments, both formal and informal, can provide insights that help determine how the child's psychological characteristics might be responsible for his or her performance status. These considerations might also affect decisions regarding types of tests that need to be administered and what environmental conditions might yield reliable and valid information. For example, if cognition is impaired, the child might not understand some of the instructions on a test or the abstract notion of exerting a maximal effort. In addition, memory functions or behavior may interfere with the test setting and with getting adequate responses that can be used to develop instructional strategies. For the adapted physical education teacher, this information may be valuable in understanding the child's psychological frame of reference or the environment in which instruction should occur. It also influences the selection of interventions and the potential to ensure learning.

SCHOOL FILES

A child's cumulative or special education file may also provide valuable information for assessment and program development. Initial files established for each student follow the child through the school years. Although the precise content of cumulative records may vary among school districts, recent test history and evaluations are available for comparisons. Updated records or assessments can provide information on recent changes in the child's condition or functional ability. Cumulative school files typically include the following:

- Name, address, family status
- IEP
- Consent for placement
- Current psychological assessment
- Copies of classroom modifications
- Release of neuropsychological assessments
- Due process forms

By directing the teacher to problems that may occur in physical education, school files can be extremely valuable in planning an adapted physical education action plan. If a child's file reveals a history of distractibility, for example, such information can help the tester decide on the types of tests to administer and conditions for testing. A child who is distractible may be tested when there are a minimum of distractions in the testing environment. If a child with diabetes is to be assessed on a physical fitness test, the adapted physical education teacher should schedule the test after lunch to avoid problems with blood sugar.

AGENCY FILES

Whenever a child is served by a particular agency, that agency typically maintains records of that client's participation. Often, the kinds of information found in health-related records and school and special education files will be reflected in agency files. Depending on the nature of the service provided by the particular agency, information specific to that agency's program emphasis will appear in the file. If the child has completed participation in a given agency's program, the teacher can review pretest results, progress reports, and posttest results recorded during the client's participation. Of particular value are insights from summary reports and anecdotal reports. Summary reports or interviews often afford information that is not apparent when reviewing quantitative assessments. For example, an assessor may place a student in a work-related setting and interview the job supervisor about the employee's work habits, ability to relate, and personality in that environment. The report may also contain information from the individual or parent concerning job satisfaction or problems encountered in that setting. Obviously, these reports may be biased by the person responding or a new person who has little knowledge of the client's background and experience.

INSIGHTS FROM PARENTS AND GUARDIANS

Parents and guardians have the right to be involved in the assessment process and should be encouraged to provide information aside from what is legally mandated. Parents can report information, typically from a naturalistic setting, about their child's history or out-of-school environment. This information may include the child's developmental history, including interviews, complete case histories, and experiences in transition situations or work environments. School personnel may have little or no knowledge of the child's past, and they typically observe behavior only within the context of the educational program. Information known only by parents may include the following:

- *Family history:* name and birth date as well as other siblings (including age and gender)
- *Birth history:* pregnancy history, birth weight, complications during or immediately after birth
- *Physical and health history:* overall health history, including present health status and physical functioning, and developmental history, including milestones (e.g., sitting, walking, toilet training, talking) or lags in development
- *Social interaction and play development:* relationships with friends and siblings; play development and interests; interaction with family, other children, teachers
- *School history:* current performance levels and progress in school; test evaluations and recommendations of teachers, therapists, doctors; current program or transition plan

Interviews should be conducted with sensitivity and their purpose made clear to the parent. The interviewer must encourage the parent or guardian to talk freely while minimizing, to the extent feasible, his or her own participation. This will facilitate the parent's or guardian's ability to reveal essential, focused insights. Interview questions should be objective and reflect the interview's focus. For example, "At what age did Amy walk?" is more appropriate than a subjective question such as, "Amy walked by age 1, didn't she?" Figure 3.2 provides a useful format for interviewing parents about their child's motor development history.

INSIGHTS FROM OTHER SCHOOL OR AGENCY PERSONNEL

Sources other than those previously cited can provide additional valuable information about a child, particularly if the child was previously in a general (i.e., unmodified) program and has only recently been referred for adapted physical education. Coworkers will be able to offer insights that shed light on how the current referral for assessment came to be deemed necessary. Classroom teachers, speech therapists, and physical educators may be able to share their observations about a child's motor development, fitness, behavioral and play history, or most efficient modality for learning. Such information can be most helpful if it is systematically recorded. Once the information has been recorded, patterns of behavior, growth, and development become more apparent and will aid in the decision-making process. For example, if Ian has a problem with attention, then this problem should be recorded and used to determine the proper assessment (see case study 2). Likewise, Mickey (case study 3) may need specific medication for his condition. Historical information from school or agency personnel may be gathered through interviews or by use of other informal measures, including rating scales or checklists (e.g., for observing a child's motor skills or social interactions during recess).

Adapted Physical Education

Gross Motor Development

Child's name: _____ Interview date: _____

Date of birth: _____ Grade/teacher: _____

Interviewer: _____

Name of parent/guardian: _____

Address: _____ Phone: _____

_____

_____

_____

		Yes	No	Unsure
A. Motor development				
1.	First walked without crawling beforehand (creeping on hands and knees)	☐	☐	☐
2.	First walked before 12 months	☐	☐	☐
3.	First walked between 12 and 18 months	☐	☐	☐
4.	First walked between 18 and 24 months	☐	☐	☐
5.	First walked after 24 months	☐	☐	☐
6.	Seemed to sit, stand, and walk late	☐	☐	☐
7.	Walks on toes	☐	☐	☐
8.	Walks flat-footed	☐	☐	☐
B. Coordination				
9.	Falls frequently	☐	☐	☐
10.	Bumps into things, people frequently	☐	☐	☐
11.	Loses balance easily	☐	☐	☐
12.	Seems to show shaky, jerky movements	☐	☐	☐
C. Body awareness				
13.	Feels uncomfortable about his or her body	☐	☐	☐
14.	Confused easily about direction (e.g., right, left, forward, sideways)	☐	☐	☐
15.	Understands basic body parts and their relationships (e.g., front, back, arm, foot)	☐	☐	☐
D. Physical fitness				
16.	Tires easily	☐	☐	☐
17.	Overweight	☐	☐	☐
18.	Seems to lack strength	☐	☐	☐
19.	Lacks vitality (energy, enthusiasm)	☐	☐	☐
E. Social and emotional development				
20.	Enjoys balls, bats, and other movement toys (jump ropes, rebounder)	☐	☐	☐
21.	Plays outdoors often	☐	☐	☐
22.	Plays vigorously with other children	☐	☐	☐
23.	Enjoys gym class	☐	☐	☐
24.	Participates in extracurricular physical activities	☐	☐	☐
25.	Enjoys playing physical games and sports	☐	☐	☐

Figure 3.2 Suggested format for interviewing parents or guardians about a child's motor development history.

Case Study 2

Ian is a 12-year-old seventh grader who has difficulty remembering the instructions for game activities. He commonly blurts out answers before the teacher is finished but has difficulty completing sequences in the proper order. After consulting with Ian's teacher, it was discovered that his homework is not turned in on time and is often incomplete. His desk is unorganized, and his academic performance is low. Ian has been given a prescription for Ritalin but does not take the medication on a regular basis.

Several red flags suggest a learning or attention disorder. The prescription of Ritalin necessitates more information from the doctor or psychologist concerning Ian's difficulties. If Ian takes the medication according to the doctor's recommendation, his problem may be remediated. If not, an alternative medication may be prescribed or more extensive neurological screenings should be utilized. In addition, the teacher should structure the environment and employ behavior management strategies to remediate Ian's performance.

Other school personnel who may provide valuable preassessment information to the adapted physical education specialist include nurses, administrators, teacher aides, and occupational therapists. The school nurse, in particular, might share information not always found in a child's school file. Often, the school nurse will have had meetings or conversations with the child's parents, doctor, or other therapists. In this context, the nurse may provide information on the use of specific medication (e.g., for a child with asthma) or on medications that could affect the child's performance or safety in physical education. Although essential information is usually documented in the health file, the insights of other school personnel should be considered along with other informal assessment information.

Nonschool personnel may also provide valuable information. If the child lives in a group home, the group home supervisor may shed some light on the child's needs, such as behavior prompts or reinforcement strategies. Likewise, an employment supervisor may provide important insights from the workplace perspective on the student's training needs, such as the amount of strength and endurance needed to lift and stack objects in the workplace.

Case Study 3

Mickey is a very active 9-year-old fourth-grader who is also very athletic. However, during physical activity he sometimes has to stop and cough. After a brief rest, he usually rejoins the activity. During physical fitness testing, he complained of being tired and could not complete a walk/run.

In this context, the teacher should be aware of any medical conditions that affect physical performance as well as any medications Mickey may need. By consulting with the school nurse, the teacher finds that Mickey has asthma and needs to take medication before exercise.

INSIGHTS FROM THE CHILD

Too often, the child is overlooked or underutilized as a valuable source of information. The student can provide information about her specific needs or self-satisfaction with her situation. Sometimes, however, a person with a disability is not perceived (by those without disabilities) as being capable of determining and articulating his own unique interests and needs (Horvat & Kalakian, 1996). Teachers need to recognize this and go directly to the child for information that typically is reported by others. Any question asked of someone else should also be addressed directly to the child, when appropriate.

It is important to establish a rapport with the child and to show genuine interest in the answers. Rapport helps alleviate anxiety and provides important information on the child's viewpoint. For example, the interviewer might say, "I've asked you to meet with me this morning to share with you what our program has to offer. Just as important, our staff is genuinely interested in what you would like to learn and do as you participate in our program." When interviewing children or persons whose social or mental ages do not roughly equate with their chronological ages, communication should match the individual's developmental status.

ROLES IN THE ASSESSMENT PROCESS

Interpretation of test data provides a major means of getting to know the child. Yet there has not always been clear determination or agreement among allied professionals regarding who assesses what. Physical education assessments of persons with disabilities have not historically been undertaken by adapted physical education personnel. It is not particularly uncommon for persons with disabilities to have been assessed for physical education by general physical education teachers, occupational therapists, physical therapists, mainstream classroom teachers, special education teachers, and sometimes psychologists. The person responsible for adapted physical education *must* be thoroughly familiar with the test, test content, and test administration procedures. The person conducting adapted physical education assessments should also be firmly grounded in adapted physical education and its relationship to special education and related services in the school setting.

At times, there will be honest differences of opinion among allied professionals regarding who assesses what. For example, flexibility is one component of physical fitness, and as such, it is typically addressed in a physical education curriculum. Flexibility is also addressed in physical therapy. The occupational therapist may assess throwing because he perceives throwing as a manipulative skill. Yet the same skill might be assessed by an adapted physical education specialist, who sees throwing skill development as being within the purview of her own profession.

Often, there are no clear-cut boundaries for determining if a given activity belongs to a specific profession. This perhaps is how it should be, since professionals who worry more about territorial imperatives than about children may be putting their professions ahead of the very persons whom the professions are trying to serve. Individuals who serve the same children must strive to create a working environment characterized by communication, mutual respect, and, foremost, the development of specific goals in the best interests of the person being served.

Assessment by the Physical Educator

Physical education teachers are involved in assessment at a variety of levels. The elementary physical educator may be responsible for conducting initial posture or scoliosis screening at the preschool or kindergarten age levels. Screening is a type of general assessment administered to all children in a class. At early age levels, motor screening becomes part of a larger, more comprehensive screening of general cognitive, affective, psychological, and social development. Children diagnosed as having disabilities at early age levels are usually referred for more in-depth diagnostic assessment.

The physical educator may also conduct screening tests at the primary and upper elementary grades. General fitness tests, such as the Fitnessgram, are often administered by the elementary physical education teacher. The health-related portion of Physical Best, however, does not offer percentile norms. Instead, it offers a single performance standard for typically developing children at each age level, 5 to 18, by gender. Since Physical Best's health-related items do not offer percentile norms, its use as a placement tool among persons who have disabilities may be of somewhat limited value. These tests, particularly when they are norm referenced, may become part of the process that determines the degree to which a student with a disability departs from typical development. For example, overall fitness data can tell the teacher how a child compares with a national average in fitness subtest areas. Teachers can subsequently make decisions and plan instruction around areas of strength and need. Results of such assessments can help determine whether a child with a disability meets entry or exit criteria for placement in adapted physical education.

At middle and high school levels, physical educators may administer tests corresponding to certain curricular units of instruction. For example, the teacher may select a soccer skills test for use at the end of a soccer unit. In a skills test, children are asked to demonstrate proficiencies in specific skills presented during the physical education class. Secondary-level physical educators may also administer group fitness tests and sometimes may administer written tests to assess knowledge of physical education concepts.

Today, most physical education curricula are objective based, with clearly defined achievement criteria for each grade level (Horvat, Eichstaedt, Kalakian, & Croce, 2003). Objective-based curricula readily lend themselves to ongoing criterion-referenced assessment. In some schools, physical education teachers must report their classes' percentage of mastery on curricular objectives taught during the school year. Objective-based programs with curriculum-embedded assessment provide a clearly defined system for evaluating programs, individualizing instruction, and monitoring pupil progress toward objectives. Objective-based instruction has had tremendous impact on physical education. Curriculum planning, accountability, and curriculum-embedded assessment are now integral parts of a field in which, for some, individualization had seemed next to impossible.

General and adapted physical educators are now faced with the challenge of conducting diagnostic tests. Assessment for diagnostic purposes requires that the teacher gather data that helps determine the specific nature of individual motor difficulties or why children are having problems in physical education.

For example, diagnostic motor testing is utilized to pinpoint particular motor development problem areas such as agility or eye–hand coordination. In-depth diagnostic assessment of motor functioning is usually administered individually. Diagnostic instruments may be formal (e.g., norm referenced) or informal (e.g., criterion referenced). Formal diagnostic tests tend to be more time consuming and may require a separate session for each objective area.

Because diagnostic tests are usually administered to children individually, it is difficult for the general physical educator to find time to test such children. In some school districts, adapted physical educators assume responsibility for all movement-related individual assessments.

The content of skills tests administered by physical educators can vary and may include tests of sports skills, fundamental motor skills, or perceptual-motor abilities. The content of these tests should directly reflect skills taught in the physical education curriculum, and skills in the curriculum should directly reflect skills needed in community- and home-based settings.

Assessments by Specialists Representing Other Therapies

In recent years, schools have become more interdisciplinary in providing opportunities for children who have disabilities. An important manifestation of this trend is that occupational therapists (OTs), physical therapists (PTs), and vocational trainers have undertaken contributing roles in public schools. Pursuant to federal mandates, these therapies are provided as related services when determined necessary to facilitate a child's special education program. When therapists are members of the child study team, portions of motor assessment can be conducted by the OT or PT. Traditionally, OTs and PTs have functioned within a medical model, while physical educators have functioned within an educational model. Physical education teachers primarily assess observable, measurable motor skills, while OTs and PTs tend to assess processes underlying movement. For example, the physical educator might assess throwing skill, while the physical therapist might assess range of motion, which to some extent underlies the ability to throw skillfully. The OT might also assess manipulative abilities that facilitate ball handling, which in turn affect throwing proficiency. OTs and PTs, like adapted physical educators, conduct both formal and informal assessments.

Occupational therapists in school settings might administer formal or informal tests to identify a student's functional performance levels in the following areas:

- Gross and fine motor skills
- Reflex and reaction development
- Developmental landmarks
- Sensorimotor functioning
- Self-help skills
- Prevocational skills
- Social interaction skills
- Ambulatory devices

Several assessment areas overlap between adapted physical education and special education. This sort of overlap of professional responsibilities has been the subject of some controversy. Therapists and educators, however, can work cooperatively to avoid gaps in both assessment and service. Upon receiving and reviewing the referral of a child for assessment, it is vital that physical educators and therapists cooperatively plan and decide who will administer each type of assessment. Each professional brings unique, relevant information to the team meeting. The interdisciplinary approach to assessment emphasizes sharing, respecting, and learning from each team member's contribution. For example, the OT, adapted physical education teacher, and vocational trainer can work together to develop the specific intervention strategies needed for the individualized transition plan (ITP) by assessing components of the tasks required in the workplace and the physical skills needed to accomplish these tasks.

In some schools, physical therapists are available to assist in motor assessment, providing valuable insights for planning appropriate physical activities. For children who have physical disabilities (e.g., cerebral palsy, muscular dystrophy), motor assessment may be based primarily on a medical model. Physical therapists can evaluate tonus and persistence of reflexes that interfere with range of motion, posture, and movement patterns. These results of a clinical evaluation by a physical therapist can then be combined with information gathered by a physical educator to develop the program plan. In cases involving physically disabling conditions when only early diagnostic information is available, an evaluation by a physical therapist may shed light on present functional capacity and subsequent implications for physical education programming (e.g., by determining head movements that may induce a reflex). In addition to identifying physiological (motor), topographical (affected parts of body), and etiological (causative) factors used in classifying physical disabilities, physical therapists can also conduct supplemental evaluations, including the following:

- Posture evaluation
- Eye–hand behavior patterns (eye dominance, eye movements, fixation, convergence, grasp)
- Visual status (sensory defects, motor defects)
- Early reflexes
- Joint range of motion and strength
- Stability skills (locomotor, head control, trunk control)
- Motor symptoms (spasticity, athetosis, ataxia, rigidity, tremors)

Although PTs can provide information vital to the physical educator, intervention becomes the point of departure for the two disciplines because of time and load constraints. Since the therapist's intervention is minimal, the adapted physical education teacher needs to translate relevant evaluative information into appropriate educational goals for each student. Within this context, the objectives defined from the evaluation of therapists and teachers must be observable and measurable, and they must be used to develop an appropriate intervention plan based on individual needs.

What You Need to Know ►►►

Key Terms

agency files	health-related records	school files
central files	parental insights	
child insights	psychological workups	

Key Concepts

1. You should understand the general role of assessment for developing the IEP and placement options.

2. You should understand medical and psychological parameters that affect the child's functioning.

3. You should be familiar with the medical concerns of a child and the safety considerations for children with disabilities.

4. You should be familiar with the child's most efficient learning modality and how it will affect assessment. How would you assess a child with a sensory disability or cognitive impairment?

Review Questions

1. What type of information is available in your local school district? Who has access to this information?

2. What information should the physical education teacher provide at the IEP meeting?

3. What essential information does the adapted physical education teacher get from other teachers or school personnel? How does that affect IEP development?

Chapter 4

Selecting an Appropriate Assessment Instrument

The purpose of conducting any assessment is to collect accurate data so that an informed decision can be made. You learned in chapter 2 that teachers need to make three types of decisions (i.e., identification, placement, and instructional) and that each of these decisions determines the type of assessment instrument that should be used. In physical education, particularly when working with children with disabilities, collecting accurate assessment data is not as simple as matching a commercially and readily available test with the type of decision that needs to be made. Consider case study 1 on page 38.

The purpose of this chapter is to provide a basic understanding of the essential criteria all assessment instruments must possess: validity, reliability, objectivity, and norms. Once you understand these factors, you can use them to evaluate assessment instruments to determine which are most appropriate for the decisions you need to make. You will also need to use these criteria when creating your own assessment instruments, which is common when working with children with disabilities.

Selecting an appropriate means of assessment is a complex process that starts with understanding the psychometric qualities of the instruments. Once you know what to look for in a sound assessment instrument, you can start the process of matching the instrument to the decision to be made and ensuring that you can

Case Study 1

A neighbor of Ms. Johanson, knowing she is a physical educator, asks her to evaluate his son Peter's running pattern to see if it is okay. He is concerned that Peter is not as fast as other boys and wants to know what he should be doing to help him.

This sounds like a simple request, but what decisions need to be made in this situation?

- Is Peter's running pattern appropriate for his age?
- If not appropriate, what needs to be worked on?
- Is his running speed appropriate for his age and gender? If not, what are the possible contributing factors, and how can they be addressed?
  - Does he lack strength?
  - Does he lack balance?
  - Does he lack coordination?
  - Is he afraid to run for some reason?

Given these basic questions, Ms. Johanson needs to determine what assessment instruments should be used to address them. Task-specific instruments often meet the demands of the task; at other times, the perfect tool cannot be found, and the physical educator must develop an instrument. On the surface, assessment appears very straightforward. If you want to evaluate students' running performance, assess how they run. The complications begin when it comes to selecting the appropriate instrument to do the assessment. Hundreds of assessment tools are available that measure some aspect of physical education. The challenge is knowing how to evaluate these tools to select the one that meets the specific demands of the assessment decision.

competently administer the test. When evaluating the appropriateness of any measurement tool, validity, reliability, and objectivity must be considered. We first define these factors and discuss their role in determining an instrument's trustworthiness. We then discuss how these factors interact with each other.

VALIDITY

Validity is a function of what is measured by the test and how the test results are used. An assessment instrument is considered valid if the scores obtained measure what the instrument was designed to measure, and there is evidence to support this judgment. In physical education, instruments are used to measure a wide range of attributes, such as beliefs, knowledge, behavior, performance, and ability, across the spectrum of physical education content, which includes physical fitness, body awareness, body management, locomotor skills, object control skills, team sports, and lifetime sports. Given this wide range of attributes and content, no one assessment instrument is universally valid. Several types of evidence can support the validity of a given instrument. Depending on the purpose of the assessment instrument and what is measured, one or more of these sources may be appropriate. Five sources of validity evidence are briefly reviewed here.

Face Validity

Face, or logical, validity is the simplest and most subjective source of validity evidence to support an assessment instrument. For face validity, there needs to be a direct connection between what is measured by the instrument and what is being assessed. For example, let's say Mr. Rodriguez is teaching a striking unit to children in third grade and wants to know if they can hit a ball off a batting tee a distance of at least 20 feet (6 meters), in fair territory, at least 8 out of 10 times. He could design an assessment instrument that provides 10 striking trials off a batting tee and record the number of times the ball lands in bounds and goes the required distance. Since there is a direct connection between what is measured by this instrument and the objective it is designed to measure, this would be considered strong face validity evidence.

Face validity is easy to judge when the instrument is limited to a few behaviors and the scoring is highly objective. In the striking example, only one behavior, striking, is measured, and the observations involve judging whether the ball is hit, whether it stays in bounds, and whether it goes at least 20 feet (6 meters). Let's look at the same skill but from a different perspective. What if the objective for conducting the assessment is to determine if the children are performing the two-hand sidearm strike correctly? The physical educator needs to create an assessment instrument like the example in figure 4.1. This instrument also appears to have face validity in that the components being observed appear to be directly connected to the objective of striking. However, there might be some issues regarding how the components have been defined and whether the number of components is appropriate. The judgments the teacher has to make are also more subjective and competency based. Instead of just judging whether the ball is hit or how far it goes, the teacher must know the seven components and judge, in the less than a second it takes for this skill to be performed, whether the student performs each correctly. For this assessment instrument, additional validity evidence is warranted to address these issues.

Content Validity

Content validity concerns collecting evidence to support that what is measured by the instrument reflects what the instrument is designed to measure. For the batting assessment in figure 4.1, what evidence shows that the seven components of a mature two-hand sidearm strike represent the essential parts of this skill and that these components can be assessed by teachers? These issues could be addressed in a number of ways. First, the person developing the assessment instrument could review the literature and cite research to support the stated components and document that these components can in fact be observed by trained teachers. A second option would be to convene a panel of experts and have them review the proposed components to judge their appropriateness. Of course, what constitutes an expert would need to be clearly defined. If the experts' ratings or the documentation from the professional literature supports the proposed components, then this would be considered evidence of content validity.

Although stronger than face validity, content validity is still subjective (i.e., it is based on subjective judgments of whether something is or is not valid). Content

Equipment and Space Requirements:

- Use a softball (12-inch circumference, official weight) with a no-sting surface, and a regulation-size metal or wooden bat that is 26"–28" in length.
- Bat in an outdoor field or large gymnasium at least 70 feet in length (10-foot staging area plus 60-foot throwing distance).

Skill Levels	Focal Points	
1. Demonstrate the mature two-hand sidearm strike. a, b c, d, e f, g	The student demonstrates the following focal points for the mature two-hand sidearm strike while batting (right- or left-handed) a softball that is thrown underhand to the student at slow speed from 20 feet, on 2 of 3 trials. A softball thrown at slow speed will travel 20 feet in 2 seconds. a. **Grip bat** with hands together, nondominant hand palm down near the base of the bat, dominant hand palm up above nondominant hand. b. **Stand sideways,** with nondominant shoulder toward pitcher, feet shoulder-width apart, weight evenly distributed on both feet, eyes on ball, bat behind dominant shoulder, hands at shoulder height. c. **Swing bat forward** in horizontal plane at waist level, with trunk rotation forward. d. **Shift weight** onto batting side foot, and step forward with opposite foot during bat swing forward. e. **Contact center of ball** with top third of the bat. f. **Follow through** well beyond ball contact. g. **Smooth integration** (not mechanical or jerky) of the previous focal points.	
2. Demonstrate the mature two-hand sidearm strike for distance.	The student with a mature two-hand sidearm strike (skill level 1) will bat a softball thrown at moderate speed from a **distance** on 2 of 3 trials. A softball thrown at moderate speed will travel 40 feet in 2 seconds, 50 feet in 2½ seconds, and 60 feet in 3 seconds.	**Striking (batting) distances:** • Grades K-1 40 feet • Grades 2-3 50 feet • Grades 4-5 60 feet
3. Demonstrate the mature two-hand sidearm strike for accuracy. 40 – 60 feet 90°	The student with a mature two-hand sidearm strike (skill level 1) and sidearm strike for distance (skill level 2) will bat a softball, thrown at moderate speed from a distance, for **accuracy,** on 2 of 3 trials.	**Accuracy criterion:** Within a 90° arc, 45° to the right or left of the student, centered on the person who threw the ball. **Striking (batting) distances:** • Grades K-1 40 feet • Grades 2-3 50 feet • Grades 4-5 60 feet

Reference Data: A baseline distance of 60 feet and a distance from the pitcher's mound to home plate of 35-40 feet is used in fastpitch softball.

Figure 4.1 Everyone CAN two-hand sidearm strike batting assessment.
From Kelly, Wessel, Dummer, & Sampson, forthcoming.

validity involves several independent judgments, providing more evidence than the single judgment made in the case of face validity. The concept of content validity can be applied to the assessment of many different aspects of physical education. For example, a paper and pencil test may be used to evaluate whether the children have acquired the necessary knowledge about physical fitness. When creating an assessment instrument to measure physical fitness knowledge, the challenge is to evaluate this knowledge with a reasonable number of questions that accurately represent the content that was taught. Evidence of content validity could be determined in this case by delineating the content taught and the emphasis given to each topic and then keying the test items to this matrix. A panel of experts could then review these materials and judge whether the items on the test accurately reflect the course content.

Concurrent Validity

Concurrent validity statistically measures the relationship between an existing instrument with established validity and a new instrument that assesses the same attribute. Your initial reaction might be why create a new instrument if there is already one that is known to be valid? The answer is usually related to time and cost. For example, Ms. Morris wants to determine the body fat of the children in her school to learn whether obesity is a problem that needs to be addressed. To answer this question, she requires a valid way to assess body fat. She could use a clinical measure that has already been validated, but it may be expensive and require travel to a lab or hospital. A simpler approach is to use a skinfold caliper to measure select skinfolds and then use a regression equation to predict the students' body fat. How does Ms. Morris know the skinfold method is valid? Validity was determined by the people who created the regression equation. They measured the skinfolds of a group of people and compared their results using a clinical measure that serves as a gold standard. By statistically comparing the results, the skinfold assessment correlates highly with the established standard and is considered strong evidence of concurrent validity.

Construct Validity

Construct validity is concerned with demonstrating that what an assessment item measures is representative of a construct. Constructs are traits such as sportsmanship, anxiety, general motor ability, and coordination. There is usually a theoretical basis for the construct and many possible potential measures. The goal is to find a series of measures that are easy and cost effective and that represent the construct. Evidence of construct validity is established by techniques such as factor analysis and tests of group differences. For example, consider an assessment instrument designed to measure coordination. One way to test its construct validity is to assess two groups of people who clearly differ (i.e., high and low) in their coordination and then see if the assessment instrument distinguishes between these two groups. If it does, this would be considered evidence of construct validity.

Criterion Validity

Criterion, or predictive, validity examines the degree to which one or more test scores can be used to predict performance on a future related event. For example, can SAT scores predict the success of college students in the United States? Can a soccer volleying test predict who makes the varsity soccer team?

To calculate predictive validity, the score on the predictor assessment (e.g., SAT) must be correlated with a score for the criterion factor (e.g., college grade point average). For example, let's say an adapted physical education tool has been created for screening all preschool and elementary children to determine if they would benefit from adapted physical education services. Depending on their scores, children are referred for additional evaluation and then ultimately placed in various settings such as general physical education (GPE), physical education with support services (e.g., aid provided), GPE with APE support, GPE with APE pullout, or separate APE. To calculate the predictive validity of our APE screening tool, the teacher correlates the students' screening scores with their performance in their ultimate placements. If the correlation is high (e.g., greater than 80%), this would be considered strong evidence of predictive validity for this instrument. The obvious advantage of having an APE screening tool with high predictive validity is that it can assist teachers and parents when making difficult physical education placement decisions, which can frequently be very subjective and prone to bias.

RELIABILITY

Reliability of an assessment instrument refers to the consistency of the result obtained over multiple administrations. On the surface the concept of reliability is very simple. If you give the same assessment twice to the same group of students, a reliable assessment will produce the same results on both administrations. For example, a physical educator could assess a child's running speed by timing how long she takes to run 50 yards (50 meters) today and then administering the same assessment again tomorrow. If the child runs approximately the same time both days, this test would be considered a reliable measure of running speed. Although the concept of reliability is simple, its application to the measurement of physical education content can be complicated because it can be affected by administration procedures, scoring precision, and student performance variability. Each of these factors is discussed in this section.

Administration procedures define how an assessment should be administered and scored. Ideally, all the conditions should be kept the same during repeated assessments so that any change detected between assessments is the result of changes in student performance. One way to reduce errors related to variability in administrative procedures is to provide explicit instructions on how each item should be set up, demonstrated, explained, and scored. While this process increases administrative consistency between assessments, it also adds to the amount of time and effort required of the teacher to learn and apply these procedures. In addition, it makes the administration of the test more formal, which sometimes adversely affects student performance. This method is most commonly used in the administration of norm-referenced instruments. Another method is to simplify the procedures for each item so that they are easier for the teacher to remember. The teacher can then administer the items in a more relaxed and potentially authentic setting. This second method is most commonly used with criterion-referenced instruments. The shortcoming of this method is that there will be minor differences between how the teacher administers the assessments on separate occasions, which may affect student performance. Consider case study 2.

Case Study 2

One day Mr. Frazier assesses his students to see how many curl-ups they can perform in 1 minute outside on the hard ground on a hot 94 °F (34 °C) day. The next day he assesses them inside on the same skill using mats in an air-conditioned gym. Do you think this change in conditions could affect their performance? To achieve high reliability, all the assessment conditions must be explicitly stated and followed. If an assessment instrument does not have explicit procedures, then teachers administering the test must record exactly what they do so they can follow the same procedures and replicate the same conditions on subsequent administrations.

Scoring precision is a function of what is measured and the amount of skill needed to make the measurement. As a general rule, high scoring precision is easier to obtain when the products of performance are being measured with mechanical tools that require minimal skill on the part of the assessor. For example, measurements of physical attributes such as height and weight tend to produce consistent results because these attributes remain constant across short time periods, and it is easy to accurately read the scores from a scale or ruler. Other examples of objective scores are distance, time, number of repetitions, and number of times a target is hit. In all these examples, what is measured can be clearly seen and scored or else measured with a device such as a tape measure or stopwatch that is easy to use.

All tests require some degree of practice before they can be administered reliably. As the nature of the attribute being measured becomes more dependent on the skill of the person administering the assessment, more attention must be placed on training to produce high reliability. For example, administering the batting assessment in figure 4.1 requires knowing the components to be observed, where to stand when observing, and what order to observe the components in, as well as skill in being able to judge when the components are being performed correctly. To achieve high reliability with these types of measures requires that the administration instructions be very specific and that the assessor be trained to an established competency level before using the instrument.

The third factor that can adversely affect reliability is performance variability. All assessments assume that when children are assessed they are fully attending to the task at hand, understand exactly what they are expected to do on the task, and give the task their best effort. These issues can be summarized as the ACE prerequisite behaviors: Attention, Comprehension, and Effort. Ideally, these factors should be addressed in the administration procedures. However, even when they are well addressed in the procedures, judging whether they are met still depends on the skill of the assessor. In other words, the physical educator must assess these prerequisite behaviors whenever he or she conducts an assessment. If a child is distracted (i.e., attention problem), appears confused (i.e., comprehension problem), or just appears to be going through the motions (i.e., effort problem), this information should be recorded along with the actual assessment score. When these behaviors appear to adversely affect performance, then this information is considered when the actual assessment score is interpreted. Figure 4.2 shows a score sheet for skill level 1 of the batting objective defined in figure 4.1. Note that three columns are provided to rate the child's ACE behaviors, and

ABC School District Class Performance Score Sheet: Batting

Teacher: _____ Start date: _____ Mastery criterion: _____

Class: _____ Grade level: _____ End date: _____

Scoring rubric: 0 = not present
1 = emerging but needs work
2 = demonstrates correct pattern consistently

ACE ratings: a = above average
b = average
c = below average

Students	Grip bat	Stand sideways	Swing bat forward	Shift weight	Contact center of ball	Follow-through	Smooth integration	Attention	Comprehension	Effort	Comments	Evaluation values					
	1	2	3	4	5	6	7	A	C	E		A	B	C	D	E	F

Directions: _____

Administrative considerations: _____

Reflections: _____

Figure 4.2 Sample Everyone CAN score sheet with ACE behaviors.
From Kelly, Wessel, Dummer, & Sampson, forthcoming.

each behavior is rated on a simple three-point scale (a = above average, b = average, c = below average).

Attention and comprehension problems can frequently be addressed by providing the children with extra practice trials, as long as this process does not negatively affect the validity of the item. Although recording ACE behaviors and providing extra practice can control for some of the obvious potential sources of error, clearly any number of other factors such as sleep, nutrition, mood, or motivation can influence the consistency of a child's performance on an assessment. This is particularly true for motor skills, where there is natural variation in ability. Consider this situation: Mr. Stevens wants to determine his students' proficiency at shooting basketball free throws. How many attempts should he give them to get an accurate measurement of their ability? What would be the effect of giving each child only 1 attempt, or at the other extreme, giving each student 100 attempts? Clearly, 1 attempt is too few and could be adversely affected by luck. A poorly skilled child could just get lucky on this 1 attempt, and a highly skilled child could be unlucky. On the other hand, 100 attempts could be adversely affected by factors such as fatigue and boredom.

Given this information, let's say Mr. Stevens decides to use 10 attempts. Will this give a consistent measurement of the students' ability? Have you ever taken 10 free throw attempts one day and hit 8 out of 10, then the next day hit only 2 out of 10? What do these scores indicate? Were you just lucky on the first day? Did you forget how to shoot free throws from one day to the next? What these results probably indicate is that getting an accurate measurement of performance on many motor skills requires multiple attempts per trial across multiple trials. The number of trials and the number of attempts per trial are functions of the complexity of the skill being assessed and the amount of performance variation. For components of fundamental motor skills, demonstrating consistency on 2 out of 3 or 3 out of 5 trials may be sufficient. For other objectives, such as affective behaviors of cooperation or sportsmanship, it may be appropriate to take several measurements a day across 2 to 3 weeks.

Remember, the goal of assessing is to obtain an accurate measurement of a child's ability. Under ideal conditions, you should probably err on the side of providing more attempts and trials. Unfortunately, in reality, a balance must be achieved between what may be ideal and what is practical given the amount of time available to conduct the assessment. The goal, then, is to determine the minimum number of attempts and trials needed to get an accurate and consistent performance. These values will probably need to be adjusted to match the developmental level of the students being assessed. As a general rule, variability tends to be higher with younger students and during the early phases of skill acquisition; it tends to decrease as age increases and during the later stages of skill acquisition.

CONTROLLING AND MEASURING RELIABILITY

Fortunately, many of the threats to reliability can be controlled via training and systematic documentation. As discussed already, threats due to administrative procedures can be minimized by identifying any potential problems and then recording how these are addressed so the assessment can be repeated under consistent conditions. Scoring threats can be addressed through training and establishing minimum competency levels before assessments are conducted.

The most challenging source of error to control for is variability, since this is not under the direct control of the teacher but is controlled by the child. These threats can be minimized by assessing the ACE behaviors and adjusting the number of attempts and trials to the student's developmental level.

Test–Retest

When an assessment instrument is created, it is customary to test for reliability and report a reliability value between 0 and 1. The simplest way to test reliability is the test–retest method, in which an instrument is administered twice to the same group of children and then a correlation, or degree of agreement, between the results is calculated. Of course care must be taken to make sure that the time interval between the two evaluations is appropriate and that no instruction or training is provided between evaluations.

Test–retest reliability can be computed by calculating a Pearson product-moment correlation. One of the limitations of this method is that if multiple trials are involved, these data must be reduced to one score per child for each assessment. This could be done, for example, by averaging the children's scores for three trials and then using the average as the final score for the correlation. Although this technique is commonly used and does provide a general indication of overall reliability, calculating an intraclass correlation coefficient is the most appropriate method for calculating reliability when motor performance tests involve two or more trials. The advantage of using the intraclass correlation method is that it uses all the data that have been collected and allows for the variance to be examined from three sources: students, trials, and the interaction of students by trials.

Alternate Form and Split Half

Two other methods for testing reliability are alternate form and split half. These techniques are most commonly used with written tests. For the alternate-form method, two equivalent forms of the test are created. They are both then administered to the same children, who are divided into two groups. The order for the forms is randomly assigned to each group. For example, the first group of students might take form B and then form A, and the other group form A and then form B. After the students finish the tests, a correlation is calculated between their scores on forms A and B. An advantage of this method is that it yields two tests; using alternate forms within a single class can address issues such as cheating. The downside is that twice as many good questions must be created, which requires more development time. A second technique that addresses the issue of test development time is the split-half method. In this case, a single test is administered to one group of children and then divided into two forms, typically by the odd and even items. Two scores are calculated for each child. These scores are then correlated to produce a reliability correlation. The obvious advantage of this technique is that it requires only one version of the test and one group of students.

OBJECTIVITY

Objectivity is a special type of reliability. Reliability as discussed previously focuses on the consistency of the results obtained by the same assessor across multiple administrations. This is commonly referred to as intrarater reliability. Objectivity is an indication of the reliability between two administrations of a test to the same group of children by different teachers. This is referred to as interrater reliability. Objectivity is affected by the same factors that influence reliability: administration procedures, scoring precision, and student performance variability. As a general rule, high intrarater reliability is easier to achieve than high interrater reliability. Theoretically, if the administration procedures for a test are well defined, two comparably trained physical educators should be able to review the instructions, practice their administration, and then administer the test to the same group of students and get the same results. The objectivity of the test is determined by totaling the number of agreements (i.e., items both raters gave the same score), dividing this sum by the total number of items on the test, and finally multiplying this number by 100. For example, if a motor skills test involves a total of 20 ratings, and the two teachers agree on 16 of the ratings, their objectivity is 80%:

$$(16/20) \times 100 = 80\%$$

One way to increase objectivity is to control the competency of the teachers using a given assessment tool. This can be done by creating or using a training video containing clips of a wide variety of students performing the skill being assessed. The clips are divided into two pools. One pool is used by the teachers to learn and develop their assessing skills; the other pool is used to test their degree of competency. The higher the competency level demonstrated by the teachers, the greater their measurement reliability and objectivity. Scoring of competitive gymnastics, figure skating, and diving at the Olympic level illustrates that, with extensive training, high objectivity can be achieved when measuring extremely complex motor skills performed at high speed and involving subjective judgments.

NORMS

Many commercially available assessment instruments provide norms to help teachers interpret how their students are performing compared with other students that have taken the same assessment. It is important to understand that *norms* does not mean normal. Norms are a description of how a sample of students performs on a test in relation to the children in the normative sample. The norms may be organized around any number of relevant factors. Simple norms can be organized around gender, grade, or age. In these cases, the values reported in the norm table represent the average score for the children in the normative sample reported by gender, grade, or age.

Table 4.1 shows the percentage of students demonstrating mastery of each of the seven components of a criterion-referenced instrument assessing batting. This is a gender (i.e., males) by age (i.e., ages 6-12) normative chart. The values in the table indicate the percentage of males at each age that have demonstrated mastery of each component. For example, 88% of the 8-year-old males demonstrated the correct grip and 66% of the males at age 10 were demonstrating the correct weight transfer. More sophisticated normative tables use values such as percentiles, z scores, and T scores. Before any norms are used, it is important to determine three things:

1. Are the norms appropriate?
2. Are they up to date?
3. Is enough information provided to judge?

Table 4.1   Percentage of Students Demonstrating Mastery of Batting

Component	Age 6	Age 7	Age 8	Age 9	Age 10	Age 11	Age 12
Grip	79	84	88	89	90	94	97
Side orientation	64	76	81	85	87	92	96
Bat position	67	77	84	88	90	94	98
Rotation	54	59	67	72	79	85	92
Weight transfer	47	49	52	58	66	73	81
Follow-through	44	46	49	57	61	69	78
Smooth integration	34	35	42	47	53	62	69

Note: Normative data for males.

The appropriateness of a set of norms is a function of how similar the children in the normative sample are to the children being assessed and of the decision the teacher wants to make. For example, Ms. Fong teaches elementary physical education twice a week to her second grade class, and she wants to evaluate how their performance on locomotor skills compares with others to see if her teaching is effective. She finds a set of norms for locomotor skills from another state and compares her children to these norms. Overall, her students are just below the means on the norms for all the skills. What does this mean? Is she a poor teacher? Are the children in her classes developmentally delayed? What if the norms were created using children that received physical education five times a week, taught by physical education specialists, and all students with disabilities were removed? Now how would you evaluate Ms. Fong's performance? Considering that she has several children with disabilities in her classes and 60% less instructional time (two times a week versus five times a week), the fact that her students are performing only slightly below the means of the norms might indicate that her instruction is very effective. The point is that you need to know the characteristics of the children used to create the norms so that you know what you are comparing your scores against. Clearly, the larger and more representative the sample used to create the norms, the more useful they are for comparisons.

When creating norms, the challenge is to maximize representativeness while balancing costs. For example, if you were creating norms for a new test, ideally you would like to include representative data on a variety of factors, such as school district size (above 10,000 versus below 10,000), geographic region (northeast, southeast, midwest, northwest, southwest), age (5 to 12), gender (male or female), and special education status (developmentally delayed, orthopedically impaired, sensory impaired, nondisabled), to name just a few. Let's say you want at least 30 children for each comparative norm. To control representativeness for just these five factors and to have 30 children for each norm, you would need 19,200 individuals in your sample (two school district sizes × five regions × eight ages × two genders × four special education categories × 30 children). If it costs $25 to assess each child in the normative sample, you would need a budget of $480,000 to create your norms. This example illustrates how costly it can be to develop norms based on large representative samples. As a result, many physical fitness and motor skills tests have norms that are based on smaller, less representative samples. This does not mean that these norms are useless. What it does mean is that you must understand the limitations of the norms when you use them to interpret student performance.

It is also important that norms be up to date. Because creating norms is so expensive, it is not uncommon for norms to be 15 or 20 years old. Since performance is reflective of the programs students participate in, and since the programs reflect the values and societal trends of the times, it is important to know when the norms were created.

To judge the appropriateness and timeliness of the norms for any given assessment, the physical educator must have access to the procedures used to create the norms. You might logically expect that this information would be provided with the tests, but this is not always the case. A compromise is frequently made between how much information is presented, to reduce costs and to make the test appear more user-friendly. It is not uncommon for a test to include a brief summary of the procedures and then refer the reader to another source, such as an article published in a research journal. It is important to track down this information and review it to determine the characteristics of the children used to create the norms and the administrative procedures and conditions of the norm data collection. In terms of the characteristics of the children in the norm sample, relevant factors include the size of the sample, how the children were selected, its representativeness, and its overall diversity. For example, a sample composed of students that volunteered for the assessment should be viewed with more caution than a sample that was randomly selected from all the students in a school.

A variety of issues should be considered when reviewing the procedures and conditions used to collect normative data. For example, who collected the data? Was it collected by the children's regular teacher, or did outside assessors come in and collect the data? How was motivation controlled for (i.e., what was done to elicit the children's best performance)? When were the data collected? Was it at the start or end of the school year? Had the students just completed a unit involving these skills? Can you see how issues such as these could affect performance? All these factors cannot be controlled, but they can be defined so that this information can be used by the test administrators in the interpretation of the results.

What You Need to Know ▶▶▶

Key Terms

ACE behaviors	criterion (predictive) validity	reliability
administration procedures	face (logical) validity	scoring precision
alternate form	intraclass correlation coefficient	split half
concurrent validity	norms	student performance variability
construct validity	objectivity	test–retest reliability
content validity	Pearson product-moment	validity

Key Concepts

1. You should know the five types of validity and be able to explain how each applies to assessment instruments in physical education.
2. You should know the three major factors that affect reliability of assessment instruments in physical education.

3. You should understand the relationship between validity, reliability, and objectivity. Which of these factors is most important when selecting an assessment instrument?

4. You should know the ACE behaviors and how they interact with student variability and reliability during assessment.

Review Questions

1. What is face validity, and why is this the most common type of validity reported for physical education assessment instruments?

2. What are some ways to improve the objectivity of an assessment instrument in physical education?

3. What factors should be considered when evaluating the norms provided with an assessment instrument or when you develop your own norms?

4. Explain how common threats to reliability of physical education assessment instruments can be controlled.

Selecting and Administering Tests

ollecting accurate assessment data is challenging because several factors interact with each other. Initially, you need to determine the type of decision required and what information is necessary to make that decision. Next, you need to select and competently administer a valid and reliable instrument that is designed to collect this information. Finally, you must interpret the test results to make an appropriate decision concerning the student's placement and program plan.

Although the focus of assessment is on evaluating one or more aspects of physical or motor performance, teachers must also consider the total child when conducting and interpreting assessment performance. In chapter 3, we focused on various information sources, such as school records and key personnel, that should be consulted to get to know the students before they are assessed. In addition, the ACE factors of attention, comprehension, and effort were introduced in chapter 4 as a method of focusing a teacher's attention on how children respond during the assessment. Factors relating to reliability and validity were also introduced in chapter 4.

The purpose of this chapter is to provide a set of rules that can be used to select the appropriate assessment instrument to match the decision that is needed. We also provide a basic set of rules that should guide the administration of any assessment.

Case Study 1

Mr. Simon has three children with disabilities in one of his fourth-grade physical education classes. He is about to start a new unit that focuses on the overhand throw. He decides to preassess the class so he can plan his instruction according to the needs of the class, and also determine whether this class placement is the most appropriate for the three children with disabilities. Mr. Simon reviews his test and measurement textbook and finds a simple assessment for throwing that can be administered to a group of children. The test, which involves averaging three throws for distance, has face validity for ages 4 through 12. He administers the assessment to his class and compares their scores with the norms provided with the test. The results indicate that the class overall is performing at the 53rd percentile. One of the three children with disabilities is performing above the class mean, while the other two children are among the lower-performing students in the class. Mr. Simon concludes that the assessment results clearly indicate the class needs to work on their throwing. However, having spent one class period conducting the assessment and another 2 hours interpreting the results, he is a bit perplexed about how to actually use this information to plan his instruction. He could form instructional groups based on how far the children can throw, but he realizes he does not have any information on why they are throwing so poorly. For example, is it because they do not know the correct throwing pattern? Or is it because they are weak and need to work on strength? In regard to the children with disabilities, one child appears to be in the right placement since she is throwing as well as half the other children in the class, but it seems that this may not be the best placement for the other two students.

Mr. Simon needs to make two decisions: an instructional decision regarding the overhand throw and a placement decision to determine if this class is appropriate for his students with disabilities. His problem is that he used a norm-referenced assessment that measured the outcome, or product, of throwing performance. What he needed in this situation was a criterion-referenced assessment instrument (CRI) designed to evaluate how the students were actually performing the throw. Had he collected this information, he would have known which components of the throw the children had mastered and which ones still needed work. He could have then used this information to plan his instruction. The criterion-referenced assessment information could have also been used to determine any unique needs the students with disabilities have on the throw objective and how these needs can be accommodated within the class. Teachers learn that they should use assessment to guide their decision making in physical education, but when they actually try to use it, some do not find the assessment results useful and subsequently stop assessing. The assessment process is not the problem; the problem is not knowing how to select the appropriate assessment tool to match the decision that needs to be made. Assessment is a dynamic process by which teachers make informed decisions, and it can be broken into the following six steps.

STEP 1: Identify the Type of Decision That Needs to Be Made

In chapter 2 it was explained that physical educators will be called on to make decisions in three categories: identification, placement, and instruction. In reality, the first decision to be made in the assessment process is which of these three types of decisions you are being asked to make.

Identification Decisions

Identification decisions involve determining whether a student's performance warrants special consideration. For example, children will qualify for a fitness award if they perform at the 85th percentile or above for all fitness items. Likewise, children may qualify for additional services if their performance is sufficiently lower than the established criteria for that age or grade. Identification decisions can be further divided into screening and qualification decisions.

Screening

Screening decisions tend to be less formal, employing assessment procedures that can be easily and quickly administered. The intent is to identify any person who may have a problem and then follow up on the initial screening with more formal assessments. For example, it is common practice in the upper elementary grades for physical educators to screen all children for scoliosis. If children are observed to have unequal shoulder and hip heights along with a gradual C curve in the spine, they would be referred to a specialist for a more formal evaluation (see chapter 8 for more information on posture screening).

Qualification

Qualification decisions tend to be more formal, requiring the use of standardized instruments and norms. A school, for example, may require that children perform or demonstrate deficiencies at least 2 years below their age on tests of motor ability or physical functioning in order to qualify for adapted physical education services. A teacher might first screen children in a class using a checklist similar to the example provided in figure 5.1. A child found to be significantly inadequate on one or more gross motor items would then be referred for a more formal assessment. In this case, the child could be evaluated using the Test of Gross Motor Development or a similar instrument. If the child's performance is 2 or more years behind his peers when compared with the test norms, he would qualify for adapted physical education.

Two critical elements come into play when making a qualification decision: (1) There must be established eligibility criteria and (2) the assessment instrument used must provide comparative standards such as norms. To qualify for special education, children must meet professionally established criteria as measured by two or more valid instruments. For physical education, the criteria for qualifying for services and the assessment instruments that are appropriate to use are less universally defined. This is in part due to the breadth of the content covered in physical education and the diversity of abilities exhibited by students with disabilities. For example, a 12-minute run for distance may be a valid measure of cardiorespiratory endurance for a child with a learning disability or who is deaf, but it would not be valid for a child with spastic cerebral palsy or spina bifida.

Placement Decisions

After a child has been identified and found to qualify for services, the next step is to determine the most appropriate and least restrictive environment (LRE) in which her physical education needs can be addressed. This is a two-part question. First, the student's physical education needs must be identified. Second, how these needs interface with the goals of the general physical education (GPE) curriculum must be determined.

Initial Observation and Referral Form

Child's name: _____ Evaluator: _____

School: _____ Date: _____

Use this form when first observing a child with a disability who has been referred for adapted physical education. Rate each item based on how the child compares with other children in his or her physical education class.

	Adequate	Needs improvement	Significantly inadequate	Not observed
Physical fitness				
Performs activities that require upper-body strength (e.g., push-ups, throwing, chest passes)	☐	☐	☐	☐
Performs activities that require lower-body strength (e.g., running, hopping, kicking)	☐	☐	☐	☐
Performs activities that require flexibility (e.g., stretching, bending, tumbling)	☐	☐	☐	☐
Performs activities that require endurance (e.g., mile run, games that involve endurance)	☐	☐	☐	☐
Body composition (e.g., child's weight and general appearance)	☐	☐	☐	☐
Gross motor skills				
Performs nonlocomotor skills (e.g., twisting, turning, balancing, bending)	☐	☐	☐	☐
Moves safely around environment (e.g., dodging, space awareness, directions)	☐	☐	☐	☐
Uses physical education equipment (e.g., balls, bats, scooters)	☐	☐	☐	☐
Performs locomotor skills (e.g., running, jumping, galloping, hopping, skipping)	☐	☐	☐	☐
Performs manipulative skills (e.g., throwing, catching, kicking, striking)	☐	☐	☐	☐
Performs dance skills (e.g., rhythm, patterns, creative)	☐	☐	☐	☐
Plays low-organized games (e.g., dodgeball, relays, tag, teacher-developed games)	☐	☐	☐	☐
Sports skills (e.g., throwing in softball, kicking in soccer, serving in volleyball, hitting a tennis ball)	☐	☐	☐	☐
Plays organized sports (e.g., basketball, soccer)	☐	☐	☐	☐
Transition to and from physical education				
Enters without interruption	☐	☐	☐	☐
Sits in assigned area	☐	☐	☐	☐
Stops playing with equipment when asked	☐	☐	☐	☐

(continued)

Figure 5.1   Block's initial observation and referral screening form.

Reprinted, by permission, from M.E. Block, 2000, *A teacher's guide to including students with disabilities in general physical education* (Baltimore, MD: Paul H. Brookes Publishing Co.).

	Adequate	Needs improvement	Significantly inadequate	Not observed
Lines up to leave when asked	☐	☐	☐	☐
Responding to teacher				
Remains quiet when teacher is talking	☐	☐	☐	☐
Follows directions in a timely manner during warm-up	☐	☐	☐	☐
Follows directions in a timely manner during skill focus	☐	☐	☐	☐
Follows directions in a timely manner during games	☐	☐	☐	☐
Accepts feedback from teacher	☐	☐	☐	☐
Uses positive or appropriate language	☐	☐	☐	☐
Relating to peers and equipment				
Works cooperatively with a partner when asked (e.g., shares, takes turns)	☐	☐	☐	☐
Works cooperatively as a member of a group when asked	☐	☐	☐	☐
Uses positive or appropriate comments with peers	☐	☐	☐	☐
Seeks social interactions with peers	☐	☐	☐	☐
Displays sportsmanship by avoiding conflict with others	☐	☐	☐	☐
Uses equipment appropriately	☐	☐	☐	☐
Effort and self-acceptance				
Quickly begins the activity once instructed	☐	☐	☐	☐
Continues to participate independently throughout activity	☐	☐	☐	☐
Adapts to new tasks and changes	☐	☐	☐	☐
Strives to succeed and is motivated to learn	☐	☐	☐	☐
Accepts his or her own skill whether successful or improving	☐	☐	☐	☐
Cognitive abilities				
Understands nonverbal directions	☐	☐	☐	☐
Understands verbal directions	☐	☐	☐	☐
Processes multistep cues	☐	☐	☐	☐
Attends to instructions	☐	☐	☐	☐

Comments regarding fitness or motor skills: _____

_____

Comments regarding behaviors and social or cognitive abilities: _____

_____

_____

Figure 5.1 *(continued)*

The purpose of physical education is to provide all children with the necessary physical and motor skills to participate in a variety of lifetime recreational sports activities that can develop and maintain their fitness and allow them to live healthy and productive lives. For the majority of people with mild and moderate disabilities, it is reasonable to assume that with appropriate accommodations and instructional modifications, the general physical education curriculum goals would be appropriate or would require only minor modifications. Unfortunately, this important factor is frequently overlooked when making placement decisions for children with disabilities. The problem is that the amount of time allocated for physical education is usually predetermined. That is, school personnel do not determine the child's physical education needs, calculate how much time is needed to achieve these goals, and then build that amount of instructional time into their school schedules. In most cases, children with disabilities are allocated approximately the same amount of physical education time as the other children without disabilities. Since time is fixed, this requires that curriculum adjustments be made to ensure that children with disabilities can learn and master functional lifetime leisure skills during the time allocated for physical education.

Case Study 2

Cassidy suffered a traumatic brain injury in a car accident when she was 4 years old. She is currently 9 years old and in third grade. She likes physical education but is 4-plus years behind her peers in motor skill development. Her physical education teacher reports that she can learn motor skills, but it takes her approximately three times as long to learn as the other students because of her cognitive processing problems. What will happen to Cassidy if she is placed in the general physical education curriculum with no adjustments to the objectives? Odds are that by the time Cassidy graduates, she will not have mastered any of the lifetime sports activities in the general curriculum. In reality she will probably have the fundamental motor skill levels of a fourth or fifth grader. The problem is that there is just too much content to learn and too little time. Given that Cassidy already has a marked delay and requires more time to learn, she will make little progress on the objectives taught in the general physical education program even when accommodations are made. By the time she starts to learn an objective, the unit will end and she will have to start working on a new objective. As a result, she will be exposed to a lot of content but will not master any of it. As she progresses through each successive grade, she will fall further and further behind and become less and less capable of learning the grade-level content because she lacks the prerequisite skills. In many cases, students like Cassidy eventually become frustrated with physical education and either stop trying or in some cases begin to act out.

Clearly, if instructional time for physical education is relatively fixed and children are starting with delays in their physical and motor development—and are going to learn motor skills at a slower rate because of their disabilities—some adjustment must be made in the amount of content that is targeted for them to learn. It is imperative that the content of their physical education curriculum culminate in the achievement of lifetime sports skills that they can use after graduation for recreation and for maintaining their fitness and health (Kelly & Melograno, 2004). If the general physical education curriculum includes 200 objectives that lead to the achievement of 10 lifetime sports skills, then a child with a disability who learns at half the rate of the children without disabilities should have a more delimited curriculum of 100 objectives that lead to the achievement of 5 lifetime sports activities. This delimited curriculum would then become the basis for creating the child's physical education IEP goals and instructional objectives.

This does not mean that children with disabilities cannot work on their delimited curricula in the general physical education setting. In most cases, the most appropriate placement for these students is in general physical education. The only difference is that they will work on fewer objectives for longer periods of time. The major accommodation that will need to be made is allowing them to substitute objectives. For example, when children without disabilities are working on running, hopping, skipping, and sliding, a child with a disability might work on just the run and hop.

So how do you determine the most appropriate physical education placement and what curriculum adjustments must be made so that students with disabilities can achieve their program goals? To answer these questions, the physical educator conducts a curriculum-based evaluation to assess where the student ranks in terms of the scope and sequence of goals established for the general physical education curriculum. The results are used in conjunction with the normative data collected during the identification process. Table 5.1 shows a sample scope and sequence chart for an elementary physical education program.

Is the GPE Curriculum Appropriate?

A curriculum-based evaluation involves comparing the performance of a child with a disability on the GPE curriculum objectives against the performance of the other students in the target placement. Although this may initially sound a bit overwhelming, it is actually very straightforward. For example, using the curriculum outlined in table 5.1, Ms. Sundstrom decides to place a new child with Down syndrome (Leon) in the general second-grade curriculum. She reviews the curriculum to see what objectives children in the general program would have achieved in first grade and also what objectives they are targeted to work on in the coming year. She then assesses the new child on these items using CRIs derived from the curriculum objectives. While she assesses Leon's motor skills, she also evaluates his behavior and learning attributes (e.g., ACE criteria). She then interprets the assessment results to determine how close his performance is to that of other children in light of any other assessment information that has been collected in the identification and qualification process. If Leon's performance is found to be similar to others and the nature of the disability does not preclude his ability to learn in the general class setting at a normal rate with appropriate support services, then the general curriculum will be appropriate. On the other hand, if his performance is markedly below class performance and evidence suggests that the nature of the disability will hinder learning and performance, then the scope and sequence of the physical education curriculum will need to be adjusted.

Is GPE the Appropriate Instructional Setting?

The second part of the question establishes the most appropriate and least restrictive environment in which the program can be implemented. The intent of IDEA is to educate all children with disabilities in the general education environment—to the maximum extent possible—using appropriate support services to achieve

Table 5.1 Elementary K–5 Curriculum Scope and Sequence

		K	1	2	3	4	5
Locomotor patterns	1.1 Run	★					
	1.2 Gallop	★					
	1.3 Horizontal jump	✓	✓	★			
	1.4 Vertical jump		✓	★			
	1.5 Hop (on both right foot and left foot)	✓	★				
	1.6 Slide	✓	★				
	1.7 Skip		✓	✓	★		
	1.8 Leap			✓	✓	★	
Object control	2.1 Underhand roll	★					
	2.2 Bounce and dribble		✓	★			
	2.3 Underhand throw	✓	★				
	2.4 Overhand throw		✓	✓	✓	★	
	2.5 Kick		✓	✓	★		
	2.6 Punt				✓	✓	★
	2.7 Two-hand sidearm strike (baseball)		✓	✓	★		
	2.8 Catch and field			✓	✓	✓	★
	2.9 Underhand strike (volleyball serve)			✓	★		
	2.10 Chest pass (basketball)		✓	★			
	2.11 Bounce pass (basketball)		✓	✓	★		
Physical fitness	3.1 Knowledge				✓	✓	★
	3.2 Training concepts				✓	✓	★
	3.3 Terminology			✓	✓	★	
	3.4 Leg strength		✓	★			
	3.5 Flexibility		✓	★			
	3.6 Abdominal strength		✓	✓	★		
	3.7 Endurance		✓	✓	✓	★	
	3.8 Arm and shoulder strength				✓	✓	★
	3.9 Agility			✓	✓	★	
	3.10 Speed				✓	✓	★
Social	4.1 Self-discipline (control)	✓	★				
	4.2 Cooperation	✓	★				
	4.3 Fair play	✓	✓	✓	★		
	4.4 Winning and losing	✓	✓	★			
	4.5 Respecting equipment and property	★					

		K	1	2	3	4	5
Body management	5.1 Nonlocomotor	★					
	5.2 Body awareness	★					
	5.3 Spatial awareness	★					
	5.4 Use of space		✓	★			
	5.5 Quality of movement	✓	✓	★			
	5.6 Relationship of body to other objects	✓	✓	✓	★		
	5.7 Basic dance patterns				✓	★	
	5.8 Forward roll					✓	★
	5.9 Rope jumping		✓	✓	★		
Game and sports skills	6.1 Following directions	★					
	6.2 Knowledge of safety and rules	✓	★				
	6.3 Member of team			✓	✓	★	
	6.4 Participating in games and sports	✓	✓	✓	✓	✓	★

★ indicates when the objective is to be mastered.   ✓ indicates when instruction will begin.

Reprinted, by permission, from L.E. Kelly and V.J. Melograno, 2004, *Developing the physical education curriculum: An achievement-based approach* (Champaign, IL: Human Kinetics), 74-75.

their educational goals. The key is that students must be working on and achieving their goals. If children cannot make reasonable progress on their objectives in the general setting with accommodations and support services, then alternative placements should be considered. A continuum of placements with corresponding support services and accommodations should be available, ranging from full-time adapted physical education (APE) to full inclusion in general physical education. Once an alternative placement is defined, it should not be viewed as a permanent placement; progress is reviewed yearly, with the possibility of modifying the alternative placement or moving children closer to a GPE placement when appropriate.

The curriculum-based evaluation process is also used to determine if GPE is the appropriate instructional setting. The focus for this question is whether the children can learn the targeted objectives in their programs. The issues here relate to the students' unique learning needs and the characteristics of the learning environment. Factors to consider are safety, the needs and attributes of the children both with and without disabilities, and potential secondary benefits of the placement. Safety concerns are relatively self-explanatory. Clearly, a child who does not possess the appropriate defensive reactions to protect herself from fast-moving objects should not be placed in a dangerous setting where she could be struck by such objects.

For children to optimally learn, they must be relaxed and comfortable in the learning environment. If a student with a disability cannot relax in his target placement, then it would not be an appropriate setting. For example, some children with autism may be overstimulated by the actions of others and subsequently unable to focus on their own learning objectives. Conversely, other children with disabilities may exhibit unusual or disruptive behaviors that distract and interfere with the learning environment. In cases where these behaviors cannot be managed by teacher aides and other support services, the placement would also be inappropriate. An ideal placement should afford children the opportunity for secondary benefits such as interacting socially with their peers, sharing common experiences, learning from their peers, and developing friendships. Since every child with a disability is unique and every class is unique, placement decisions are highly individualized. In all cases, every attempt should be made to address any minor placement issues with appropriate accommodations. However, when an appropriate learning environment cannot be attained with reasonable accommodations, then alternative placements should be considered.

Instructional Decisions

Once a child is placed, the last type of decision that must be addressed is instructional. These decisions involve determining what objectives are targeted for instruction, what learning and behavioral characteristics should be considered when delivering instruction, and how the children should be grouped. Instructional decisions are made almost exclusively with CRIs. Referring back to table 5.1, let's assume that children are scheduled to work on the skip and overhand throw objectives first. The teacher would conduct a preassessment activity that involves the children in an activity, game, or drill that features these objectives. She would then observe the children and assess which components of each objective they can already perform using a score sheet similar to figure 5.2. In addition, the teacher would observe and record the students' ACE (attention, comprehension, effort) behaviors as well as any other pertinent learning and behavioral information. She might note that Diana appears to be more of an auditory than a visual learner, José is self-conscious and does not perform as well as he can in front of some of his peers, and finally that Asha is totally distracted by Denise. The teacher interprets the recorded data to make a variety of instructional decisions such as what components to focus on, how to group the children, and what instructional activities to use.

Conducting instructional assessments is a relatively straightforward process. First, the physical educator needs to know what content the children are expected to learn. This information is provided in the curriculum, such as the example shown in table 5.1. Once the instructional content is targeted, the next step is identifying an assessment instrument to measure this content. Referring to table 5.1, let's assume the objective being worked on is the overhand throw. The teacher would find an assessment item to measure this objective. It is common for these assessments to be included in the curriculum materials (Kelly & Melograno, 2004). Figure 5.3 shows a sample Everyone CAN CRI for the overhand throw. Note the CRI indicates the basic administration instructions as well as the specific components that must be observed.

Although the primary focus of most instructional decisions is learning physical, motor, and cognitive objectives, it is not uncommon for children with disabilities to also have behavioral objectives. These might involve learning behaviors such as attending to a task, learning not to scream when excited, or looking at the teacher when spoken to. In all these cases, the process is the same. First, the behavior must be clearly defined in terms of what behavior is desired and in some cases what behavior is being inhibited. Next, a baseline is established that shows the

ABC School District Class Performance Score Sheet: Overhand Throw

Teacher: _____   Start date: _____   Mastery criterion: _____

Class: _____   Grade level: _____   End date: _____

Scoring rubric:
0 = not present
1 = emerging but needs work
2 = demonstrates correct pattern consistently

ACE ratings:
a = above average
b = average
c = below average

Students	Nondominant side toward target 1	T position 2	Throwing arm above shoulder 3	Weight shift 4	Ball release toward target 5	Follow-through 6	Smooth integration 7	Attention A	Comprehension C	Effort E	Comments	Evaluation values A	B	C	D	E	F

Directions: _____

Administrative considerations: _____

Reflections: _____

Figure 5.2   Sample Everyone CAN CRI score sheet for the overhand throw.
From Kelly, Wessel, Dummer, & Sampson, forthcoming.

Equipment and Space Requirements:

- Use a tennis ball (2.5-inch diameter) for skill level 1. Use a softball (12-inch circumference, official weight) with a no-sting surface for skill level 2 and skill level 3.
- Use a 4-foot square vertical target placed 2 feet off the ground (target markings may be taped to a wall).
- Throw in an outdoor field or large gymnasium at least 70 feet in length (10-foot staging area plus 60-foot throwing distance).

Skill Levels	Focal Points	
1. Demonstrate the mature overhand throw. a, b c, d e, f, g	The student demonstrates the following focal points for the mature overhand throw while throwing a tennis ball toward a target with the dominant hand (right or left) on 2 of 3 trials. a. **Side orientation,** standing with nondominant side toward target, weight evenly distributed on both feet, feet shoulder-width apart, eyes on target, ball held in dominant hand at waist level in front of body. b. **T position** with almost complete extension of the throwing arm, with trunk rotation back. c. **Throwing arm passes above shoulder,** with body rotation forward. d. **Weight shift** to throwing arm side foot during extension of throwing arm, and weight shift to foot on the opposite side of the body as throwing arm passes above shoulder. e. **Ball release toward target,** palm facing downward, knees and hips slightly flexed, trunk near vertical. f. **Arm follows through** well beyond ball release toward target. g. **Smooth integration** (not mechanical or jerky) of the previous focal points.	
2. Demonstrate the mature overhand throw for distance.	The student with a mature overhand throw (skill level 1) will throw a softball for **distance** on 2 of 3 trials.	**Throwing distances:** • Grades K-1 40 feet • Grades 2-3 50 feet • Grades 4-5 60 feet
3. Demonstrate the mature overhand throw for accuracy. 60 ft 50 ft 40 ft	The student with a mature overhand throw (skill level 1) and overhand throw for distance (skill level 2) will throw a softball for **accuracy** on 2 of 3 trials.	**Accuracy criterion:** Hit a 4 foot square vertical target placed 2 feet off the ground. **Throwing distances:** • Grades K-1 40 feet • Grades 2-3 50 feet • Grades 4-5 60 feet

Reference Data: A baseline distance of 60 feet is used in fast pitch softball.

Figure 5.3 Sample Everyone CAN CRI for the overhand throw.

From Kelly, Wessel, Dummer, & Sampson, forthcoming.

current strength, or how often the desired behavior is exhibited. A plan is then created to develop and reinforce the desired behavior and, when appropriate, to extinguish the undesired behavior. The children are then periodically observed and the frequency of behavior recorded to show their progress.

STEP 2: Understand the Unique Attributes and Needs of the Child

Now that you understand what type of decision you need to make, the next step is to understand the unique needs of the child you are assessing. (This topic is addressed in chapter 3.) You cannot select or administer an assessment instrument without knowing the needs and attributes of the child you are going to assess. For example, what information does a physical educator need to select an appropriate assessment test to measure physical fitness? Would knowing just the age and gender be sufficient? Or would it also be important to know that the child is nonverbal, has asthma, uses a wheelchair for mobility, is latex sensitive, and has anxiety attacks when under pressure? This is a relatively extreme example, but it illustrates the importance of knowing the attributes of the child being assessed before a test is selected and administered. In general, the students' needs and attributes should be considered in five areas:

1. Communication
2. Cognitive
3. Physical and motor—limitations and assistive devices
4. Social and behavioral
5. Medical

Clearly, you must be able to communicate to the child what you want her to do during the assessment as well as understand any questions she may have during the assessment. This may involve using an interpreter for a child who is deaf, if you cannot sign, or a computerized language board for a student with a neurological condition. The bottom line is you must recognize any communication limitations in order to select an appropriate test. For example, if Mr. MacNeil wants to use a shuttle run to measure agility, he would need to explain how the test is performed, that it is important that the students run as fast as they can, and that the time does not stop until they cross the finish line. Although he may be able to communicate the basic test by demonstrating the skill, it would still be necessary to communicate some information about how the test should be performed. Once the teacher knows the child's communication abilities and the nature of the test he plans to use, he can then make any appropriate accommodations (e.g., getting an interpreter) to ensure that the test can be administered appropriately.

A child's level of cognitive functioning is closely related to her ability to communicate but has greater implications regarding test selection and administration. For a child to perform adequately on a test, she must know what she should do and why she is doing it—and she must also want to do well. Many children with low cognitive abilities do not understand the concept of a test.

In these cases, if what the teacher is asking them to do does not make some functional sense to them, they probably will not comply. Others may grasp the basic task but not understand the need to perform the task quickly, accurately, or to the best of their ability. The teacher must know students' level of cognitive functioning to select appropriate test items as well as to interpret their performance on the items.

Many children have physical and motor limitations as a result of their disabilities that require special consideration when selecting tests. For example, when evaluating running ability, the physical educator may need to select a test that allows some variations, such as using a wheelchair or providing guide wires for children who are blind. For students with neurological impairments, factors such as range of motion and degree of motor control can impose limits on how fast or how intensely they can move.

Although not as obvious as cognitive and communication needs, social and behavioral issues must also be considered when selecting and administering tests. An assumption underlying most assessments is that the children want to do well on the test. In other words, there is a general social expectation that when a test is given, you should do your best. For many children with disabilities, this is not a shared social expectation. They have taken hundreds of tests and have not typically done well. As a result, their expectation may be, *Here is another test I am going to fail.* Since they do not believe they can succeed, they may underperform because they lack motivation. Other children have learning or behavioral problems that interfere with their testing ability. For example, some children may have difficulty attending to instructions, so they get incomplete information on what they are supposed to do and then perform inappropriately. It is important to know whether what you are observing and assessing is their best ability for the skill you are assessing or their best guess as to what it is they think you are assessing.

Many children with disabilities also have secondary medical conditions or take medications that can have an adverse effect on their ability to perform physical and motor skills. For example, before giving a test to measure cardiorespiratory endurance, it would be important to know if a child has a heart or respiratory condition. Other children may take medications that impose limitations on their ability to perform. For example, a child with seizures may take medication that controls his condition but has a side effect of impaired balance. Other children may need to adjust (e.g., children with diabetes) or supplement (e.g., children with asthma) their medications in preparation for certain types of tests, necessitating a thorough understanding of medical conditions and any medications.

STEP 3: Identify the Dimensions of Physical Education That Need to Be Evaluated

This step may initially seem rather odd. If you want to evaluate how well a child can catch, you would select a test that measures catching. The question becomes more complicated when you want to assess whether a child is physically educated, well skilled, or physically fit. The problem is that physical education includes a number of fundamental skill areas (e.g., locomotor skills, object control skills, body awareness, body management, posture, and fitness) as well as numerous complex motor skills, where fundamental motor skills are combined to perform team and individual sports skills. In addition, physical education also teaches a wide range of cognitive objectives, such as fitness training principles and sports rules, as well as values such as ethical play and sportsmanship. The problem is that proficiency in one area is not necessarily correlated with proficiency in another. For example, a child can be physically fit but not well skilled or well skilled but not very knowledgeable about how games and sports are played. It is important therefore to know what aspects of physical education you want to evaluate and then to pick assessment instruments that include these dimensions.

STEP 4: Select or Create an Appropriate Assessment Instrument to Match the Decision to Be Made

Most assessment instruments are selected based on very practical considerations such as how easy they are or how much time they require to administer. Although these are important issues, many other factors should also be taken into account. Table 5.2 outlines a number of questions that should be considered when selecting an assessment instrument to make different types of assessment-based decisions. The questions in the table parallel the issues addressed thus far under the first three steps of the assessment process, as well as the psychometric qualities covered in chapter 4. The common assessment-based decisions made in physical education are listed down the left side of the table, and the various factors that should be considered when selecting an assessment instrument for each decision are listed across the top of the table. To help you read the table, each factor abbreviated across the top of the table is briefly explained here.

• *Decision.* What decision needs to be made: identification, placement, or instruction?

• *Type of decision.* This column identifies the focus of the decision. For identification decisions, the focus is either on screening to identify children that may require special attention or on qualification of children who have been referred for further evaluation. For placement decisions, the subquestions focus on the child's physical education needs—based on present level of performance—and on the least restrictive physical education setting where these needs should be addressed. Although these questions are directly linked, they can require different assessments to be answered. For example, it may be appropriate to administer an individual motor ability assessment to evaluate a student's present level of performance when determining his physical education needs. But to determine whether these needs can be addressed in the general physical education setting, it may be appropriate to observe this student in a general physical education setting to evaluate how he attends, behaves, and interacts in a class setting.

• *What needs to be evaluated.* This factor parallels the previous question and identifies what aspects of physical, motor, cognitive, and social behavior need

Table 5.2   Decision Matrix for Selecting Assessment Instruments

Decision	Type	Preliminary questions					
		What needs to be evaluated	Reference standard needed	Type of administration	Type of data needed	Equipment and space	Skill to administer
Identification	Screening	General motor ability Physical fitness Locomotor skills Object control skills Body awareness Behavior Knowledge	Norms or criteria, but usually norms	Individual or group, usually group for screening	Product or process, usually product	Do you have the necessary equipment and space to administer the test?	Do you have the prerequisite skills to administer the test?
Identification	Qualification	General motor ability Physical fitness Locomotor skills Object control skills Body awareness Behavior Knowledge	Norms	Individual	May include both process and product measures but most focus on product measures	Do you have the necessary equipment and space to administer the test?	Do you have the prerequisite skills to administer the test? Should the test be given by an APE specialist?
Placement	PE goals	Present level of performance Learning rate Long-term physical and motor needs	Combination of NRI and CRI	Individual	Product and process, with more emphasis on process	Do you have the necessary equipment and space to administer the test?	Do you have the prerequisite skills to administer the test? Should the test be given by an APE specialist?
Placement	L R E	Content in the GPE curriculum Performance levels of the students in the target placements	Physical education curriculum, local norms, and performance criteria	Group	Product and process, with more emphasis on process	Normal instructional space and equipment	Do you have the prerequisite skills to administer the test?
Instructional		Where the student ranks on the content targeted for instruction in the curriculum	CRI for each objective taught in the curriculum	Individual or group, usually group	Product and process, with more emphasis on process	Normal instructional space and equipment	Do you have the prerequisite skills to administer the test?

Test selection criteria				
Validity	**Reliability**	**Objectivity**	**Norms appropriate for disability**	**Sample sources**
Is the test valid for each student's disability, age, and gender?	Is there evidence to support the test's reliability?	Is the test being administered by more than one person?	Are the norms applicable to the students being evaluated?	These tend to be commercial tests such as the New York State Posture Test. See chapters 7 and 8.
Is the test valid for each student's disability, age, and gender?	Is there evidence to support the test's reliability?	Is the test being administered by more than one person?	Are the norms applicable to the students being evaluated?	These tend to be commercial tests such as TGMD. See chapters 6 and 7.
Is the test valid for each student's disability, age, and gender?	Is there evidence to support the test's reliability?	Is the test being administered by more than one person?	Are the norms applicable to the students being evaluated?	These can be commercial or teacher-developed tests. See chapter 7.
Is the test valid for the students?	Is there evidence to support the test's reliability?	Is the test being administered by more than one person?	Local norms created on the students in the program	These can be commercial or teacher-developed tests. See chapter 6.
Is the test valid for the students?	Is there evidence to support the test's reliability?	Is the test being administered by more than one person?	Local norms can be created for when mastery is demonstrated of the criteria for each objective	These can be commercial tests such as Everyone CAN CRIs or teacher-developed tests. See this chapter.

to be evaluated to address the decision that needs to be made. Some of the challenges in physical education include the tremendous amount and range of content covered and the lack of comprehensive assessment instruments that measure all aspects of this content. As a result, it is frequently necessary to administer several different assessment instruments to get a comprehensive understanding of a child's abilities so that an appropriate decision can be made.

- *Reference standard needed.* What are the reference standards for the decision being made? If, for example, the decision is a determination of whether a student qualifies for special education services, then the assessment used must have normative standards. For other decisions, such as what aspect of an objective to focus on during instruction, the assessment must have specific performance criteria that indicate what aspects of the skill the student being assessed can and cannot perform.

- *Type of administration.* Can the assessment be administered individually, or can it be administered to a group of children? The underlying issue is time. Although it would be ideal to individually assess every student, this is not practical in many situations. As a result, screening instruments are used to evaluate large groups of students, and then individual assessments are used to make follow-up identification and placement decisions. For instructional decisions, it is most common to select instruments that can be used with entire classes. When needed, these instruments can also be individually administered.

- *Type of data needed.* This question is closely related to the reference standard discussed previously and the type of decision that needs to be made. The issue here is whether the data collected by the instrument provides information on how (i.e., the process) skills are performed or focuses on the outcome of the performance. For example, does the instrument collect information on how the child threw, such as whether she stepped with the opposite foot or followed through in the intended direction of the throw, or does it just measure how far she threw the ball?

- *Equipment and space.* This is a practical consideration. Do you have the space and equipment required to administer the assessment instrument?

- *Skill to administer.* Do you have or can you develop the skills necessary to administer the instrument? This issue is addressed in more detail in step 5 of the assessment process, learn and administer the instrument.

- *Validity.* Is the instrument valid? An instrument must be valid for a given child's disability.

- *Reliability.* Is the instrument reliable? Reliability issues can usually be addressed with training.

- *Objectivity.* Objectivity is an important consideration if two or more teachers will be administering a given instrument to the same students. How consistent are the results?

- *Norms appropriate for disability.* Are the norms appropriate for the child's disability? It is important to carefully review the information provided with the assessment instrument to make sure it is appropriate for the decision and students you plan to use it with.

- *Sample sources.* The last column provides examples or sources for finding assessment instruments to match the various types of decisions made in physical education. More detail is provided on a variety of these assessment instruments in other chapters in the book. You can also find additional information on assessment instruments in many physical education elementary and secondary methods books as well as test and measurement books.

The purpose of table 5.2 is to guide you through a series of questions that will help you select the most appropriate assessment instrument for the decision you need to make. Unfortunately, in many cases when evaluating children with disabilities, there may not be a commercially available test that meets your needs. In these situations, you will need to develop your own instruments.

STEP 5: Learn and Administer the Instrument so That Valid and Reliable Data Are Collected

A critical factor to consider in instrument selection is the training and preparation required to administer the instrument. Regardless of whether a standardized NRI or a teacher-developed CRI is being used, attention must be given to both preparation and administration of the instrument. For most NRIs, these procedures will be clearly defined in the manual and must be followed exactly in order to use the interpretative data provided. Most CRIs offer teachers a little more latitude, but certain rules must be followed to ensure the data collected are both valid and reliable. A general set of guidelines that can be applied to most assessment situations follows.

1. Review and know how to administer the instrument well enough so that you can focus your attention on the child being assessed and not on the mechanics of administering the items (e.g., reading the instructions or reviewing the performance criteria to be observed).

2. When using an instrument for the first time, plan for a few pilot tests. Practice giving the test to one of your children or a neighbor's child. These practice trials will help you internalize the procedures and will most likely identify other potential administration problems that can be addressed and prevented.

3. When possible, set up any necessary equipment in advance, and anticipate any potential problems. Be prepared with backup equipment, such as stopwatches and targets, that is critical for administering a given item.

4. When using instruments that focus on the process of a skill (e.g., throwing), identify where you need to stand (how far away and at what angle) so that you can see the components that need to be performed.

5. Choose an appropriate assessing activity or organizational format so that the students are actively engaged and you are free to move as needed to conduct the assessment.

6. Develop an efficient method to accurately record the assessment data you need to collect.

7. Remove all environmental factors that may interfere with performance, such as unnecessary equipment or audience effects.

There is no substitute for good planning and preparation when assessing. Although being aware of the child's attention, comprehension, and effort during assessing will improve the validity of the data collected, teachers must also employ common sense. Here are a few simple rules that should be followed when assessing.

1. When in doubt, do not give credit. Given the complexity and subjective nature of many of the behaviors assessed in physical education, it is not uncommon for there to be some ambiguity as to whether a student is consistently demonstrating a given motor skill or behavior pattern. Whenever there is doubt, the rule to follow is to not give the child credit for mastery of the behavior in question. If you err in this direction, the worse that can happen is that you will continue work on this behavior. If the child has actually mastered the behavior in question, the worst he can experience is success and maybe a little boredom until you reassess. On the other hand, if you err in the direction of giving credit for the behavior, you will not focus any additional instruction on this behavior. If the child has not mastered this behavior, she now will potentially fail or at a minimum practice the incorrect pattern until you reassess her and catch your error.

2. Make sure the testing conditions do not compete with or confound the performance. If you want to assess a child's qualitative throwing performance, then the assessment task should require the child to throw the ball both hard and far. Because of space and motivation considerations, it is not uncommon for teachers to use a throwing task that requires students to throw at a small target that is relatively close. If students misinterpret the task, they may decide it is more important to hit the target than to throw hard. In this case, they may modify their throwing pattern to maximize accuracy at the expense of correct form. The end result is that the teachers get an assessment of how well the students can modify their throwing pattern to do well on an accuracy task rather than an accurate assessment of their throwing pattern.

3. Make sure the children know what you are asking them to do. When using NRIs, teachers usually do not have much flexibility in how the instrument is administered. However, if while administering an instrument you observe that the students appear confused by the instructions, you should question the validity of the data you collect. With most CRIs, teachers have a little more flexibility in how the items are administered. If a child appears confused, follow up and ask the child if she understands what is being requested.

4. Be aware of any potential audience effects. Because most assessments in physical education must be administered in a public setting, there is always a threat that one or more environmental factors may negatively affect performance. If children know they are going to perform worse than other students, they may just dismiss the assessment and act as if they do not care. Unfortunately, if the students do not give their best effort, you do not get an accurate assessment of their ability. Therefore it is critical that assessments be conducted in such a fashion that children do not feel they are being "tested." One of the best ways to deal with test avoidance is to make assessment an ongoing process and to integrate it into natural activities in the class.

5. Do not teach while formally assessing. Periodically, at least at the beginning and end of units of instruction, it is important to assess children to rate them on the objectives being taught. One of the toughest things to do while formally

assessing children is to not immediately use the assessment information to give instructional feedback. Again, one of the best ways to conduct this form of assessment is to observe the children in a naturalistic setting, such as a game where they are applying the skills being assessed and can be observed without the expectation of immediate feedback.

6. Give general positive feedback. Inevitably, students know they are being evaluated in some situations, and they will naturally look to the teacher after each performance for feedback. If you say nothing, it is possible that the children will interpret this as negative feedback and try to alter their performance. In these instances, it is probably best to give a general positive statement such as "Well done."

7. Devise and use a method that allows you to record performance data as soon as possible. Probably the single greatest complaint teachers have about assessment relates to the time involved in collecting and recording assessment data. Develop innovative ways to quickly and accurately record assessment data.

8. Be prepared. All assessments require some amount of practice to administer efficiently. To be effective, teachers must internalize the components of the skills they are going to observe. If you need to refer to your checklist while assessing to review the components of a skill, you are not ready. It typically requires about an hour of practice to memorize the components of most motor skills and to see them accurately. After several hours of practice, you will begin to see the skill in terms of the components. At that point, instead of looking at the skill and mentally comparing the performance with the checklist, you will see the performance in terms of which components are performed correctly and incorrectly.

STEP 6: Interpret the Assessment Data Collected and Make an Appropriate Decision

The last step in the assessment process is interpreting the data and making a decision. An identification decision typically involves looking up raw scores or a composite score in the normative tables provided with the instrument and obtaining a percentile or age-equivalent score. The teacher then compares this value to the established eligibility criteria. If the value meets or exceeds this standard, the student would be deemed eligible. For children with disabilities, this type of decision must be made to determine if they qualify for special education services. Children are typically assessed on a number of factors such as motor skills, IQ, and adaptive behavior; they must be found to have delays greater than two standard deviations below the mean for their age and gender. Remember that test scores are only indicators that sample specific dimensions of ability. When making identification decisions, physical educators need to look at the total child in the context of the setting and the decision they are making. When the scores do not add up or are inconsistent, do not be afraid to add a little common sense to the equation.

The process for placement decisions is similar to procedures described for identification decisions. The major difference is it may be appropriate to use either an NRI or a CRI test, depending on the nature of the placement decision. In GPE, a placement decision could involve whether a new student should be placed in an intermediate or advanced tennis class. To address this question, it is necessary to know the prerequisite objectives for the intermediate and advanced classes as well as what objectives are targeted for instruction in each. The new child can then be assessed on these prerequisite and target skills and her results compared with the performance levels of the students in the intermediate and advanced classes. A decision can then be made as to which class the child would be most successful in.

For children with disabilities, a common placement decision physical educators need to make is determining the most appropriate and least restrictive physical education setting. The law requires that students be placed in the general educational setting to the maximum degree possible as long as their instructional needs can be met and they can be successful. To make this decision, you need to know what skills the children in the general physical education class already possess and what skills they are targeted to learn. You must then assess the child with the disability on these objectives to determine his present abilities. After comparing the results, you can judge whether this child's needs can be accommodated in this setting with appropriate support services. Again, it is important to interpret the assessment results in the context of the total child. Although your expertise is in the motor domain, you must be sure the placement is appropriate based on the child's cognitive, personal, and social needs as well.

Interpreting assessment data for instructional decisions has several dimensions. At the start of the unit, initial assessment data are used to determine the students' skill level on the content targeted for instruction. This information in turn guides a variety of decisions, such as the focus of instruction for the next class; how students should be grouped for instruction; and what games, drills, and activities should be planned. The data are also used to set target expectations for both the students and the teacher. Children should be informed of what they have achieved in terms of content and what they need to focus on during instruction to improve. During instruction, assessment data are used every time children are observed and feedback is given. Finally, reassessment and postassessment data are used to evaluate and make decisions regarding student progress, teacher effectiveness, the appropriateness of instructional methods, and the overall merit of the program. Although instructional assessment is presented here as a stand-alone process, it is also an integral part of all instruction. To give children instructionally relevant feedback, you must continually observe and assess. Use the assessment data to tell the children what they are doing correctly and what aspects of the skill they now need to focus on.

What You Need to Know ▶▶▶

Key Terms

criterion-referenced
    instruments
curriculum-based
    evaluation
identification decisions

instructional decisions
norm-referenced instruments
objectivity
placement decisions

qualification decisions
reliability
screening decisions
validity

Key Concepts

1. You should understand the six steps in the assessment process.

2. You should know the five areas of students' needs and attributes to be considered when selecting an assessment instrument in physical education.

3. You should understand the factors to be considered when selecting a physical education assessment instrument.

4. You should know the seven guidelines that ensure the assessment data you collect are both valid and reliable.

Review Questions

1. What is curriculum-based evaluation, and when is it used in physical education?

2. If during your assessment you have some doubt whether students have demonstrated mastery of a skill component, why is it recommended that you not give them credit?

3. Compare norm-referenced and criterion-referenced instruments in physical education in terms of the time needed to learn the instruments and administer them correctly.

4. What are the step-by-step procedures you would follow to determine the LRE placement for a new student with autism that is entering your school? Specifically, what instruments would you use and why?

Chapter 6

Assessing Motor Development and Motor Skill Performance

The focus of overall development should be on relevant information regarding placement and the determination of functional capabilities of persons with disabilities. Several sources of information contribute to identifying specific developmental landmarks, reflex movements, and voluntary movements that are used for ambulation, stability, and object control. Later these movements become patterns and are used in conjunction with other movements to accomplish specific functional tasks, or are performed on an individual basis or in a competitive format as sports activities. In this chapter, the focus is on development of movement and coordination, including tests of motor development, reflexes, motor ability, perceptual-motor skills, sports skills, and balance assessments.

Motor development tests are designed to evaluate progression of typical motor functioning on a continuum. The use of developmental norms assumes that comparing the performance of a child with disabilities against norms for typical development is appropriate, and deviations from the norm are indicative of a delay or problem in development, or are associated with a physical or cognitive disability. Developmental scores, including age and grade equivalents, compare performances across age or grade peer groups and can detect potential movement dysfunctions. These data are useful in clinical case studies, initial motor development screening, and longitudinal research on motor development. The use of a developmental approach assumes that all people progress through the same series of motor development tasks, although they may encounter landmarks at various time intervals in the developmental process.

It is important that teachers quickly determine which children qualify for their special education services. Once it has been established that a child has a significant gross motor delay, the cause of the delay should be established in order to focus on program intervention. For example, a child with a neurological condition may still encounter some primitive reflex activity that affects or disrupts movement. Likewise, lack of strength or the presence of a sensory impairment may also affect motor functioning. With the assistance of the programming team, the teacher can identify these limitations, determine what might be causing the delay, and develop a program plan to guide intervention.

Case Study 1

Mr. Kozlov was recently hired as the adapted physical education specialist for the Block County Public Schools. He was told by the county's director of special education that his adapted physical education caseload would include preschoolers with disabilities who demonstrate significant motor delays. Mr. Kozlov is concerned because there are more than 40 children with disabilities in the school system who require a special needs pre-school program. It would not be feasible for a teacher to service all 40 preschoolers plus his typical load of school-aged children with disabilities, so he needs a specific method to determine which children qualify as having significant motor delays.

Mr. Kozlov must determine if his preschoolers have a neurological or sensory deficiency, lack of motivation, or developmental disorder that may affect performance. In each context, his selection of tests may rely on the specific characteristics of each child and how to quantify a significant delay.

REFLEX TESTS

Reflexes are involuntary subcortical movement reactions exhibited after sensory stimulation such as head movement, light, touch, and sound. The primary purpose of reflexes is for infant protection and survival and to stimulate the central nervous and muscle systems (Gabbard, 2004; Payne & Isaacs, 2005). Most reflexes appear in infancy (and some even during late prenatal development), and these reflexes usually are inhibited or disappear by 6 months of age in typically developing children. For example, an infant's strong grasp reflex (i.e., grasping onto anything after stimulation to the palm of the hand) is enjoyable for a parent during the infant's first few months of life. However, by 6 months, the grasp reflex should all but disappear, allowing the child to demonstrate more voluntary grasping and releasing abilities.

Sherrill (2004) contends that of all the reflexes that affect motor behavior, only 10 principal reflexes are closely aligned with movement performance. These include the hand grasp reflex; asymmetrical tonic neck reflex; Moro reflex; symmetrical tonic neck reflex; foot grasp reflex; tonic labyrinthine reflex, supine; tonic labyrinthine reflex, prone; crossed extension reflex; extensor thrust reflex; and positive support reflex. Spinal-level reflexes, such as the crossed extension and extensor thrust, are for protection and nourishment of the infant. Brain stem reflexes, such as tonic neck, labyrinthine, and associated reactions, are tuning reflexes that affect muscle tone rather than produce specific movements. See table 6.1.

In addition, other reactions or responses appear during later infancy and early childhood. These responses include righting reactions (keeping one's head in line with the body), tilting reactions (keeping oneself from falling over when balance

Table 6.1   Reflexes

Reflex or reaction	Stimulus	Response	Persistence
Brain stem reflexes			
Asymmetrical tonic neck	Turn or laterally flex the head	Increased extension on chin side, with accompanying flexion of limbs on head side	Difficulty in rolling because of extended arm Interferes with holding the head in midline, resulting in problems with tracking and fixating on objects Evident in catching and throwing when one elbow is bent while the other extends because head position rotates or tilts to track a ball
Symmetrical tonic neck	Flex or extend the head and neck	With head flexion, flexion of arms and upper extremities, with extension of the legs Backward extension of head results in extension of arms and flexion of legs	Prevents creeping because head controls position of arms and legs Retention prohibits infants from flexing and extending legs in creeping patterns Also interferes with catching, kicking, and throwing since changes in head position affect muscle tone and reciprocation of muscle groups
Tonic labyrinthine (prone and supine)	Stimulate vestibular apparatus by tilting or changing head position	In prone position, increased flexion in the limbs; in supine position, extension occurs in limbs	Affects muscle tone and ability to move body segments independently into various positions, such as propping the body up in a support position before crawling or rolling
Positive support	Touch balls of the feet to a firm surface in an upright position	Extension of the legs to support weight in a standing position	Disruption of muscle tone needed to support weight or adduction and internal rotation of the hips, interfering with standing and locomotion
Spinal reflexes			
Grasping (palmar and plantar)	Apply pressure to palm of hand or hyperextend wrist Stroke the sole of foot	Flexion of fingers to grasp, then extension to release Toes contract around object stroking foot	In hand, causes difficulty in releasing objects, in throwing and striking, and in reception of tactile stimuli
Crossed extension	Stimulate ball of foot	Flexion followed by extension and adduction of opposite leg	Coordination of leg movements in creeping and walking impeded by stiffness and lack of reciprocal leg movement

(continued)

Table 6.1 *(continued)*

Reflex or reaction	Stimulus	Response	Persistence
Spinal reflexes *(continued)*			
Moro reflex	Change head position; drop backward in a sitting position	Extension of arms and legs, fingers spread, then flexion of arms; addition of arms across chest	Interferes with ability to sit unsupported and to perform locomotor patterns or sports skills with sudden movements (e.g., abduction of arms and legs during gymnastics interferes with balance)
Body righting	Rotate upper or lower trunk	Body segment that is not rotated follows to align body	Interferes with ability to right oneself when head is held in a lateral position
Neck righting	Turn head sideways	Body follows head in rotation	Cannot align head with neck when body is turned Impedes segmental rolling
Labyrinthine righting	Limit vision or tilt body in various directions	Head will move to maintain upright position	Unable to reorient head in proper body alignment and position Interferes with head control in movement
Optic righting	Tilt body in various directions	Head will move to maintain upright position	Unable to reorient head in proper body alignment and body posture
Parachute reactions	Lower infant forward rapidly or tilt forward to prone position	Extension and abduction of legs and arms to protect from fall	Lack of support to prevent body from falling
Tilting reaction	Displace center of gravity by tilting or moving support surface	Protective extension and muscle tone on downward side Upward side has curvature of trunk and extension of extremities	Lack of support to prevent body from falling Clumsiness and awkwardness resulting in loss of balance, muscle tone, and falling

Data from C. Gabbard, 2004, *Lifelong motor development*, 4th ed. (New York: Pearson/Benjamin Cummings); K.M. Haywood, & N. Getchell, 2005, *Life span motor development*, 4th ed. (Champaign, IL: Human Kinetics); S.B. O'Sullivan & T.J. Schmitz, 2001, *Physical rehabilitation: Assessment and treatment*, 4th ed. (Philadelphia: F.A. Davis Company).

is lost), and protective reactions (putting arms out to prevent injury during a fall). These responses, which are controlled cortically and thus reflect higher neurological development, remain throughout the life span; they provide righting or protective reactions that allow the infant to assume some movement control and coordinate various body positions, such as lifting the head and turning the body. For example, if a child is standing and is pushed forward, she might tilt her head away from the direction of the push in order to maintain balance (righting reaction). If the push is hard enough that the child feels she may fall, she may put her arms and even one leg out in an effort to maintain balance (tilting reaction). And if the push is hard enough that the child actually falls, then she will put her arms out to break the fall (protective reaction).

Reflexes that persist can be a sign of neurological problems and may ultimately prevent a child from demonstrating voluntary movement. For example, the asymmetrical tonic neck reflex (ATNR) can be stimulated by turning the infant's head to one side. The face-side extremities will extend, while extremities on the other side will flex. This reflex is common in infants up to 6 months, but the reflex is usually subtle in most normally developing infants and does not appear every time the child's head is turned to the side. On the other hand, in infants with neurological damage (such as cerebral palsy), the ATNR may be very strong when the child's head is turned, may appear every time the child is stimulated around the head, and may persist well into early childhood (and even later childhood in children with severe neurological damage). Infants with persistent ATNR will have difficulty exploring their bodies with their hands, bringing their hands to midline, and rolling over; children with persistent ATNR will have difficulty with movements that require symmetry, such as walking and using two hands together.

Similarly, equilibrium and protective responses need to appear in late childhood for normal development to occur. If these responses do not develop, such skills as sitting, standing, and walking will be delayed or may not appear at all because of the child's inability to maintain balance in response to changes in the center of gravity (O'Sullivan & Schmitz, 2001). Equilibrium, tilting, and protective responses are evaluated by equilibrium platforms or therapy balls to assess tilting reactions and the infants' adjustments to maintain balance.

Reflex assessments are not commonly performed in most schools unless it is clear that a child has persistent neurological problems such as cerebral palsy or a head injury. However, awareness of persistent reflex behaviors is imperative to understand if the reflex is detracting from a child's motor development and performance. For example, the teacher can avoid movements that initiate a reflex (such as turning the head, which stimulates the ATNR) and implement strategies (such as strengthening neck muscles) that can help the child avoid some reflex actions. For children with disabilities, the teacher should be able to identify the level of reflex functioning and then provide appropriate tasks to facilitate reflex inhibition. The adapted physical education teacher should participate in reflex testing to learn more about how reflexes are affecting a particular child and to determine if these reflexes are affecting the child's development.

Scoring of reflexes is generally subjective, using a scoring key to denote absence or changes in the movement. Scoring may range from 0 (normal) to 1 (decreased), 2 (absent), 3 (exaggerated), or 4 (sustained). Several common reflexes that may be helpful in determining potential motor behavior problems are included in table 6.1 (Gabbard, 2004; Haywood & Getchell, 2005; O'Sullivan & Schmitz, 2001).

Milani–Comparetti Neuromotor Developmental Examination

The Milani-Comparetti assessment is available in most settings to evaluate the neurological maturity of infants from birth to 24 months in two areas: spontaneous behavior and evolved responses (Milani-Comparetti & Gidoni, 1967). Spontaneous behaviors include many developmental landmarks such as head control, body control, and active movements such as standing. Infants from birth to 24 months are assessed for primitive reflexes and for righting, parachute, and tilting reactions. Scoring ranges from 1 to 5 points, with 5 indicative of typical functioning, 3 or 4 indicative of mild to moderate abnormal functioning, and 1 or 2 indicative of severe dysfunction or motor delays. Assessment is related to the months that reflexes or reactions should occur given typical development and can be used to develop a profile for children at specific ages (Gabbard, 2004). Sherrill (2004) recommends that outside a clinical setting, absence or presence of a landmark reflex or reaction should be noted using the letters *A* or *P* as appropriate. Payne and Issacs (2005) feel this assessment is suitable to monitor motor functioning during medical checkups and is useful for children with motor delays.

Fiorentino Reflex Test

Fiorentino has long been associated with reflex testing in typical and atypical development. The focus of the Fiorentino Reflex Test is directly related to understanding and analyzing factors that contribute to atypical development through the retention of primitive reflexes. This test is especially useful for persons with severe involvement and for individuals with cerebral palsy. According to Fiorentino (1981), the tester should be able to interpret a child's functional behavior in typical development and identify patterns of incoordination that interfere with typical development. A criterion-referenced plus (+) or minus (–) score indicates presence or absence of a reflex or reaction that may result in abnormal muscle tone and positive or negative motor delays that are processed in lower brain centers.

Primitive Reflex Profile

An instrument developed by Capute, Palmer, Shapiro, Wachtel, and Accardo (1984) quantifiably assesses primitive reflex behaviors (asymmetrical tonic neck, symmetrical tonic neck, and the Moro reflex). Primitive reflexes were selected because their role in the development of typical functioning makes them the most indicative of atypical development. The scale, which follows, employs a 5-point classification scoring system, not only to observe typical and atypical movement responses but also to note the strength of the reflex. To quantify the reflex, the following scores are assigned:

- 0 = absent
- 1 = small change in tone
- 2 = physically present and visible
- 3 = noticeable strength and force
- 4 = strong

MOTOR DEVELOPMENT TESTS

A major premise in motor development is that certain behaviors emerge through maturational processes and then develop through learning and practice. Problems may interfere with this process, resulting in failure to achieve appropriate developmental landmarks. For example, watching a child develop the ability to creep on his hands and knees is a visible change from the child's previous ability to simply crawl on his belly. Factors that have led to this change in motor behavior might include increased strength, postural control, and ability to coordinate the limbs for movement; understanding of his body; and awareness and desire to explore his surroundings. In terms of assessment, most motor development tests examine the visible changes, or "motor milestones," a child achieves from birth to around 6 years of age (depending on the specific test) as opposed to the processes that underlie the development of these milestones. Most motor development tests also include accompanying age norms describing when most children should achieve a particular milestone. The following is a list of typical motor behaviors found in most motor development tests, along with estimated ages when children are expected to achieve these behaviors:

Estimated age	*Motor behavior*
2 to 3 months	Lifts head from floor when placed in prone position
4 to 5 months	Reaches for and grasps rattle
5 to 6 months	Sits independently
6 to 7 months	Rolls over
7 to 8 months	Crawls on belly
9 to 10 months	Creeps on hands and knees
10 to 11 months	Stands independently for a few seconds
11 to 12 months	Takes first independent steps
1 1/2 to 2 years	Fast walk in attempt to run
2 to 2 1/2 years	Jumps so both feet are off the ground at same time
2 1/2 to 3 years	Basic gallop with one foot leading other
3 to 3 1/2 years	Catches (scoops) playground ball when ball is tossed to child
3 1/2 to 4 years	Basic hop on one foot
4 to 5 years	Throws ball overhand and hits target in two out of three trials
4 to 6 years	Basic skipping pattern

Motor development is often divided into two categories: gross motor development and fine motor development. Gross motor skills, which make up gross motor development, refer to skills controlled by large muscles or muscle groups, such as the muscles in the legs (locomotor patterns) and in the trunk and arms (object control skills). Fine motor skills, which make up fine motor development, refer to skills controlled by smaller muscles or muscle groups, such as movements with the hands (grasping and releasing, cutting with scissors, stringing beads, holding a crayon, and drawing) (Gallahue & Ozmun, 2006). Adapted and general physical educators as well as physical therapists are more concerned with gross motor development, while special education and classroom teachers as well as occupational therapists tend to be more concerned with fine motor development. Early identification and intervention are critical in order for children with disabilities to develop to their fullest potential (Bricker, 2002).

The most effective way to determine if children experience motor delays and require motor intervention programs is to screen children using a test that measures motor development and compare the results with what is typically expected during development. Such tools are known as developmental assessment tests. Developmental tests tend to be standardized, with very clear directions and criteria. These instruments also tend to be norm referenced, allowing a teacher to compare the development of the child she is testing with a sample of similar-aged children. For example, a child who is 5 years old might score at a 3-year-old's motor level on a developmental test. The teacher would know that the child has a 2-year motor delay in overall development and would clearly qualify for early intervention services.

Developmental tests tend to examine the acquisition of motor milestones such as the appearance of reflexes, sitting posture, creeping, crawling, rolling over, standing, walking, jumping, and balance (Burton & Miller, 1998). With few exceptions, test items are graded as pass or fail based on whether or not a child can accomplish a particular milestone. The pass or fail format and clear criteria (e.g., can the child stand on one foot for 3 seconds) make these tests easy to administer, but unfortunately, they do not generally examine the quality of movement patterns except for a few select items (e.g., walking up stairs alternating feet, throwing overhand versus underhand).

The study of typical development and the creation of norms for when infants and toddlers should achieve certain motor milestones form the basis of most motor development tests (Burton & Miller, 1998). In this context, the development of the central nervous system during infancy and early childhood proceeds in a normal hierarchical pattern that can be seen in the appearance of certain motor milestones. The appearance of these milestones at certain times indicates normal development, while delays in their appearance might indicate potential problems in development (Payne & Isaacs, 2005). For the physical education teacher, being able to identify potential problems that interfere with development will facilitate intervention and program planning based on individual needs. Therefore, the children in case study 1 can be assessed to identify problem areas that lead to placement decisions and an intervention plan. Several of the common tests used to assess developmental landmarks are outlined in this section.

Peabody Developmental Motor Scales 2 (PDMS–2)

The Peabody Developmental Motor Scales 2 (PDMS-2) were designed to assess fine and gross motor skills from birth to 7 years of age (Folio & Fewell, 2000). Like other global developmental tests, the PDMS-2 is standardized and norm referenced. But unlike global developmental tests, the PDMS-2 focuses solely on motor development, with gross motor and fine motor subsections. The gross motor subsection has 151 items divided into four categories: reflexes, stationary, locomotion, and object manipulation. The fine motor section, which is popular with occupational therapists, has 98 items divided into two categories: grasping and visual-motor integration (Folio & Fewell, 2000). The PDMS-2 is included in a sample write-up in appendix A.

All items on the PDMS-2 are scored on a 3-point scale. A score of 2 indicates passing at the set criteria for the test item; a score of 1 indicates the child shows a clear resemblance to the skill but cannot perform the skill to the set criteria; and a score of 0 indicates that a child cannot or will not attempt the item, or the attempt does not show the skill is even emerging (Folio & Fewell, 2000). For example, when scoring the item in which the child stands for 5 seconds on one foot with the nonstanding leg held parallel to the ground, the child would receive a 0 if he could not stand on one foot at all, or only very briefly. But if this child stood on one foot for 2 or 3 seconds with hands on hips part of the time or perhaps keeping his leg not quite parallel to the floor, then he would receive a score of 1. And finally, if the child could stand on one foot for 5 seconds using the criteria set in the item, then he would receive a score of 2. This 3-point scoring system is more sensitive than the simple 2-point pass or fail measure typically used in most developmental tests. The examiner can give credit to children whose skills might be emerging but who have not quite mastered the skills.

As noted earlier, the gross motor portion of the PDMS-2 is divided into four categories. Scores from all the categories can be combined to calculate an overall gross motor age, which can then be used to determine if the child is on age level or delayed. More important, these categories can be calculated separately, allowing a teacher to determine if a child has strengths or weaknesses in particular motor areas. For example, a child might have good locomotor and stationary skills but score poorly on object manipulation. This indicates that her motor problems revolve around eye–hand coordination or upper-body coordination problems. By identifying submotor areas where a child has problems, the teacher can create a more focused intervention program (see table 6.2 for a sample of items from the locomotor subarea).

Because this test is widely accepted in early intervention and is easy to use, we recommend its consideration for infants and toddlers with disabilities. Folio and Fewell (2000) indicate that the PDMS-2 does not include norms for children with disabilities but provides vital information that is valid and useful for identifying developmental needs. The performance of children with physical disabilities may be compromised on the PDMS-2, but the test is still recommended. The accompanying curriculum is also helpful in early movement analysis and program planning. From personal observations and use in clinical and school-based settings, the Peabody and the Brigance Inventory of Early Development are two functional tests that provide useful information on motor development.

Brigance Inventory of Early Development II (IED–II)

The Brigance IED-II (Brigance, 2004) is a criterion-referenced (curricular objectives directly related to instruction) and norm-referenced (age benchmarks) developmental test designed for children from birth to 7 years of age. The IED-II can serve as a diagnostic instrument and criterion-referenced assessment (Brigance, 2004). Note that the norm-referenced benchmarks in the Brigance do not come from a norm sample but rather are developmental milestones derived from

Table 6.2   Sample Items in the Locomotor Section of the Peabody Developmental Motor Scales 2

Item	Age in months	Item name	Highest scoring criteria (2 points)
47	21-22	Walking sideways	Walks sideways 10 ft (3 m) with same foot leading
48	21-22	Walking line	Walks with 1 foot on line for 6 ft (2 m)
49	23-24	Jumping forward	Jumps forward 4 in. (10 cm), maintaining balance
50	23-24	Jumping up	Jumps up 2 in. (5 cm) with feet together
51	23-24	Jumping down	Jumps down without assistance from 7 in. (17.5 cm)
52	23-24	Walking up stairs	Walks up 4 steps without support (1 or both feet on step is okay)
53	25-26	Walking down stairs	Walks down 4 steps without support (1 or both feet on step is okay)
54	25-26	Walking backward	Walks backward 10 ft (3 m) without heels touching toes

From M. R. Folio and R.R. Fewell, 2000, *Peabody developmental motor scales,* 2nd ed. (Austin, TX: Pro-Ed).

various developmental references. The Brigance is a global developmental test covering a broad range of areas, including the following:

- Preambulatory motor skills and behaviors
- Gross motor skills and behaviors
- Fine motor skills and behaviors
- Self-help skills
- Speech and language skills
- Social-emotional development

Scores are recorded as pass or fail for specific items. As long as the child is successful, she can proceed until the highest item is completed correctly. In addition to its use as a diagnostic tool, the Brigance can also be used as "an instructional guide with objectives stated in functional and measurable forms, as a monitoring process, as a tool for communicating individual placement, and as a resource for developing age-equivalent scores for parents/caretakers and professionals in child growth and development" (Brigance, 2004, p. xvii).

Of most interest to the adapted physical educator are the motor subsections and the social-emotional subsections on the Brigance IED-II. The two gross motor sections are (1) preambulatory motor skills and behaviors and (2) gross motor skills and behaviors. A nice feature of the Brigance IED-II is the comprehensive skill sequence presented for each developmental area. This skill sequence includes all the items on the Brigance, including milestone skills as well as other secondary items, along with the expected age when these skills appear in normally developing children. The skill sequence can easily be used to chart developmental progress as well as to estimate the developmental level of a child. This method is recommended when testing children with more significant delays and disabilities. Teachers can also choose to use the accompanying developmental record book, which focuses on primary milestones that are appropriate for most children.

In both types of assessments, the examiner reviews the list of developmental items and determines an entry level for assessment (a subjective rating of where the child ranks developmentally), then engages the child in play, encouraging him to demonstrate the behaviors on the test. The examiner circles the items the child can demonstrate and underlines the items the child cannot demonstrate. A color-coding system is suggested for tracking progress. After the first round of assessment, use a regular black lead pencil to circle items that have been mastered and a blue pencil to underline items (simply underline the item number) that will be targeted for immediate instruction. After completing the second assessment, use a blue pencil to circle all items that have been mastered during this second marking period. Then use a red pencil to underline items that are targeted for immediate instruction in the next marking period. After completing the third assessment, use a red pencil to circle all items that have been mastered during this marking period. This type of color-coded marking record allows teachers and therapists to easily note the child's level when he started the program, skills targeted for instruction after each assessment, and skills mastered between the first and second and then second and third marking periods. Since each task on the Brigance has a developmental age associated with it, it is also easier for the examiner to interpret the results of the Brigance in terms of developmental norms and whether or not the child has a developmental delay.

Denver II

The Denver II is a revision of the Denver Developmental Screening Test (DDST) to assess development in children up to 6 years (Frankenburg, Dodds, & Archer, 1990). By design, the test is simple, quick to administer, and inexpensive. It assesses development in four areas:

1. Gross motor (e.g., sitting, walking, broad jumping, throwing a ball overhand, balancing on one foot)
2. Fine motor–adaptive (e.g., stacking blocks, reaching for objects, drawing a person)
3. Language (e.g., responding to sounds, imitating speech sounds, recognizing colors, counting)
4. Personal-social (e.g., smiling responsively, feeding self, dressing)

The Denver II contains 125 items, with approximately 32 items on the gross motor scale, and proceeds in a developmental progression. Each child is tested individually and is scored as pass, fail, refusal, or no opportunity (because of parent or guardian restrictions). The norms show a range of ages by month during which a particular behavior could appear, as well as charts that reflect the age at which 25, 50, 75, and 90% of the children can achieve certain behaviors. A child is considered "delayed" on those items for which achievement does not compare with age-group peers. Children who demonstrate one or more delays on the test are considered for further evaluation.

The original version of the test was criticized for being unrepresentative because of its standardization sample and test reliability (Horvat & Kalakian, 1996). The revision of the test includes stability reliability and interrater reliability between 80 and 100% for most items. Validity of the Denver II is based on a regression analysis and standardization data of more than 2,000 subjects (Frankenburg, Dodds, Archer, Shapiro, & Bresnick, 1992). This version has overcome many of the original concerns of the DDST and is a valuable screening tool for young children with developmental delays.

Bayley Scales of Infant Development II (Bayley II)

The Bayley Scales of Infant Development II (Bayley II) is the revision of the 1969 Bayley Scales, designed to determine current developmental status and the extent of deviations from expected peer-group development. The Bayley II provides a three-part evaluation of the developmental status of infants and preschoolers at risk: mental (sensory-perceptual acuities, discrimination), motor (fine and gross), and behavior (attention and arousal, orientation and engagement, emotional regulation, motor quality). The motor scale results are expressed as a standard score (Psychomotor Development Index) measuring body control, large muscle coordination, finger manipulation, dynamic movement, dynamic praxis, postural imitation, and stereognosis.

The Bayley II was renormed on a sample of 1,700 (850 boys, 850 girls), aged 1 month to 42 months, in 1-month intervals. As a departure from the earlier stated design of assessing typical motor development, the primary use of the current Bayley Scales is with at-risk children or those who are expected to be at risk (Bayley, 1993). The instructional manual reports that information regarding validity was extrapolated from clinical samples of at-risk children who were premature, have the HIV antibody, were prenatally drug exposed, were asphyxiated at birth, are developmentally delayed, have frequent otitis media, are autistic, or have Down syndrome (Bayley, 1993).

The test manual is written clearly and provides normative data to compare performance with age-group peers, along with follow-up evaluations for the clinician. Test administration is suggested for a single session, or two sessions if needed. The scoring procedures allow the examiner to determine a child's developmental age for each domain (Bayley, 1993). Score possibilities include pass, fail, or other (omitted, refused, or reported by parent), with subsequent conversions to the Psychomotor Development Index.

In contrast to the Denver II, the Bayley II is a more expensive test requiring special equipment and stimulus materials. However, the Bayley II appears to be a welcome revision for assessing the developmental status of infants, especially children who are at risk for developmental delays. A companion to the Bayley II, the Bayley Infant Neurodevelopmental Screen (BINS), is a screening test designed to measure basic neurological functions, as well as social and cognitive processes, on a pass or fail basis. The BINS is often helpful for teachers to use as a quick screening device before administering another test of motor development.

Assessment, Evaluation, and Programming System (AEPS) for Infants and Children

The Assessment, Evaluation, and Programming System (AEPS) is an activity-based instrument that links assessment, intervention, and evaluation for children with disabilities or those at risk for developmental delays (Bricker, 2002). The updated second edition assesses and monitors six developmental areas in children from birth to 6 years of age, including the following:

- Fine motor
- Adaptive
- Gross motor
- Social communication
- Cognitive
- Social

According to the AEPS test manual (Bricker, 2002), each developmental area is subdivided into a progression of skills (including strands of general skill areas) and goals for specific skills, as well as instructional objectives that are task analyzed and designed to meet overall goals. Scoring on each item is based on 0 (does not pass), 1 (inconsistent performance), or 2 (passes consistently). Specific comments also are used in what Bricker (2002) terms qualifying notes to emphasize performance scores.

According to Bricker (2002, p. 89), the gross motor domain measures skill acquisition in the following areas:

- Moving body parts independently of each other and positioning the body in supine and prone positions to facilitate movement and locomotion
- Maintaining balance and moving in a balanced sitting position
- Maintaining balance and moving in an upright position
- Using coordinated actions while moving

The teacher selects items from each of the four strands that have specific objectives. For example, in strand A (balance and mobility), goal 1 is to run while avoiding obstacles, and goal 2 is to alternate feet while walking up and down stairs. The teacher can then score the item (0, 1, or 2) and add a qualifying note, such as "assistance provided" or "adaptation needed."

This test is highly recommended for teachers of young children—especially since the assessment is linked to activities—as well as for developing the IEP and individualized family service plan (IFSP).

FUNDAMENTAL MOTOR PATTERN TESTS

A subcategory of motor development is the development of fundamental motor patterns. Fundamental motor patterns refer to movement patterns that are necessary, or fundamental, for participation in sports. For example, soccer players need to run and kick; softball players need to throw and catch; and basketball players need to dribble, shoot, and catch. Children who do not develop mastery of these fundamental motor patterns will be unable to successfully and effectively participate in sports in middle and high school (or as adults) (Payne & Isaacs, 2005).

Fundamental motor skills are usually divided into two categories: locomotor skills and object control skills. Typical locomotor skills that are taught and mastered in elementary school include the run, gallop, jump, slide, hop, and skip. Typical object control skills include the throw, catch, two-hand sidearm strike (like a baseball strike), one-hand sidearm strike (like a forehand shot in tennis), kick, punt, soccer dribble, and basketball dribble. Although many preschool-aged children can demonstrate rudimentary patterns of these skills, it is not until elementary school (and even middle school) that most children are expected to master many of these patterns. Unlike tests of early motor development that examine whether or not a child has reached a particular motor milestone without concern for the pattern, tests of fundamental motor patterns focus on how the child performs the skill. In other words, what does the child's movement pattern, or qualitative aspects of the pattern, look like when he is throwing a ball? Tests of fundamental motor patterns are designed to identify differences in the development of various qualitative aspects of the patterns.

As children reach elementary school and early childhood (5 to 10 years), developmental tests may no longer be appropriate. Motor milestones seen in infancy and early childhood follow a fairly set developmental course, both in terms of the sequence of skills (i.e., the order in which they develop) and when these skills appear. Because of a variety of factors such as interest level, culture, socioeconomic status, youth sports participation, and gender, the development of movement patterns at the elementary age level is much more variable, both in sequence and time of appearance (Payne & Isaacs, 2005). For example, some children might acquire a fairly skilled throwing pattern by age 6 because they practice at home or compete in youth sports programs, while children with disabilities may not have the opportunities to practice or learn specific skills.

Most tests of fundamental motor patterns are criterion-referenced instruments based on observational assessment. That is, the focus of the test is to determine whether or not a child displays the prescribed pattern for a motor skill without regard to the child's age. It is clearly anticipated that younger elementary-aged children may not be developmentally ready to master some of these skills (e.g., they do not have the upper-body strength or coordination to demonstrate mastery of the overhand throw). Nevertheless, a teacher can determine how close a child is to achieving mastery of various fundamental movement patterns and gauge whether a child is delayed by comparing her performance to that of others in the school.

Case Study 2

Peter, a 7-year-old second grader, has been referred for an evaluation. The adapted physical education teacher asks him to perform various locomotor and object control skills, noting that he has mastered most of the locomotor patterns—with the exception of skipping—but has not mastered any of the object control skills. Although mastering object control skills is not necessarily typical for second-grade children, this child is not even close to mastering many of these skills. During testing, Peter does not attempt to step when throwing, and he allows the ball to hit his chest rather than try to use his hands to catch it.

In comparison to the rest of the children in his second-grade class, Peter is less advanced. The teacher can provide some extra opportunities for him to practice, or if the problem persists, recommend neurological screening, sensory screening, or placement in adapted physical education.

Tests of fundamental motor patterns tend to focus on the qualitative aspects of each skill (what the skill looks like) rather than on the outcome of the skill (how many times a child catches or hits a ball or how far a child throws a ball). When examining the qualitative aspects of a motor skill, two models tend to be followed. In the first model, various developmental levels of a particular skill are examined. This can be done by examining whole-body movement (e.g., the throwing pattern is at an initial, elementary, or mature level [Gallahue & Ozmun, 2006]) or examining the development of each component of the skill.

With the component model, the physical educator examines the various developmental levels of the arm action, trunk action, and leg action of a movement such as the overhand throw. For example, the leg component of the overhand throw could be broken into four developmental levels: no step, stepping with same-side foot (same side as throwing hand), short step with opposite foot, and long step with opposite foot (Roberton & Halverson, 1984). Each component of the throw (e.g., arm action, trunk action) is broken down into similar developmental levels. When a child is tested, the examiner notes which level the child displays for each component. This model allows an APE specialist to determine the child's current pattern and then target and determine a logical progression for the next step in instruction. For example, a child who is not stepping at all would not be taught how to take a long step when throwing. Rather, a teacher might want to focus on intermediate-level instruction of leg action for the overhand throw, such as shifting weight and taking a short step. On the downside, the level of detail in this model requires a keen eye and a fair amount of time to watch and classify developmental components of each skill.

In the second model, the overhand throw is broken down into qualitative components, but only the most skillful level (mastery) is outlined for assessment. For example, the components of a skillful basketball bounce might include the following:

- Eyes on ball
- Ball bounces slightly to side of foot (of hand that is dribbling)
- Ball is pushed with fingertips rather than slapped with palm
- Ball is pushed with motion from shoulder rather than motion from elbow
- Ball consistently bounces to belt level

With this as the target for mastery, the examiner simply watches the child's performance and marks yes if the child displays mastery of a component and no if the child does not. The advantage to this model is it provides a simpler and quicker way to qualitatively screen children's fundamental motor skills, which is particularly important when screening several children. The teacher still has the ability to clearly determine which components a child has not yet mastered and thus should be targeted for instruction.

Several models and resources are available for teachers to use as observational assessments to classify students at the initial, elementary, or mature stage of development. In addition to the previously mentioned assessments, teachers should consult *Fundamental Movement* (McClenaghan & Gallahue, 1978) and *Fundamental Motor Patterns* (Wickstrom, 1983). Each is an excellent reference that can be used to develop program plans and checklists for assessing specific motor patterns.

Test of Gross Motor Development 2 (TGMD–2)

The Test of Gross Motor Development 2 (TGMD-2) is an individually administered norm- and criterion-referenced test that measures the gross motor functioning of children 3 to 10 years of age. This is one of the few tests that examine qualitative components of fundamental motor skills that are based on a normative component. This normative component allows teachers to quickly and more accurately determine if a child has delayed fundamental motor patterns compared with other children of the same age.

The TGMD-2 contains 12 gross motor patterns frequently taught to children in preschool and elementary school. The locomotor subitems include the run, gallop, hop, leap, horizontal jump, and slide. The object control subtest measures the two-hand strike, stationary dribble, catch, kick, overhand throw, and underhand roll. Each of these motor skills has been broken down into three to five components (Ulrich, 2000). The following shows a sample of how a locomotor skill and object control skill are broken down into components on the TGMD-2:

Horizontal jump	1. Preparatory movement includes flexion of both knees, with arms extended behind the body.
	2. Extends arms forcefully forward and upward, reaching full extension above the head.
	3. Takes off and lands on both feet simultaneously.
	4. Brings arms downward during landing.
Two-hand strike	1. Dominant hand grips bat above nondominant hand.
	2. Nondominant side of body faces the tosser, feet parallel.
	3. Rotates hips and shoulders during swing.
	4. Transfers body weight to front foot.
	5. Bat contacts ball.

The examiner analyzes the fundamental motor skills on the TGMD-2 to determine if a component is present (1) or not present (0). Results are then tallied across two trials and totaled for locomotor and object control subtests. Finally, each subtest score is compared with a normative sample for analysis (Ulrich, 2000). Results can be presented in two easy ways for parents and teachers to understand. The first is to present a percentile ranking comparing a child's score with other children of the same age. For example, 8-year-old Chandra scores 32 on the locomotor portion of the TGMD-2. This puts her at the 5th percentile, which means 95% of the children Chandra's age would be expected to perform better than she does on locomotor development. Such a low percentile ranking would most likely qualify her for adapted physical education. Another way to present results is to calculate a developmental motor age, or age equivalent. A child who scores 32 on the locomotor portion of the TGMD-2 would have an age equivalent of 5 years, 3 months. This means that Chandra has a delay of more than 2 years and thus would likely qualify for APE services.

The TGMD-2 is straightforward and easy to administer. This instrument is helpful in identifying areas of motor weakness and allows the APE specialist to translate the test results to IEP goals as well as specific targets for instruction. For these reasons, the TGMD-2 is one of the most popular motor tests used by adapted physical educators and one that we highly recommend. (See appendix B for a sample write-up using the TGMD-2.)

I CAN

The I CAN program is not a test but a curriculum with a built-in assessment system (Kelly & Wessel, 1990). I CAN is a task-analyzed physical education system that is a criterion-referenced measure of the current level of performance. The I CAN curriculum offers a set of diagnostic-prescriptive teaching resource materials with a curriculum structure designed for use with primary school children. It provides a system for training teachers in planning, assessing, prescribing, teaching, and evaluating student progress in physical education. The program is individualized and flexible enough for a variety of settings. The instrument facilitates communication with parents and provides a management tool for teachers. I CAN addresses activities in the following skill areas:

- *Primary skills:* fundamental skills, body management, health and fitness, aquatics
- *Secondary skills:* backyard and neighborhood activities, team sports, outdoor activities, dance, individual sports
- *Preschool skills:* locomotor skills, object control skills, play equipment skills, body control skills, play situation skills
- *Associated skills:* self-concept, social skills

Scores on specific motor skill objectives are marked on a performance score sheet, which is also used to score progress on objectives. Skills are assessed in levels performed with assistance; levels performed without assistance; movement patterns; and distance, speed, or accuracy.

Advantages of I CAN and its criterion-referenced assessment are relevance and ability to track continuous progress. Disadvantages include lack of comparative test data (percentiles), lack of reliability and validity information, time required to assess each objective, and relatively high cost. It should also be noted that

I CAN is based on task analyses of mature patterns of movement, so beginning or entry-level components of the pattern may not be addressed. However, I CAN assessment is relevant to instructional and program planning for most motor and fitness skills of young children.

The I CAN preschool and primary skills assessment materials are most useful for elementary physical education teachers and for physical education teachers of children with mild to severe disabilities. The leisure and recreation assessment materials are most useful with secondary school students and adults with disabilities.

Currently the I CAN materials are being revised and integrated with the Achievement Based Curriculum model to form Everyone CAN. Everyone CAN will provide assessment items in the areas of locomotor skills, object control, body awareness, body control, health and fitness, rhythm and dance, and learning and social skills. These materials will include assessment items for each objective, with accommodations for children with disabilities.

MOTOR ABILITY TESTS

When testing children with disabilities to determine if they qualify for services, motor abilities should be considered. Motor abilities are general capacities or characteristics that are related to the ability to perform motor skills such as running, jumping, throwing, or catching. These capacities or traits are assumed to be fairly stable and not easily changed with short amounts of practice or experience. In other words, each child possesses a certain level of balance and speed and coordination that is difficult to change. In addition, these motor abilities directly relate to a child's ability to perform locomotor and object control skills. For example, a child needs a certain level of dynamic balance (a motor ability) to successfully hop and skip (motor skills). Similarly, a child needs a certain amount of eye–hand coordination to be able to catch.

Motor ability assessments tend to include items not commonly seen or practiced by children, such as stringing beads (manual dexterity), jumping while clapping the hands (general coordination), catching a tennis ball with one hand (eye–hand coordination), and standing on a balance beam (static balance). Unlike motor milestones and fundamental motor skills, tests of motor abilities provide a glimpse into why a child might be struggling with motor skill development. For example, Ricardo does not step when throwing, striking, or receiving a ball. Although it is clear that he has not mastered these fundamental skills, why he is missing these particular components is left to speculation. With a test of motor ability, a subtest of balance might indicate that he has trouble with both static and dynamic balance. Now by examining the missing qualitative components of throwing, catching, and striking along with the information that Ricardo has some underlying balance problems, the adapted physical education teacher can make a stronger case that the child's balance problems are why he is unable to step when performing these fundamental motor patterns.

Motor abilities include balance, postural control, agility, bilateral coordination (using two hands together), eye–hand and eye–foot coordination, and dexterity (fine motor skills), as well as specific types of strength and flexibility that are needed for successful motor skill performance (Horvat, Eichstaedt, Kalakian, & Croce, 2003). Each of these motor abilities is tested with relatively novel tests. For example, in the Bruininks-Oseretsky Test of Motor Proficiency (Bruininks &

Bruininks, 2005), eye–hand coordination and speed are measured by having the child sort cards that feature either a blue circle or red square. The challenge for the child is to sort as many cards as possible, correctly, in 15 seconds or less. A child who scores well on such a test item is assumed to have good eye–hand coordination and speed, which in turn suggests she should perform well in skills requiring that type of motor ability, such as returning a serve in tennis or hitting a pitched ball in softball.

One of the strengths of motor ability tests is that they tend to be highly standardized, with clear administrative directions that increase reliability and are easy for an examiner to follow. Another strength is that they are usually norm referenced, allowing comparison with children of similar ages. As noted earlier, norm comparisons help the teacher quickly determine if a child is performing at her developmental age level or is delayed in comparison to her peers. In addition, results such as percentile rank or developmental motor age are easily communicated to parents and other teachers.

Bruininks–Oseretsky Test of Motor Proficiency 2 (BOT–2)

Of the various motor ability tests, the Bruininks-Oseretsky Test of Motor Proficiency (BOT) was one of the most widely used in adapted physical education. The current version, the BOT-2, is an individually administered norm-referenced test that assesses the motor functioning of children and adults from 4 to 21 years of age. The complete battery for the new version has 53 items divided into eight subtests: fine motor precision, fine motor integration, manual dexterity, upper-limb coordination, bilateral coordination, balance, running speed and agility, and strength. The long form takes about 60 minutes to administer and generates either a battery composite score or a composite score for one of the four motor areas (fine motor control, manual coordination, body coordination, and strength and agility). The short form of the BOT-2 consists of 14 items, with at least 1 item taken from each of the eight subtests. The short form is often used to quickly screen a child to see if further testing is required. It takes about 15 to 20 minutes to administer and also yields a composite score. Scoring varies from item to item, including drawing a number of objects, number of repetitions, or time required to complete a task.

After tallying the raw scores on the BOT-2, teachers can analyze the results in several different ways. The easiest way is to convert the raw data to points for percentile rankings and age equivalents. Norm tables are provided to enable the examiner to locate percentile rankings and age equivalents for the total test, battery composite, or motor composite. Norms are also available separately for the short form composite score, as well as each test item. This allows the examiner to determine if a child has deficits (or strengths) in a particular motor area. In addition, the BOT-2 provides percentile rankings and age equivalents for each subtest in the motor areas. For example, the teacher would be able to determine if a child is on age level or significantly behind her peers on each of the four motor composites, allowing the teacher to pinpoint delays and instructional needs.

The BOT-2 was standardized on a representative sample of 1,520 individuals from 4 to 21 years of age. The original version was one of the first motor tests to be developed from stringent standardization procedures. Test–retest reliability coefficients for the long form and the short form are generally high, but need to be replicated. Validity data presented in the test manual are considered to be measures of content and construct validity. These results support the use of the test to screen children for motor difficulties. However, the test does contain scores that are compared to the normative sample for developmental coordination disorder (ages 4-15, n = 50), mild-moderate mental retardation (ages 5-12, n = 66), and autism/Asperger's Disorder (ages 4-20, n = 45). Our opinion is that the BOT-2 is an appropriate assessment of motor ability, but further study is needed to determine whether the revisions are appropriate for individuals with disabilities.

In addition, the motor skills inventory (MSI) and the accompanying motor development curriculum for children developed by Werder and Bruininks (1988) can be used to give a criterion-based assessment on a pass (+) or fail (−) basis. Werder and Bruininks indicate that the BOT can be administered at the beginning and end of a program, with the MSI administered more frequently throughout the year for periodic assessments of each skill to document progress. (See appendix C for a sample of the Bruininks-Oseretsky Test of Motor Proficiency 2.)

Movement Assessment Battery for Children (MABC)

The Movement Assessment Battery for Children (Movement ABC, or MABC) is a revised version of the Test of Motor Impairment (TOMI), which was designed to measure motor impairment in children from the ages of 4 to 12. The assessment has two parts: an individually administered test requiring the child to perform a series of motor tasks and a checklist designed to be administered by a parent or teacher who is familiar with the child's functioning (Henderson & Sugden, 1992). Groupings are categorized by the following age bands:

Age band 1	4 to 6 years
Age band 2	7 to 8 years
Age band 3	9 to 10 years
Age band 4	11 to 12 years

According to Henderson and Sugden (1992), Movement ABC is a comprehensive assessment that yields normative and qualitative measurements of manual dexterity, ball skills, and balance (static and dynamic). Major categories include manual dexterity items such as threading nuts on bolts, shifting pegs by rows, turning pegs, making cutouts, and other fine motor items; ball skills including throwing beanbags and balls, catching a bounced ball, catching off a wall with one hand, and hitting a target; and static and dynamic balance items such as using balance boards, beam walking, jumping over a cord, and clapping. Henderson and Sugden indicate that task requirements in each level are identical but vary slightly with each age band. In addition, for each age band a qualitative observation is available to note variables that relate to the child's behavior during testing, such as concentration, confidence, posture, and control.

Items are scored at the age level of the child based on, for example, the number of seconds to complete a trial or the number of catches executed out of 10 attempts. If a child does not start a task, the score is recorded as a failed attempt (F), inappropriate for the child (I), or a refusal to attempt a task (R). A shorter version (the Movement ABC Checklist) provides an opportunity to screen and monitor children on a daily basis; it includes 48 questions in four sections, with responses from 0 (very well) to 3 (not close).

The following sections detail movement over what Henderson and Sugden (1992, p. 25) refer to as more complex interactions:

Section 1   The child is stationary and the environment is stable.

Section 2   The child is moving and the environment is stable.

Section 3   The child is stationary and the environment is changing.

Section 4   The child is moving and the environment is changing.

Section 5   Behaviors related to physical activity.

Section 5 of the checklist provides behavioral information that may influence performance and movement competence on sections 1 to 4 (Henderson & Sugden, 1992). For example, section 5 is used to interpret or consider if a behavior or environment may contribute to an inappropriate response.

The first four sections are then scored to determine if children are at risk (15% of the population) or have definite movement problems (5% of the population). Behavior factors from section 5 are ranked high, medium, or low as contributing factors to the child's performance.

According to Henderson and Sugden, once the checklist is used to validate movement competence in a one-on-one setting, the performance test will provide a more detailed diagnostic procedure and aid in long-term planning. Croce, Horvat, and McCarthy (2001) administered this test to 106 children and recommend the instrument as a valid assessment of motor behavior. They believe the MABC has two distinguishing components that appeal to practitioners. One is the checklist that helps in the assessment and management of motor problems in an educational setting. The other is that the MABC is comprehensive for identifying motor impairments in children and links test results to individual needs (Croce et al., 2001). In addition, the MABC is particularly popular among clinicians and therapists for identifying children with developmental coordination disorder (Clark, Smiley-Oyen, & Whitall, 2004). This revision of the Test of Motor Impairment (TOMI) provides a promising screening and diagnostic assessment procedure that can be used to compare children at various ages on motor skill performance, identify potential movement problems, and provide accurate information for program planning.

PERCEPTUAL–MOTOR TESTS

Similar to motor abilities, perceptual-motor abilities are traits—in this case, specifically sensory and perceptual traits—that underlie the ability to perform various motor skills. Being able to accurately receive information (sensation) and then accurately interpret this information (perception) is critical for virtually all movement. There are six different perceptual modalities: visual (sight), auditory (hearing), kinesthetic (body awareness), tactual (touch), olfactory (smell), and gustatory (taste). Of these, visual and kinesthetic perception are most critical to physical educators and therapists because these two areas are most directly related to successful motor skill performance (Gabbard, 2004).

Visual perception has several subareas, including perceptual constancy, spatial orientation, figure-and-ground perception, depth perception, field of vision, perception of movement, and visual-motor coordination. Kinesthetic perception refers to the ability to sense, or to be aware of, movement and body position. Unlike the visual system, which receives information from the environment, the kinesthetic system receives information from within the body through sensory receptors in the muscles, tendons, and joints as well as through the vestibular system (balance system) located in the inner ear (Gabbard, 2004; Payne & Isaacs,

2005). Perceptual-motor tests are designed to evaluate the normal development of the visual and kinesthetic perceptual systems and to determine if a child has a significant deficit in one or more subareas within these systems.

Case Study 3

Kala, an 8-year-old second grader, sees her partner about 10 yards (10 meters) away from her. She sees that her partner is getting ready to toss a yarn ball, about the size of a tennis ball, to her. She also sees that her partner is winding up to throw the yarn ball overhand. What is occurring that will help Kala execute the appropriate movement? At this point, Kala is sensing what is happening, or basically taking in information through her visual senses. She prepares herself to receive the ball by getting her hands ready and looking at the ball in her partner's hand. When the ball is thrown, the girl quickly perceives if it is tossed high or low as well as to the right or left. She also perceives the speed and trajectory of the ball. Then she compares what she sees with her own abilities to catch. Kala quickly realizes that the ball is tossed high and to the right, so she adjusts by moving her body and her hands to the right. She continues to track the trajectory and speed of the ball, making slight adjustments to her hands. All that has happened is the interpretation of the visual information she has and is receiving. When the ball arrives, she senses it touching her hands, and she perceives that she needs to quickly grasp the ball to successfully make the catch.

Receiving, perceiving, and then acting on information from the environment takes a split second in real time. But being able to accurately perceive information from the environment (ball coming toward you) and then select a movement to match what is happening in the environment (where to move to catch the ball) is critical for a child to perform motor skills successfully. In our case study Kala is doing all the right things in trying to catch the ball. For children who are unable to process sensory information and select the appropriate movement, a specific test of perceptual-motor functioning should be used.

Children who have difficulty receiving information, making sense of the information they receive, or forming a movement to match the information from the environment ultimately will demonstrate movement problems. Several tests assess perceptual-motor abilities and development. Many of these tests are used in laboratory and clinical settings and are often difficult to generalize to a school setting for developing program plans. The Purdue Perceptual-Motor Survey, the Developmental Test of Visual Perception 2, and the Sherrill Perceptual-Motor Screening Checklist are perceptual-motor tests that are useful for teachers.

Purdue Perceptual–Motor Survey (PPMS)

One of the first and most popular perceptual-motor tests is the Purdue Perceptual-Motor Survey (PPMS). The PPMS was developed at a time when perceptual-motor development was linked to academic performance; it was constructed to determine if a child who has academic problems might have related perceptual-motor deficits. Today, the test is used to quickly screen children to determine if motor skill deficits might be related to some type of underlying perceptual problem. However, Roach and Kephart caution that the survey is "not designed for diagnosis . . . but rather to allow the clinician to observe perceptual motor behavior in a series of behavioral performances" (1966, p. 11). If results of the

PPMS indicate perceptual-motor problems, the clinician should refer the child for more in-depth testing.

The PPMS was designed to evaluate children aged 6 through 10 years. The survey contains 22 items divided into five categories: balance and posture, body image and differentiation, perceptual-motor match, ocular control, and form perception. Each item is presented to the child and then scored on a criterion-referenced scale from 1 (completely unsuccessful) to 4 (meets highest level of criteria), with scores of 2 and 3 indicating that the child met part of the criteria. For example, one of the balance items on the PPMS is walking forward, sideways, and backward on a balance beam. The 4-point scoring system for walking forward follows:

4 The child walks easily and maintains balance throughout

3 The child has occasional difficulty but is able to regain balance each time

2 The child steps off the beam more than twice or pauses frequently

1 The child cannot perform or more than 25% of his performance is out of balance

The PPMS was validated in the early 1960s on 200 children. Although test–retest reliability results were high (95%), the limited number of subjects in the sample as well as the limited standardization procedures make the true reliability of this test a bit suspect. In terms of validity, the PPMS—along with other tests of its time—has been shown to not be valid in terms of identifying children with learning disabilities. However, the first two sections of the test (balance and body image) do provide a fair indication of which children have problems in these perceptual-motor areas and who should be referred for further testing by an occupational therapist or other specialist.

Developmental Test of Visual Perception 2 (DTVP–2)

The Developmental Test of Visual Perception 2 (DTVP-2) is a revision of Frostig's original Developmental Test of Visual Perception. Based on updated theories of perceptual development, the test is designed to measure visual perception and visual-motor integration skills in children aged 4 to 10 years (Hamill, Pearson, & Voress, 1993). The DTVP-2 includes the following eight subtests: eye–hand coordination, figure and ground, copying, visual closure, spatial relations, visual-motor speed, position in space, and form constancy. The entire test takes approximately 35 minutes to administer. Norm tables included in the examiner's manual allow raw scores on each subtest to be converted to age equivalents and percentile rankings. Composite scores for general visual perception, motor-reduced visual perception, and visual-motor integration also provide age-equivalent and percentile scores. These norms were created when the DTVP-2 was standardized on 1,972 children from 12 states, with a fair representation of gender, geographic region, ethnicity, race, and urban or rural residence.

One of the strengths of the DTVP-2 is its strong reliability and validity. Internal reliabilities and test–retest reliabilities exceed 80% for all ages. Criterion and construct validity are supported through correlation studies with similar tests. Testing also shows that children who were previously identified as having perceptual difficulties do poorly on the DTVP-2 (Hamill et al., 1993). This is one of the few perceptual-motor tests on the market with strong reliability and validity as well as a large enough sample to create valid norm tables.

Sherrill Perceptual–Motor Screening Checklist

Teacher-developed perceptual-motor tests are probably more popular than standardized tests. There really are no current standardized perceptual-motor tests on the market that are appropriate for adapted physical education teachers. However, testing some of the basic foundations of perceptual-motor abilities does make sense if teachers want to gain a better understanding of why a child might be having problems with motor skill performance. As was the case with the PPMS, children who score poorly on these teacher-developed screening tests should be referred to specialists for more detailed testing and perhaps diagnosis of specific problems, such as a visual impairment or vestibular system dysfunction.

Sherrill (2004) created a simple-to-administer perceptual-motor screening checklist that can quickly indicate to the APE specialist that a child is having perceptual-motor problems. The criterion-referenced checklist contains 46 items that are scored "present" or "not present." Sherrill recommends that a child who has 10 items or more scored as "present" be referred for a more comprehensive examination.

Other Perceptual Components

Other perceptual components can also be assessed to determine various problems encountered by children. Many are available in perceptual-motor tests, while others may be specific to deficiencies required for developing and initiating a program plan. Most can be used in a checklist to note the presence or absence of the component.

- *Spatial relations:* the ability to perceive the relationship of an object in space to another object or to the person. Crossing the midline is a spatial relations phenomenon, as is putting movements in the right order (e.g., positioning the arms, legs, and trunk in relation to executing a movement). Test questions may involve standing next to the teacher or leader, moving to the other side of the gymnasium or playground, crossing the midline using a bat that can be grasped with two hands, or throwing a ball or skipping.

- *Form constancy:* the ability to detect differences in form and shape, such as between a football and basketball, or differences in contrast (i.e., identifying the object if it is placed in various positions such as upside down, left, or right). Tactile, visual, and verbal information should be used to initiate movements.

- *Position in space:* the ability to perceive laterality or directionality when objects are placed in different positions in relation to the child (e.g., balls or other objects in various locations). Fitness or motor assessments may require lifting the arms above the head or the foot from a balance beam.

- *Depth perception:* the ability to judge distance when climbing stairs, overshooting or undershooting while reaching for an object, or misjudging a step or curb. Difficulties may require compensation techniques or the use of other sensory modalities to provide correct information. Vertical disorientation may also affect motor performance, especially in posture and gait, since everything seems tilted or distorted. Movement through the environment may be affected if the person does not compensate.

- *Agnosia:* the inability to recognize familiar objects in one modality while recognizing the object through another modality. Modalities may be intact yet not functioning because of interruption of the transmission of sensory input. Common agnosias include visual, auditory, or tactile. Assessments can be implemented by identifying objects, such as a basketball; by touching or bouncing the ball; or in the case of auditory agnosia, by identifying sounds with the eyes closed.

- *Apraxia:* the inability to perform purposeful movements, although functional strength, attention, and coordination may be appropriate. Generally, apraxia is the result of dominant-hemisphere lesions and may be associated with language difficulties or aphasia. The corresponding dysfunction in the motor domain disrupts skilled movements and motor planning required for movement execution. Initiation of postures and limb movements are common techniques in the assessment of apraxia.

- *Body schema:* the awareness of body parts and their functions. Parietal and temporal lobe dysfunctions may interfere with performing appropriate movement sequences on one side or from the opposite side. Initiation of movement sequences should be utilized, as well as statements concerning body awareness (e.g., placing hands above the head or below the waist). Right–left discrimination difficulties may also be evident if the person cannot execute movements when given commands for a specific direction. For example, the child may be asked to point to specific body parts (e.g., touch your left ear, right foot) or to identify body parts from a visual model (e.g., poster) of a person.

SPORTS SKILLS TESTS

Sports skills are simply those skills required in specific sports. Most sports require some object control skills (e.g., throwing and catching) and locomotor skills (e.g., running and sliding). For example, to be successful in football, a player needs to be able to throw and catch (and in some cases, kick and punt) as well as run, slide, or gallop (when backing up to play defense to cover a receiver) and jump (to catch or knock down a high ball). Sports skills are specific to each sport, although many sports share some similar skills. Catching, for example, is common to basketball, baseball, and lacrosse. However, a basketball player catches a ball with two hands, a baseball player catches a ball with a glove, and a lacrosse player catches a ball with a lacrosse stick. Skill assessment should therefore be specific to the sport a child is playing or may play in the future.

As children reach middle school and beyond, the focus of physical education and recreation turns to individual and team sports and physical fitness. (Physical fitness testing is covered in chapter 7.) Sports skills testing becomes the most appropriate form of testing for middle- and high-school-aged youngsters. This type of testing can have multiple purposes. First, a child with suspected motor problems could be compared with peers in his class or school on various sports skills to determine if he is delayed. For example, Ms. Beals could test a child on the basic skills needed to play sports that are popular in a particular community—say volleyball, basketball, and soccer. She could test all the children in each grade on skills within these sports to create a norm sample. Then she could compare how well the targeted child did in relation to his peers on these sports skills. Ms. Beals might find that 90% of children in ninth grade can demonstrate the basic skills in each of the selected sports. However, the targeted child has mastered only 20% of the sports skills tested. This might be enough of a delay to indicate that he qualifies for adapted physical education (see appendix D).

Another use of skill testing is determining which sports skills a child with disabilities has interest in learning and has the potential to learn. In other words, a child who has already qualified for APE services could be tested on skills in several different individual and team sports to gauge the child's abilities and interest in particular sports. Results might indicate that a high schooler with Down syndrome has some well-developed basketball skills and seems to enjoy the sport. Goals could then be created that might eventually allow this student to play in a community basketball league, a special basketball program such as Special Olympics, or even just in the driveway of his group home when he comes home from work.

Finally, sports skills testing can be used to guide the development of IEP objectives and lesson plans. For the older individual in the previous example, the APE specialist could create and administer a qualitative basketball skills test to determine exactly what skill components this child can perform well and what components need to be targeted for instruction. For example, the qualitative breakdown of shooting that follows indicates that the target of instruction for this child should be coordinating his shooting action and his follow-through.

Shooting	Yes	Eyes on basket, feet shoulder-width apart, knees flexed
	Yes	Marked flexion of knees before shooting
	Yes	Shooting hand under ball with fingers apart; ball held slightly off center of forehead, shooting-hand side; elbow directly under ball, pointed down; nondominant hand on side of ball
	No	Coordinated extension of knees, hips, and ankles while flexing wrist and fingers to guide ball on release
	No	Follow-through with the shooting hand remaining briefly in the release position toward basket

Special Olympics Sports Skills Assessment

Special Olympics provides guides that contain sports skills tests for each sport they offer. These criterion-referenced tests break down skills into progressions of competency rather than into component parts, as the TGMD or other qualitative tests do. In addition, there are two levels for each sports skills test: level I for beginners and level II for athletes with higher skill levels. A nice feature of the Special Olympics skills assessments is the inclusion of a knowledge component (understanding of the rules) and a social component (participation). Although these components are basic, they do indicate how much a child understands the game and how to play it.

Each item on the test is graded as a pass, or successful (score of 1), or fail, or unsuccessful (score of 0). A child who successfully performs at least 30 items on the level I test is then given the more advanced level II test. A scoring mechanism allows the coach or examiner to tally the scores from each item of the test to get a total score. This total score can be used to group athletes and to chart progress.

Teacher–Developed Sports Skills Assessment

It is often easier and more realistic for the adapted physical education teacher to create his or her own sports skills checklist that breaks down various sports skills into components. This could be done independently or with the help and cooperation of other teachers in the school district. By working together, adapted physical education teachers can ensure that the test is valid and useful for all teachers in the district. In addition, many teachers are also coaches who have expertise in the sports and games. Skills can be broken into four or five components or into even more detail. Figure 6.1 provides an example of a volleyball skills test that was created by the physical education staff of a school district.

Volleyball Skills Test

Underhand Serve

1. Preparatory position: face net, feet shoulder-width apart; 45° forward trunk lean; hold ball in nondominant hand, with arm extended across body at waist height in front of serving arm.
2. Hold serving arm straight; pendular swing back at least 45° to initiate serve; then bring serving arm forward with pendular arm motion.
3. Stride forward with opposite foot in concert with forward motion of striking arm.
4. Heel of striking hand strikes center of ball held at or below waist height in line with back foot and in front of serving foot.

Overhead Pass

1. Preparatory position: face oncoming ball, feet (set) staggered shoulder-width apart, knees slightly bent, arms and hands hanging by knees; eyes are on ball.
2. Move to get under ball, with head tilted back, legs flexed; move hands to just above forehead.
3. Hand position: palms out, fingers apart and slightly bent.
4. Upon contact, keep head in tilted position, eyes focused on ball; hyperextend wrists and flex fingers to form a diamond or triangle to absorb force of the ball.
5. Extend knees and arms upward on follow-through.
6. Pass ball to above net height.

Forearm Pass

1. Ready position: face ball, feet shoulder-width apart, knees slightly bent; arms hang below waist and extend in front of body, palms facing up.
2. Preparatory hand position: one hand placed in the other hand, with thumb of lower hand placed across fingers of upper hand, forearms together.
3. Eyes are on ball.
4. Move to meet ball by transferring weight forward, arms together, knees bent.
5. Contact ball with flat side of forearms.
6. Upon contact, extend knees to raise the arms upward.
7. Complete pass standing straight up, arms parallel to floor; hands stay together throughout the entire motion.
8. Pass ball to a height of at least 8 ft (2.5 m) to stationary teammate.

Figure 6.1 Checklist showing skills broken down into 4 simple components (underhand serve) and into more detailed components (6 for the overhead pass, 8 for the forearm pass).

From Albemarle County Public Schools, 1995, *Albemarle County Middle School physical education curriculum.*

A sports skills test can also be created in the form of a rubric that contains specific criteria or standards to evaluate performance and progress, providing the teacher or therapist with detailed guidelines for making scoring decisions (Block, Lieberman, & Connor-Kuntz, 1998). Rubrics are part of the authentic assessment model, which involves measuring performance in real-world settings on functional skills that a child needs in order to be successful in physical education, recreation, and community sports (Block et al., 1998). For example, Ms. Anderson wants to assess 12-year-old John's present level of baseball skills so she can better prepare him to play on a Challenger Baseball team in the community. Instead of using a standardized test such as the Bruininks-Oseretsky Test or even the Test of Gross Motor Development, she can create a simple rubric for baseball. The rubric can include important skills such as running the bases, fielding (see figure 6.2 for an example), hitting a ball off a tee, and throwing to a teammate. Ms. Anderson can create the rubric in such a way that John's present level as well as progress toward higher-level skills can be recorded.

Rubric for Fielding a Ground Ball

Little Leaguer

- Does not react to ball, even with verbal cues
- Pays attention to batter 25% of the time or less, even with verbal cues
- Involved in self-stimulatory behavior or may not stay in proper position 75% of the time or more

Minor Leaguer: A Ball

- Reacts to ball if provided verbal cue
- Pays attention to batter 50% of the time with verbal reminders
- Involved in self-stimulatory behavior or may not stay in proper position 50% of the time

Minor Leaguer: AA Ball

- Reacts to ball (looks at ball) and will walk to retrieve ball if given verbal reminder
- Pays attention to batter 75% of the time and needs only occasional verbal reminders
- Displays appropriate waiting behavior 75% of the time, with occasional verbal reminders

Minor Leaguer: AAA Ball

- Reacts to ball and walks to retrieve hit ball independently 4 out of 5 trials
- Pays attention to batter independently 4 out of 5 trials but may not display ready position
- Displays appropriate waiting behavior independently 4 out of 5 trials but may not cheer teammates

Major Leaguer

- Reacts to ball independently by quickly walking or running to where ball was hit
- Pays attention to batter and displays ready position
- Displays appropriate waiting behavior, including proper positioning and cheering on batter or teammates

Note: Category names (minor leaguer, major leaguer) are made up and can be anything from colors to numbers to letters to names of teams.

Figure 6.2   A teacher-created rubric is an alternative to a standardized test.

This type of rubric assessment can be easily translated into goals for this child as they relate to baseball. John, who has autism, tested at a "Minor Leaguer: A Ball" level. Recall from figure 6.2 that this means he reacts to the ball if provided verbal cues, pays attention to the batter about 50% of the time with verbal reminders, and is involved in self-stimulatory behaviors or may not be in proper position 50% of the time. Our logical goal for this child is to get him to the next level on the rubric, Minor Leaguer: AA Ball. So, his IEP might read as follows:

Goal: John will show significant improvement in fielding skills as noted by mastery of the following objectives:

Objective 1: John will react to ball (looks at ball) and will walk to retrieve ball within 5 seconds of a verbal cue in three out of four trials.

Objective 2: John will pay attention to the batter (watch batter) 75% of the time, independently, with only one verbal reminder during a batter's turn at the plate, in three out of four trials.

Objective 3: John will display appropriate waiting behavior (stands in correct position, does not walk around field, does not exhibit any self-stimulatory behaviors) 75% of the time, with one to three verbal reminders in a 5-minute period, in three out of four trials.

Notice how easy it is to set appropriate, achievable, and meaningful IEP goals when rubrics are created. Finally, when assessing John on the rubric, Ms. Anderson could make this a truly authentic assessment by assessing him while he plays modified games of tee ball in physical education or by watching him while playing a game of Challenger Baseball over the weekend.

BALANCE TESTS

Balance is an essential component of movement efficiency and is included in many motor ability, development, and perceptual tests. For example, balance is measured in all the listed tests of motor development as well as the BOT-2 and Movement ABC. In addition, some form of balance is required for perceptual-motor functioning, as measured in the Purdue Perceptual-Motor Survey and the Developmental Test of Visual Perception.

Case Study 4

Christa is a 7-year-old, second-grade girl with Down syndrome who is experiencing difficulty walking up and down stairs and coordinating her movement. She is clumsy and often trips or falls during play activities. Both her vision and hearing screening are within acceptable limits, yet her movement continues to be disordered.

Christa's teacher knows that balance is multifaceted, and he wants to determine which components may be affecting Christa's balance. For example, the teacher has already determined that Christa's lower-extremity strength is deficient in the quadriceps and plantar flexors. He's hoping that a strengthening program of these muscles will help Christa, but he wants to gather some additional information on balance.

Balance is also a vital component of all sports and movement skills, especially functional tasks such as standing, walking up stairs, and lifting objects. In this context, teachers should utilize balance assessments in conjunction with other measures to determine if the underlying component is affecting task performance, as illustrated in case study 4. For example, balance is multifaceted and not dependent on one factor. Several components of our sensory system affect balance, including the auditory, visual, vestibular, and somatosensory systems. The eyes, ears, vestibular apparatus of the inner ear, and muscle spindles all provide information that is transmitted via afferent nerve fibers and spinal tracts for analysis so that movement can be initiated and controlled (Shumway-Cook & Woollacott, 2001).

Vision provides information on head movement and keeps us aware of our body position and relationship to the environment. The visual system works concurrently with the vestibular system concerning velocity and rotation from the vestibular system to provide a reference for postural control (Shumway-Cook & Woollacott, 2001). If vision is restricted, compensations and adjustments can be made from other sensory modalities to maintain stability. Vestibular input is used for movement and stabilization of the head during gait patterns. In conjunction with the visual system, the vestibular system stabilizes the eyes and maintains posture. Vestibular problems contribute to a loss of balance and affect the ability of the nervous system to mediate contradicting sensory information (Shumway-Cook & Woollacott, 2001).

Proprioceptive and tactile input also provide critical somatosensory feedback regarding body sway, position in space, and environmental shifts or surface changes. We use a combination of tactile and proprioceptive information to continually adjust to postural changes and maintain stability. For some children, balance or stability may be affected by a developmental disorder or loss of sensory function. Neurological or neuromuscular function may be compromised in older children. In many ways, balance disorders in children parallel the loss of function seen with aging, strokes, head injuries, or Parkinson's disease. With this in mind, many of the tests discussed in this chapter have components of balance. Table 6.3 (page 104) provides several examples from a multitude of balance tests that can be used in physical education. Once the teacher has eliminated muscular weakness or sensory dysfunction, the functional component of balance can be addressed.

◼ W̲hat You Need to Know ►►►

Key Terms

agnosia	fine motor skills	protective reactions
apraxia	form constancy	reflex movements
ATNR	fundamental motor patterns	righting reactions
authentic assessment	gross motor skills	spatial relations
body schema	motor abilities	spinal-level reflexes
brain stem reflexes	motor development	sports skills
depth perception	perception	tilting reactions
developmental landmarks	position in space	

Table 6.3   Selected Balance Tests

Test	Procedure
Functional Reach Test (Duncan et al., 1990; Donahoe et al., 1994)	Child stands with feet shoulder-width apart, with one arm raised to 90° of flexion. She reaches as far forward as possible without losing balance and moving the feet. The maximum the child can reach beyond her extended arm length while maintaining a fixed position is recorded.
Berg Balance Scale (Berg, 1993)	Child is measured on 14 functional tasks including the following: sitting to standing unsupported; transitions such as sitting to standing, standing to sitting; variations in standing such as eyes open or closed, feet together, turning, picking up objects. A total score of 56 is derived from 0 to 4 points for each item, with 4 designating that criteria are met, while a 0 score is an inability to meet task requirements.
Romberg Test (Blumenfeld, 2001)	Child stands with heels and ankles together 3 ft (1 m) from a wall, with the eyes focused on a visual target. Arms are across the chest and hands touch the shoulders. Balance is recorded for 30 s with eyes open and then closed. Test is terminated if feet or hands move or if eyes open.
Sharpened Romberg (O'Loughllin, 1993)	Child stands with feet in tandem (one foot in front of the other), arms across the chest and hands touching the shoulders. Balance is recorded for 30 s with eyes open and then closed. Test is terminated if feet or hands move or if eyes open.
Single-Leg Stance (O'Loughllin, 1993)	Child stands on one leg, with arms across the chest and hands touching the shoulders. Eyes are focused on visual target from a distance of 3 ft (1 m). The number of seconds is recorded with eyes open and then closed, then test is repeated with the opposite leg. Test is stopped if legs touch, foot on floor moves, foot touches floor, arms move, or eyes open.
Standing on Foam Surface	Child stands on a padded surface, with hands on hips, or in a single-leg stance procedure, eyes open and then closed. Balance is recorded for 30 s on each leg. Test is terminated if hands or feet move, foot touches floor, or eyes open.

Key Concepts

1. You should understand the differences between reflex assessments, developmental assessments, and tests of motor behavior. Describe when each test is appropriate.

2. You should be able to use tests of motor development, behavior, and sports skills to develop an instructional plan. If specific tests do not fit your population, how would you create a rubric for a specific sports skill?

3. You should be familiar with testing protocols, scoring, and safety procedures for various assessments. Practice administering tests to children of various ages or disabilities and describing their performance. What would be usable to develop their instructional programs?

Review Questions

1. If a child has a visual-perceptual problem, would you change the method in which information is presented? If yes, how would this be accomplished?

2. For children who are lacking motor skills, would you develop a home program or pair the child with a peer for additional practice?

3. If a child continues to have difficulty with balance in class, would you recommend this child for additional testing? What test would you recommend?

4. What testing or modifications are needed for children with perceptual impairments?

Chapter 7

Assessing Physical Fitness

Among the major goals of physical activity—including adapted physical education—is providing all individuals with the opportunity and desire to lead physically active and independent lifestyles. We want to emphasize the importance of physical fitness for many tasks that affect functional development and that are needed in community- and work-related settings. Clearly, physical fitness is a great facilitator of these goals. One could argue that physical fitness is *the* great facilitator for enjoying activity and increasing the functional capabilities of persons with disabilities. Physical fitness generally makes activities more enjoyable and translates to independence in the community and at work.

Achieving and maintaining a functional level of physical fitness through activity should become a lifelong reality and an essential component of adapted physical education and rehabilitation programs. For this to occur, adequate assessments should be utilized to determine specific levels of fitness and the effects of intervention programs designed to develop and maintain physical fitness. For example, Marty is a participant in your high school physical education class. What fitness capabilities does he require to finish school and prepare for a job at the local supermarket? If Marty participates in sports, he may want to increase aerobic capacity, strength, or power to perform in competition. Finally, moving about, rising from a chair, carrying groceries, and throwing a ball all require the ability to maintain a level of physical fitness. In this chapter, we define and discuss the components of fitness as well as present a sample of fitness test items and batteries.

FITNESS AMONG PERSONS WITH DISABILITIES

Always proceed with caution in making generalizations about persons with disabilities. People with disabilities, *as a group,* typically do not manifest fitness levels characteristic of their nondisabled counterparts. Historically, many factors have prevented persons with disabilities from achieving optimal, and sometimes even minimal, fitness levels.

A major factor often limiting achievement of fitness potential among persons with disabilities is underexpectations on the part of others, including parents, teachers, coaches, or potential employers. The focus on the disability undermines the goals or ability to achieve. In addition, underexpectations can be transmitted consciously or subconsciously and learned by persons with disabilities. The limited opportunities for play or engaging in physical activity may be a result of anxious or overprotective parents, but in some cases, opportunities for children to participate may be restricted.

People with disabilities may comprehend that others perceive them as being limited, which may contribute to low self-esteem. Perhaps one of the most viable avenues to improved self-esteem is maintaining parameters of fitness that promote a positive, active lifestyle that stresses independence and the capabilities of the person. Being fit means being active, and being active is positive and healthy; it generalizes to independent living and integration in community- and work-related settings. The net result can be a sense of feeling good that promotes positive self-esteem, self-reliance, and functional fitness. Further, fitness that promotes an active lifestyle emphasizes accomplishment rather than what cannot be accomplished.

FITNESS DEFINED

Although there is widespread consensus that fitness is important (and, therefore, should be assessed), the components that comprise fitness are more open to debate. Historically, fitness components have been divided into two major categories: physical (i.e., health-related) fitness and performance fitness, or motor fitness. In recent years, interest in fitness, specifically health-related fitness, has addressed attributes that facilitate day-to-day function and health maintenance (e.g., muscular strength and endurance, flexibility, cardiorespiratory endurance, and body composition) as well as health components as they relate to function or functional fitness, especially for persons with disabilities. In this context, functional fitness is being able to accomplish daily living tasks such as lifting, stretching, or moving to promote overall function and independence.

Health-related fitness and functional fitness are the major focus of this chapter, while elements of motor fitness, such as balance, are included in chapter 6. Since power results from a combination of strength and speed, it is included in this chapter. The term *explosive strength*, or *power*, is often used synonymously to describe the muscles' ability to exert maximal force in the shortest possible time. More specific examples of fitness tests are included in table 7.1 and are designated laboratory based, field based, or a combination of both.

MULTIDIMENSIONALITY OF FITNESS:
Implications for Selecting Test Items

Fitness is multidimensional, and it is required for many developmental, performance-related, and work-related tasks. In addition, various components of physical fitness tend to exist exclusively of one another. This mutual exclusivity requires that physical educators use different test items (i.e., items representative of each proficiency) to measure task-specific performance with respect to each component. For example, if Ms. Rogers wants to measure how many times

Table 7.1 Fitness Components and Appropriate Tests by Setting

Fitness component	Laboratory based	Combination	Field based
Muscular strength and endurance	Isokinetic dynamometer (Cybex, Humac) Cable tensiometer	Free weights, 1RM bench press, curls, lat pull-downs Variable resistance, 1RM 50% of 6RM to fatigue (Fleck & Kraemer, 2004) Manual muscle testers (Horvat, McManis, & Seagraves, 1992; Horvat, Croce, & Roswal, 1993) Hand-grip dynamometers Back and leg dynamometers	Pull-ups Modified pull-ups Flexed arm hang (The Cooper Institute, 2004) Curl-ups (ACSM, 2005) Sit-ups Isometric push-ups (Johnson & Lavay, 1988) Medicine ball throw Push-ups (ACSM, 2005) Sit-to-stand (Rikli & Jones, 2001)
Flexibility	Leighton flexometer (Leighton, 1955)	Goniometer (Norkin & White, 2003) Length of muscle groups (Kendall, McCreary, Provance, Rogers, & Romani, 2005) Inclinometer (American Medical Association, 1988)	Sit-and-reach (AAHPERD, 1988) Modified sit-and-reach (Hoeger, Hopkins, Button, & Palmer, 1990) V sit-and-reach (Golding, 2000) Back-saver sit-and-reach (The Cooper Institute, 2004) Modified back-saver sit-and-reach (Hui & Yuen, 2000)
Body composition	Hydrostatic weighing Potassium whole-body counting Bioelectrical impedance X-ray absorptiometer Air displacement plethysmography Anthropometry Near-infrared interactance	Skinfolds (The Cooper Institute, 2004)	Body mass index (Corbin, Lindsey, Week, & Corbin, 2002) Girth measurements (Heyward & Wagner, 2004) Waist-to-hip circumference ratio
Cardiorespiratory endurance	$\dot{V}O_2$max treadmill (ACSM, 2005) $\dot{V}O_2$submax cycle ergometer (ACSM, 2005) Max arm-crank ergometer (ACSM, 2005) $\dot{V}O_2$max Schwinn Airdyne (Pitetti & Tan, 1990)	PWC 170 (Bar-Or, 1983) Stair-climbing submax test Rowing ergometer submax test	9 min or 12 min run for distance 1 mile run/walk (The Cooper Institute, 2004) 20 m Pacer test (The Cooper Institute, 2004) 20 min shuttle run (Montgomery, Reid, & Koziris, 1992) Bench step-test pulse recovery (Golding, 2000) Rockport walking test (Kline et al., 1987)
Explosive strength (power)	Vertec	Wingate peak power test (Bar-Or, 1983) Margaria-Kalaman leg power test (Margaria, Aghemo, & Rovelli, 1966)	Vertical jump (Clarke & Clarke, 1987) Long jump (Clarke & Clarke, 1987) Sargent jump (Sargent, 1921) Shot put or medicine ball throw (McCloy & Young, 1954)

Chris can lift a weighted box and stack it on a table, she needs to measure the strength and endurance of his upper body. Likewise, when measuring any given component, more than one test item may be necessary to ensure that proficiency has been thoroughly addressed. When measuring strength, for example, arm strength is not necessarily predictive of trunk or leg strength. For the sake of thoroughness, teachers should administer test items that make valid assessments of strength in each specific muscle group that is deemed relevant, and more important, task specific. Since the components of fitness tend to be mutually exclusive, each component should be addressed separately to adequately document function. Teachers may also want to test both sides of the body and develop a combination, or composite, score to give a representation of upper-body or lower-body strength.

Case Study 1

Ron is a 17-year-old boy with Down syndrome who is scheduled to graduate from high school in 2 years. What is needed for him to successfully work at a local supermarket? The teacher knows several things about the situation:

- Ron will need to stay on the job for a minimum of 5 hours.
- Most of his tasks will involve lifting, stacking, and carrying items.
- He is sedentary and seldom participates in any physical activity.

For Ron to be successful, the teacher needs to analyze the functional fitness requirements of his job. The job-specific tasks require a minimal amount of strength to lift, carry, and place objects such as boxes in a specific location. Therefore, the teacher needs to assess Ron's muscular strength in the muscle groups required to initiate task movements in the upper and lower extremities. Next, she needs to gauge his endurance, or ability to repeat the movements on a continual basis. Since he is sedentary, the teacher may recommend a physical activity program that emphasizes strength and conditioning to improve his overall functioning.

COMPONENTS OF FITNESS

Muscular strength and endurance, flexibility, cardiorespiratory endurance, body composition, and power are all measurable aspects of fitness. This section describes these components and provides examples of how each is assessed.

Muscular Strength and Endurance

Muscular strength and muscular endurance are separate entities that can significantly increase the functional capabilities of persons with disabilities. These essential components of fitness correlate highly with self-sufficiency, job performance, and work productivity (Croce & Horvat, 1992; Zetts, Horvat, & Langone, 1995). However, the link between strength and endurance often blurs, in part because of how these proficiencies are often measured. *Strength* is defined as maximal muscular exertion of relatively brief duration; it is generally measured by the amount of force a person can exert in a single maximal effort. *Muscular endurance* is defined as submaximal exertion that extends over a relatively long period of time. Where muscular strength involves a brief, all-out effort, muscular endurance involves a submaximal, extended effort. For individuals who may rely on their physical skills, such as strength and endurance, to perform job-related tasks, enhanced physical capabilities can make a significant contribution to their overall vocational and social development. For Ron in case study 1, the development of strength and endurance is a priority to accomplish work-related tasks. Lack of strength may interfere with the ability to throw a ball, jump, or repeat a swimming stroke across the pool. Therefore, it is imperative that teachers accurately and reliably ascertain strength and endurance and how they relate to specific function in children with disabilities.

Case Study 2

Stewart is a 10-year-old fifth grader with spastic hemiplegia affecting the left side of his body. He tends to favor his left side and initiates all his action with the right. He is hesitant when walking up and down stairs, leading with the right side and then moving his left leg to the same step. How can his physical education teacher assess Stewart to discover why his gait pattern is affected in this manner? What intervention would you suggest?

The teacher must determine the strength discrepancy between the two sides of the body. He can assess and compare the affected side with the nonaffected side and base his treatment on strengthening both sides of the body. He can also analyze Stewart's gait to see if strength is affecting his ability to maintain balance and initiate movements. After the assessment, the teacher can provide a conditioning program that includes range of motion (ROM) exercises, strength exercises, and specific movements to emphasize an appropriate gait.

Several methods are available to assess the strength and endurance performance of persons with disabilities. In laboratory settings, cable tensiometers, free weights, and isokinetic devices can be used to assess muscular strength. However, these tests are impractical in field-based settings or when many people must be tested in a short time period (see table 7.1).

To accommodate these situations, more economical and practical tests must often be employed. For example, upper-extremity assessments in field-based settings commonly use push-ups, pull-ups, or some modification of these tests. When measuring the strength and endurance of the lower extremities, the most commonly used field-based tests are the long jump and vertical jump. Although some researchers consider these tests to be measures of power, each of these field-based tests is considered a relative measure of strength (Pate & Shepherd, 1989).

In children and persons with disabilities, strength and endurance measures, such as the pull-up, often result in zero scores or, at best, inaccurate indicators of actual strength or functional capability. Body size and weight can also restrict or strongly influence physical performance (Shepherd, 1990). To offset these problems, researchers have attempted to minimize the effect of body weight and to eliminate zero scores in upper-body measures by developing modified pull-up tests or by using the flexed arm hang (Woods, Pate, & Burgess, 1992).

Field-based tests are widely variable in comparing children and persons with disabilities. Variations based on levels of strength, body structure, and the rate and extent of growth at different developmental stages are available (Woods et al., 1992). Most of these tests are not specific enough to isolate individual muscles; instead, they test groups of muscles that work synergistically (Horvat, Croce, & Roswal, 1993).

Typically, physical educators measure muscular strength and endurance in practical settings using items including, but not limited to, pull-ups, sit-ups, push-ups, the flexed arm hang, and parallel bar dips. A major problem in using these items is that the relative fitness level of the person with the disability determines whether strength or endurance is being measured. If strength is best measured by a single maximal effort, then multiple repetition test items similar to those just cited are of questionable validity as strength measures. For example, a child able to execute only one pull-up is demonstrating strength (albeit limited) in specific arm and shoulder girdle muscles. In contrast, being able to execute numerous repetitions demonstrates muscular endurance. As a general rule, when the task's difficulty limits repetitions to 10 or fewer, strength tends to be measured; repetitions beyond 10 begin to measure muscular endurance. According to Corbin, Lindsey, Week, and Corbin (2002), strength and endurance are on a continuum, with 1 repetition indicating muscular strength and the opposite end of the continuum (multiple repetitions) indicating endurance. Scores in the middle signify a combination of strength and endurance. We can infer from this premise that if 1 to 10 repetitions of any given activity develops strength, then that number—if the effort is maximal—also measures strength.

Strength can be measured more purely (according to the definition cited previously) by using one or more of a number of devices that measure force exerted in pounds or kilograms. Examples of such devices include cable tensiometers, hand-grip dynamometers, and back and leg dynamometers. These tools enable measurement of single all-out efforts. In other settings, physical educators can determine 1-repetition maximum (1RM) using a universal gym, bench press, forearm curl, or latissimus dorsi pull-down and convert it to a composite strength score. Endurance tests using 50% of the person's 1RM values (Berger, 1970) or 50% of 6RM for younger children can also provide a composite endurance score for the total number of repetitions (Fleck & Kraemer, 2004; Kraemer & Fleck, 1993).

When interpreting strength measures, a factor to consider is the force exerted in relation to body weight. For example, if a 125-pound (57 kilogram) person applies a given amount of leg strength to a leg dynamometer, and another person weighing 100 pounds (45 kilograms) applies the same force, the second person would be judged the stronger. When assessing strength, teachers must look beyond raw strength and interpret strength measures in terms of *strength per pound or kilogram of body weight.* Some people may have inert body weight from sitting in a wheelchair, and comparisons can be made across muscle groups or from an upper- or lower-body composite score. The importance of assessing strength per pound of body weight is underscored by Rarick and Dobbins (1975), who determined that among the various fitness components, muscular strength correlates most highly with motor skill development in children.

Strength can be measured (and developed) isotonically, isokinetically, and isometrically. When measuring isometric strength, it is important that repeated assessments of the same person or between individuals occur at precisely the same point (i.e., degree of angle at the joint) in each person's range of motion. This is critical because strength within the same muscle or muscle group differs, often dramatically, when measured at different points throughout the muscle's or muscle group's range of motion. When measuring strength isotonically or isokinetically, examiners must ensure that subjects repeatedly exert force through the same range of motion. Typically, the best standardization procedure is to have each person exert force through his or her entire range of motion. Getting someone with a disability to exert force through an entire range, particularly when considering fatigue or lack of motivation or attention, is sometimes difficult. In addition, some persons with low levels of strength will respond by producing their peak strength at angles that are not normally advantageous. If that can be determined, it is important to plan the intervention to develop strength across a full range of motion.

Depending on a person's fitness level, sit-ups, push-ups, and the flexed arm hang often provide better evaluations of muscular endurance than of strength. This is particularly true when such measures require substantially less than a single all-out effort. Repetitions of any given item as a measure of muscular endurance can be scored in two ways. A test item can require the subject to execute as many repetitions of an activity as possible (e.g., the bench press) or repetitions can be performed within a given time limit (e.g., sit-ups). Items requiring maximum repetitions without regard to time may be more precise as measures of endurance, although they may not be time effective. Items with time limitations may increase time effectiveness, but they may also introduce the unwanted element of muscle contraction speed or skill, which could contaminate a score believed to represent only endurance.

Muscular Strength and Endurance Assessments

Static (isometric) strength and muscular endurance are commonly measured with dynamometers, cable tensiometers, or load cells, while free weights and isokinetic machines can be used to measure dynamic strength and endurance.

Isometric Strength and Endurance

We recommend handheld dynamometry as a reliable and objective measure of functional strength. Handheld dynamometers are designed to quantify peak force output when manually testing various muscles (Aufsesser, Horvat, & Croce, 1996). Instead of applying a graded subjective rating of 0 (no contraction) to 5 (full movement and resistance), which occurs when manually testing a particular muscle or muscle group (Kendall, McCreary, Provance, Rogers, & Romani, 2005), handheld dynamometers provide a quantifiable measurement of muscle force, usually in kilograms of force, or Newtons. This essentially eliminates the subjective and often unreliable values obtained from standard muscle testing.

Extensive research supports the reliability and objectivity of handheld dynamometry with nondisabled adults, nondisabled children, and persons with neuromuscular disorders (Aufsesser et al., 1996; Horvat, McManis, & Seagraves, 1992). In addition, this research has been extended to investigate the reliability and objectivity of handheld dynamometry in persons with disabilities (Aufsesser, Horvat, & Austin, 2003; Horvat, Croce, et al., 1993).

Handheld dynamometers (figure 7.1) quantify isometric muscle strength and are designed to measure forces between 0 and 199.9 kilograms or forces exerted in fractions of a pound. Each unit is placed between the tester's hand and the subject's limb. Muscle force is then determined by either a make or break test procedure. In a *make* test procedure, the examiner holds the dynamometer

Figure 7.1   A handheld dynamometer.

Courtesy of Hoggan Health Industries.

stationary while the tested individual exerts a maximum effort against the device. This contrasts with a *break* test procedure, where the tester exerts a force against the tested person's limb segment until the tested person's effort is overcome, and the limb segment gives or breaks. Bohannon (1988) concludes that the reliability of make and break tests is similar (i.e., differing by less than 1.5%), so one testing method cannot be interpreted as clearly superior to the other. Horvat and Croce (1995), however, recommend the make test as a more efficient procedure for children and persons with disabilities.

When using the handheld dynamometer on persons with disabilities, the adapted physical educator should familiarize the subjects with the testing protocol, test positions, and instrumentation to minimize effects of practice efforts on test performance (Croce & Horvat, 1992). The tester should place subjects in the appropriate testing positions and allow practice trials with the instrument until they are able to perform the testing protocol on cue. Test positions for measuring strength are commonly based on those outlined by Kendall et al. (2005) or by manufacturers of the testing devices.

According to Horvat et al. (1993), to ensure consistency in testing, the tester should use consistent body joint and dynamometer positioning; stabilize movements; give consistent verbal feedback to subjects during data acquisition; provide the opportunity for subjects to visualize tested body parts; and place the dynamometer perpendicular to the limb segment on which it is applied. The final point ensures that the measured force against the instrument is maximal. The testing procedure requires minimal experience with handheld dynamometry (i.e., less than 5 hours of practical experience).

A final consideration for testing protocol involves the number of test trials. Most researchers recommend from two to four trials (Bohannon, 1990). An advantage of multiple trials is that test variability can be observed and judgments made regarding sincerity of the subject's effort. This becomes even more important when testing persons with disabilities because performance variability is often encountered with this population. Consequently, it is recommended that the mean of three trials of dominant and nondominant sides be used.

An important aspect of muscle testing is the versatility of measuring several muscle groups on both sides of the body; the sum of several muscle groups; or a composite strength score that can address overall functional ability. Clinically, we have used muscle testing to evaluate pre- and posttest performance on strength measures of high school youths with intellectual disabilities and have correlated strength with work performance as indicators of individual capabilities (Seagraves, Horvat, Franklin, & Jones, 2004). In this context, we recommend using handheld dynamometers for the ease and versatility of accessing numerous

Figure 7.2 A hand-grip dynamometer is used to examine hand and arm strength.

muscle groups in a relatively short time period. In addition, the strength composite can yield an overall level of strength rather than strength in one extremity.

Another tool for measuring static strength is the hand-grip dynamometer (figure 7.2). The subject grips the appropriate apparatus and squeezes as hard as possible to elicit maximal force. The dynamometer measures forces between 0 and 100 kilograms (up to 220 pounds) and usually has an adjustable handle to accommodate hand size differences. Corbin et al. (2002) provide norms for hand-grip isometric strength in young adults 18 to 30 years of age. The Brockport Physical Fitness Test (BPFT) uses a dominant grip-strength procedure, and similar scores can be obtained with a back and leg dynamometer or cable tensiometer to record arm lifts, arm presses, or back lifts. Back and leg dynamometers use a platform while the participant flexes at the knees, grips a hand bar, and exerts force with a pulling motion. Scores are generally recorded as peak force in pounds and converted to kilograms. Baumgartner, Jackson, Mahar, and Rowe (2003) report that static strength measures correlate highly with work productivity tasks—such as pushing and pulling forces, shoveling rate, and carrying weighted objects—and can be used to document strength values in specific muscle groups. Endurance can also be assessed by sequencing a grip dynamometer as hard as possible for 60 seconds and comparing the initial force with the force executed at 60 seconds (Heyward, 2002). Although the hand-grip dynamometer has been used extensively, it measures a specific component of strength (grip strength) that does not generalize to the larger muscles in the body.

Dynamic Strength and Endurance

Strength can also be assessed by the ability to apply force in a maximal or near-maximal contraction. Strength in this context is used to lift oneself off the ground onto a wheelchair or to transfer from a wheelchair to an automobile seat. Endurance relates to performing the activity for an extended time such as throwing a baseball, pushing a wheelchair, or lifting and stacking boxes in a work setting.

To measure absolute strength or endurance, the greatest amount of weight lifted for the specific exercise in one complete repetition (1RM) can be documented. For absolute endurance, a specific weight can be selected for multiple repetitions—for example, 80 and 35 pounds (36 and 16 kilograms) for males and females, respectively, in the YMCA bench press (figure 7.3) and 40 pounds (18 kilograms) for men and 25 pounds (11 kilograms) for women in the YMCA curl test (Golding, 2000).

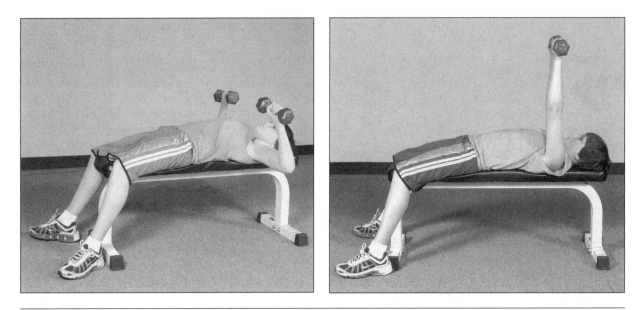

Figure 7.3   The bench press can be used to measure absolute strength or endurance.

Johnson and Lavay (1988) recommend the bench press for persons 13 years of age or older using a 35-pound (16-kilogram) barbell. The child repeats the action until fatigue or until 50 repetitions (for males) or 30 repetitions (for females) have been completed. For younger children and schools without bench press equipment, the flexed arm hang or isometric push-up can be substituted. To perform the push-up, the child holds his body in the up position (arms extended) of the push-up for as long as he can. The BPFT uses the isometric push-up, pull-up, modified pull-up, dumbbell curl, reverse curl, and trunk lift as measures of strength and endurance. Further, the BPFT recommends the wheelchair ramp test or 40-meter push/walk as alternatives for strength testing. Another task that is often used in clinical settings, the seated push-up, requires the participant to lift the body 12 inches (30 centimeters) for a maximum of 20 seconds. This assessment is very useful because the movement is similar to the functional skills needed to accommodate transfers.

Scoring for 1RM tests commonly documents the maximal amount of weight lifted, while absolute endurance records the number of repetitions or time maintained in a particular position. Other endurance tests can utilize a percentage of repetition maximum to document the number of repetitions completed during various tasks such as the bench press, curls, and lat pull-downs. The versatility of repetition maximum tests is useful for persons who use a wheelchair or who have limited function or deficiency in some muscle groups.

Lower–Extremity Strength

Isometric, isokinetic, and weight training equipment can be used to measure strength in the lower extremities. A 1RM strength test for the leg press or leg extension can determine maximal values of weight lifted or moved. For individuals with disabilities, it may be advantageous to use manual muscle testing (Horvat, Croce, et al., 1993) or a percentage of the repetition maximum to document the number of repetitions for the leg press, leg curl, or leg extension. In persons with weakened extremities, the ability to lift and move the leg may be indicative of the level of function that is present, providing a baseline for developing the instructional program. For example, in case study 2, Stewart demonstrates a strength discrepancy between the right and left sides of the body that ultimately affects his gait. After determining his level of functioning, the teacher can develop a program plan emphasizing exercises that can remediate the discrepancy. Another recommended test is the 30-second chair sit-to-stand, which consists of counting the number of times a person can rise from a sitting to a standing position without using the arms. The test has proven to correlate very well with lower-extremity strength in persons with visual impairments and is highly recommended for other populations (Horvat, Ray, Nocera, & Croce, 2006; Rikli & Jones, 2001).

Upper–Extremity Strength

Several measures of upper-body strength are usually included in fitness batteries. Procedures such as the flexed arm hang and pull-up are the most common. However, since these scores have a variety of problems, including zero scores and unaccounted differences in body weight, several modifications can be employed. As mentioned earlier, Johnson and Lavay (1988) include the isometric push-up, while other sources use a modified pull-up. A modified pull-up is accomplished with an adjustable horizontal bar. The child's feet are in contact with the floor, and she extends the hips and knees while performing the pull-up. Children perform as many repetitions as possible to determine strength and endurance of the arms and shoulder girdle (Baumgartner et al., 2003). These types of assessments often hinder children because of moving their body weight and zero scores. Some of the modifications, such as the modified pull-up, are helpful, but we suggest using other measures, for example, handheld dynamometry, to document functional strength.

Abdominal Muscular Strength and Endurance

The most common test to measure the strength and endurance of the abdominal region is the sit-up, or curl-up, with the hands placed in a variety of positions. In the BPFT battery, the modified curl-up is used; the hands slide along the thighs until the fingertips contact the knees (Winnick & Short, 1999) (figure 7.4). The YMCA uses a half-sit-up test, or abdominal crunch, designed to keep the back flat and negate the hip flexors. The total number of repetitions or the number completed within 60 seconds can be recorded. In the Physical Best test battery,

Figure 7.4 The most common test to assess abdominal muscular strength and endurance is the curl-up. The modified curl-up is shown here.

the subject places the hands on the chest and flexes the knees to eliminate as much of the hip flexors as possible. Johnson and Lavay (1988) recommend terminating the test if the person stops for 4 seconds, quits, or completes 50 sit-ups. They also recommend removing the time limit to eliminate the motor efficiency factor. Any of these assessments seem appropriate and are recommended to assess abdominal strength and endurance.

Flexibility

Flexibility is defined as the ability to move the body and its parts through a wide range of motion without stress. A muscle that is not flexible can heighten the likelihood of strain, not only at attachment sites but also in the muscle itself. Lack of flexibility can lead to decreased strength and loss of functional capabilities.

When measuring flexibility, individual differences in threshold of discomfort must be recognized to ensure that testing does not put a subject at undue risk of muscle strain. Perception of discomfort is very subjective and unique to every person. Recognizing this threshold is particularly critical if the test subject is limited by muscle disease. For example, a person with Duchenne muscular dystrophy may be more susceptible to muscle strain during testing because of a lower level of muscular strength than someone whose relative inflexibility is not a function of underlying muscle disease.

Flexibility is important for a variety of reasons. Significant inflexibility places a person at a disadvantage in functioning and common everyday tasks. For example, reaching for an item on a high shelf or pushing a wheelchair may be difficult for individuals with contractures or spastic cerebral palsy. Discomfort and a loss of flexibility may promote a sedentary lifestyle and contribute to a cycle in which the person's sedentary lifestyle precipitates further losses of flexibility and other components of physical function.

Corbin et al. (2002) indicate that flexibility in any given muscle group will vary depending on environmental conditions and psychological state. Variables affecting flexibility include motivation to put forth maximum effort, degree of relaxation, warm-up, muscle soreness, and environmental temperature. These conditions should be kept as stable as possible when assessing flexibility. Controlling such variables facilitates valid judgments when score comparisons are an issue. In this context, flexibility measures should be based on the type and severity of disability. The assessments discussed here are all functional and specific but may vary according to the population.

People with disabilities, perhaps because of inopportunity or lowered expectations of themselves and from others, may not be as flexible as the general population. Flexibility, too, is a function of muscle fitness. Typically, fit muscles, provided they have been exercised through normal ranges of motion, are flexible muscles.

A number of disabilities often militate against flexibility. For example, spastic cerebral palsy is characterized by hypertonicity and contractures in affected muscle groups. How flexible the person with spastic cerebral palsy is at any given time may be determined, to varying degrees, by ambient temperature, level of arousal, and medication. An individual with spastic cerebral palsy who is in a warm room, calm, and taking muscle relaxants is likely to demonstrate more flexibility than if he or she were cold, were excited, and had neglected to take prescribed muscle-relaxing medication. Persons with Duchenne muscular dystrophy often experience decrements in flexibility owing to the dystrophic muscles' diseased state, while children with juvenile rheumatoid arthritis typically are inflexible because of joint pain that compromises movement. This pain, to the degree it discourages movement, inevitably results in some loss of range of motion.

Flexibility Assessments

Flexibility is highly specific. A tester cannot make generalizations about overall flexibility by measuring range of motion at one site only. In fact, the only valid way to determine range of motion in any joint is to specifically measure range of motion at that joint.

Many flexibility measures, even some venerable ones, may be questionable in terms of validity. Take, for example, the sit-and-reach test as a flexibility measure. At least three factors could influence the score: back flexibility, hamstring flexibility, and the ratio of arm length to leg length. It is often difficult to precisely determine the degree to which each factor has contributed. Further, the slightest flexion at the knee joint will render a sit-and-reach score invalid because the hamstrings, the major muscle group being stretched, cross the knee joint.

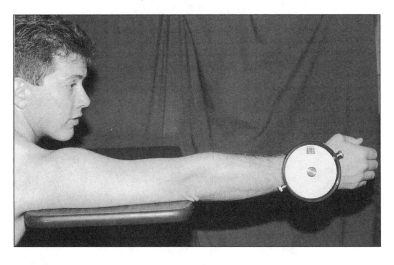

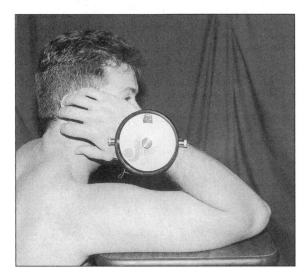

Flexibility scores may be reported as linear measurements or rotary measurements. Although each is efficient, linear measurements probably have greater applicability in practical settings. Typically, linear measurements require little more than some form of ruler or sit-and-reach box, in which flexibility of a particular muscle group (hamstrings) or range of motion (shoulder) is noted. Several recommended variations include the modified sit-and-reach that incorporates a finger-to-box distance to control limb-length biases; the back-saver sit-and-reach; the YMCA Flexibility Test; and the YMCA Older Adult Flexibility Test. Each of these tests may be appropriate for persons with disabilities, not only to eliminate limb-length bias but also to circumvent problems of excessive tightness or weakness associated with certain disabilities.

Rotary measurements usually require instruments more typically seen in laboratory settings, such as flexometers or goniometers (figures 7.5

Figure 7.5 Range of motion at the elbow joint can be measured using a Leighton flexometer.

and 7.6). In addition, specific actions (figure 7.7) can be used to document movement through an arc of 0 to 180°. Specific flexibility can be determined through range of motion in the extremities; rotation of the limbs; or movements in planes around the horizontal, vertical, or coronal axis (Norkin & White, 2003).

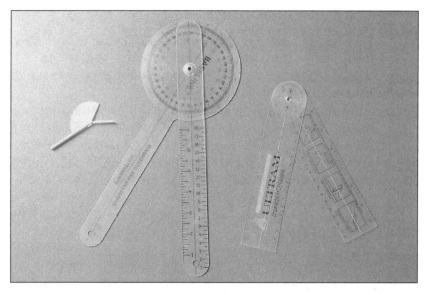

Figure 7.6 Examples of different types of goniometers used to be measure range of motion.

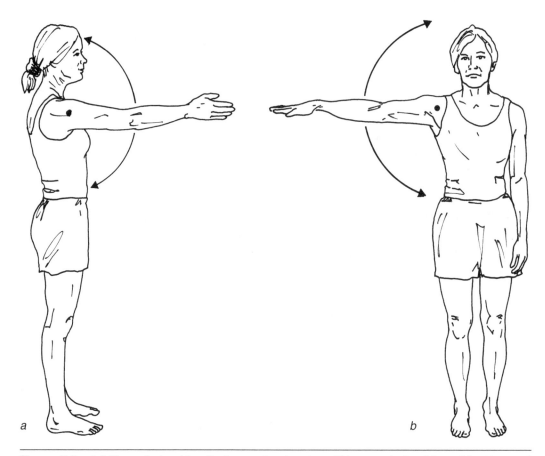

Figure 7.7 *(a)* Normal shoulder flexion and extension; *(b)* normal shoulder adduction and abduction.

Lower-Extremity Flexibility

The most common test for lower-extremity flexibility is the sit-and-reach, which is included in most test batteries. Subjects sit with their heels flat against a bench or box that is 12 inches (30 centimeters) high and reach as far forward as possible. The farthest point reached on the fourth trial counts as the score. A modified sit-and-reach test includes a sliding measurement scale. Subjects slide the scale along the top of the sit-and-reach box until the zero point of the scale is even with the fingertips (Hoeger, Hopkins, Button, & Palmer, 1990; Hui & Yuen, 2000). This finger-to-box distance establishes a zero point that accommodates limb-length variations in children and may more accurately portray the lower-limb flexibility of persons with disabilities.

Kendall et al. (2005) also assessed the length of the hamstrings by placing the subject's pelvis in a neutral position, anchoring the supporting leg, and lifting the other (a straight-leg raise). Normal hamstring length (70 to 80°), excessive length (110°), and short hamstring length (50°) can be detected (as shown in figure 7.8). This technique may be especially helpful for persons with disabilities because range of motion in joints may be linked to functional capabilities. For example, in paraplegia, tightness in some muscles enhances muscle function, while in quadriplegia, tightness of lower-trunk muscles aids in maintaining sitting postures by increasing trunk stability. In contrast, other persons may require flexibility to complete many functional tasks, such as transfers or dressing. The excessive flexibility in Down syndrome may result in ligament instability that affects activities of daily living and muscle development, or causes imbalances. Other functional measures of flexibility can utilize a goniometer to document range of motion in the joints or simply to document specific movements through

Figure 7.8 Hip flexion and hamstring length assessment.

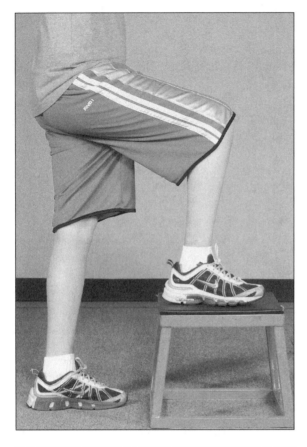

Figure 7.9 Hip flexion.

a 180° range of motion during flexion and extension. In addition, rotary movement, as measured by a goniometer, can be used to measure head, arm, or leg flexibility in the frontal, horizontal, or sagittal planes (Norkin & White, 2003).

Palmer and Epler (1990) have provided illustrations of functional muscle movements, such as hip flexion, in which the person stands and places the foot of the test limb on an 8-inch (20-centimeter) step, then returns it to the floor (figure 7.9). The examiner can document the movement through the specific range needed to climb stairs or document muscle strength by the number of repetitions, from 0 (nonfunctional) to 5 (functional).

Upper-Extremity Flexibility

The Target Stretch Test includes a series of stretches through a range of motion including wrist extension, elbow extension, shoulder extension, shoulder abduction, shoulder external rotation, forearm supination, and forearm pronation. Several other measures such as the shoulder stretch and modified Thomas test, as used in the Brockport Physical Fitness Test, can also be used to assess upper-extremity flexibility.

Cardiorespiratory Endurance

Many people equate fitness with the ability to effectively meet challenges requiring cardiorespiratory endurance. Such challenges include cycling, power walking, jogging, or swimming.

Cardiorespiratory endurance is an important component of fitness, particularly when the potential for promoting a healthy lifestyle is the primary criterion by which fitness components are judged, given its potential for reducing heart disease and obesity. Historically, the standard for measuring cardiorespiratory endurance has been maximum oxygen uptake ($\dot{V}O_2$max). However, precise measurement of $\dot{V}O_2$max requires expensive and sophisticated equipment. To evaluate $\dot{V}O_2$max in practical settings without elaborate laboratory equipment and procedures, researchers have constructed tests whose results correlate significantly with laboratory assessments of $\dot{V}O_2$max. If a field test for cardiorespiratory endurance correlates with its laboratory test counterpart, the field test can be assumed to validly measure cardiorespiratory endurance.

Typical cardiorespiratory endurance field tests call for the subject to run a prescribed distance (e.g., 1 or 1.5 miles [1.6 or 2.4 kilometers]) for time or run a prescribed period of time (e.g., 9 or 12 minutes) for distance, while other measures rely on pulse recovery after a prescribed level of exertion. Some tests may rely on cadence (e.g., use of a metronome) or a cassette, as in the

Pacer test, for standardizing workloads. Items requiring the subject to maintain cadence may be inappropriate if, for example, the person has a mental disability or attention-deficit/hyperactivity disorder.

Some older test batteries that relied on either the 300- or 600-yard (274- or 549-meter) run as a measure of cardiorespiratory fitness have been found invalid because outcomes do not correlate significantly with their $\dot{V}O_2$max laboratory test counterparts (Fernhall & Tymeson, 1988).

When pulse counting provides the basis for determining cardiorespiratory fitness, the test administrator and test interpreter must consider a number of variables. Pulse rate for any given level of exertion can be affected by factors such as environmental temperature and the subject's level of arousal. Counting heartbeats, particularly when pulse is rapid immediately after exercise, can sometimes be difficult. While postexercise heart rate is being counted, pulse rate will be recovering toward normal. As a result, if postexercise pulse is taken over too long a time period (e.g., 60 seconds), the tester will record a pulse rate lower than that which was occurring at the moment exertion ceased. To remedy this problem, most postexercise pulse measures are of either 6 or 10 seconds in duration. When pulse is taken for 6 seconds, the tester need only add a zero to the number of beats counted to determine beats per minute. When pulse is taken for 10 seconds, the tester multiplies the number of beats counted by 6. The major drawback of the 6-second method is that an inaccurate pulse count of only 1 heartbeat results in an error of 10 beats per minute. Heart and pulse monitors can record heart rates in intervals and are more precise. Unfortunately these devices may not be available in field-based settings, although they are recommended in the Brockport Physical Fitness Test and in field-based studies on activity for individuals with mental retardation (Lorenzi, Horvat, & Pellegrini, 2000; Horvat & Franklin, 2001).

Ideal places for taking the pulse are at the radial artery (located immediately proximal to the wrist joint between the finger flexor tendons and the radius) and the carotid artery (located at the side of the larynx midway between the shoulder and jaw). Two fingers (do not use the thumb), with just enough pressure to palpate the pulse, work best.

By their very nature, most tests of cardiorespiratory endurance can be relatively time consuming. Often the number of persons needing to be tested and the degree to which those being tested can assist in their own scoring (e.g., counting heartbeats) will determine the specific measure used. Generally, in field-based settings, group tests use a timed run for distance or a 1-mile (1.6 kilometer) run for time. Fernhall and Tymeson (1988) report an 88% correlation between $\dot{V}O_2$max and the 1.5-mile run in subjects with mental retardation. The BPFT uses a 20-meter Pacer, a 16-meter Pacer, the Target Aerobic Movement Test (TAMT), and a 1-mile run/walk as the primary aerobic functioning measures. The Pacer participants run back and forth across the distance and progressively pick up the pace, which increases each minute. The number of laps completed is recorded. The TAMT encourages participants to exercise at a recommended target heart rate using various physical activities to accommodate persons who are nonambulatory or who use supportive devices. Alternatives to running tests include the YMCA 3-minute step test and the cycle ergometer test, which have been used to test aerobic fitness with adequate results.

In addition, physical educators must adequately prepare children for testing and ensure they are free of cardiorespiratory or joint disease. For example, persons with Down syndrome, as a group, manifest certain heart defects or atlantoaxial instability requiring consultation with the appropriate medical personnel to answer the following questions:

- Does the child have any exercise-induced allergies or respiratory or circulatory complications?
- Has the child ever experienced faintness, dizziness, shortness of breath, or chest pains during or after exercise?
- Does the child have any bone, joint, or spasm disorders that may be aggravated by testing?

In certain cases, the person may use a wheelchair, hands, feet, or assistive device for testing, as in the TAMT. Any special circumstances relevant to mobility should be noted, and retests should be conducted under precisely the same conditions as the original. Wheelchairs, in particular, can have a significant effect on any timed test, whether the test alleges to measure cardiorespiratory endurance or speed. Wheelchair frame rigidity, weight, and state of repair are all critical factors. If there has been a change in wheelchairs or a change in the chair's state of repair between tests, test results should not be compared. In addition, using a combination of arms and legs, as with a Schwinn Airdyne cycle ergometer, may elicit values higher than expected because more muscle mass is involved (Pitetti & Tan, 1990). Variations in the level or extent of disability may also affect remaining or functional muscle mass. For this reason, comparing scores among wheelchair users is often of limited value.

One problem inherent in cardiorespiratory endurance testing is that the person being tested may be disinclined to endure the degree of discomfort necessary to produce a valid cardiorespiratory endurance score. In such instances, the tester must determine what motivates each person, as often seen in run/walk tests (Lavay, Reid, & Cressler-Chaviz, 1990). In extreme cases, the tester may find herself running with and encouraging the individual(s) being tested. Obviously, in this scenario, group testing is preferred. Further, if the person administering the test is going to participate alongside the subject, that tester must be consistent with the applications of motivational devices and be physically able to complete the test. Pitetti and Fernhall (2005) recommend an extensive familiarization of the testing protocol to ensure participants are comfortable with their surroundings and understand the task that is required.

Cardiorespiratory Endurance Assessments

One of the most difficult components of physical fitness to measure in children and persons with disabilities is cardiorespiratory endurance. The amount of time, motivation, and ability needed to generate a maximal effort is difficult to sustain, causing the measures to vary with the population assessed. Some protocols will reduce the amount to be run or walked from 900 to 600 to 300 yards (or meters). These distances may not be sufficient to document cardiorespiratory fitness (Baumgartner & Horvat, 1991). Pitetti and Fernhall (2005) provide an excellent review of measuring cardiorespiratory endurance of persons with mental retardation that should be viewed as the gold standard for adapted physical education. In addition, Bar-Or (1983a) has provided test data on individuals with cerebral palsy. Based on these investigations, the following field-based tests should be considered.

Run/Walk Test

Distance runs may be utilized to record time or distance. Running tests include the 1-mile run (found on the Fitnessgram), 1.5-mile run, and 12-minute run. The Fit Youth Today (FYT) battery uses a 20-minute steady-state jog, with distance recommended as the criterion score (American Health and Fitness Foundation, 1986). Baumgartner et al. (2003) indicate that 1-mile and 9-minute runs are valid tests of cardiorespiratory function based on the relationship of time to oxygen uptake. Johnson and Lavay (1988) employ an aerobic movement procedure that includes running; jogging; marching; walking; and propelling a wheelchair, exercise bicycle, scooter board, or walker. This procedure is highly recommended since it provides many variations for children with disabilities.

Rockport Walking Test

The Rockport Walking Test (Kline et al., 1987) estimates $\dot{V}O_2$max from walking 1 mile and monitoring heart rate, while Ross and Jackson (1990) have developed a regression equation for estimating $\dot{V}O_2$max based on weight (pounds), mile walk (time), exercise heart rate (beats per minute), and age. Pitetti, Rimmer, and Fernhall (1993) extend the equation for predicting cardiorespiratory fitness from the Rockport Walking Test to persons with disabilities as

$$\text{peak } \dot{V}O_2 = 101.92 - 2.35 \text{ (mile time)} - 0.42 \text{ (weight)}$$

based on earlier investigations (Fernhall & Tymeson, 1988; Rintala, Dunn, McCubbin, & Quinn, 1992).

Step Tests

The Canadian Standardized Test of Fitness (CSTF) step-test item, measuring cardiorespiratory endurance, has been modified by Montgomery, Reid, and Koziris (1992) and Reid, Montgomery, and Seidl (1985). The subject ascends and descends two 8-inch (20 centimeter) steps at a preestablished cadence; heart rate is utilized to predict aerobic capacity according to the Jette, Campbell, Mongeon, and Routhier (1976) formula. Depending on the heart rate elicited, additional 3-minute bouts of stepping are performed until the person's target heart rate is achieved. Reid et al. (1985) report that only 53% of subjects stopped the test because target heart rate had been achieved, while Montgomery et al. (1992) indicate that the CSTF overestimates peak oxygen consumption. Reid et al. (1985) also report that lack of motivation tends to be a significant factor in subjects' failure to achieve respective target heart rates, a finding of many investigations of persons with disabilities. Pitetti et al. (1993) indicate that muscular coordination and agility can also affect step-test performance. The YMCA Step Test (Golding, 2000, 2002) may provide an alternative measure, although this test has not been used for persons with disabilities.

Shuttle Run

Another test that has been used for persons with intellectual disabilities is the modified Leger and Lambert (1982) shuttle run. Montgomery et al. (1992) modified the first-stage speed of the Leger and Lambert protocol (8.5 kilometers per hour) to 7 kilometers per hour before proceeding to the level of 8.5 kilometers per hour. According to Pitetti and Fernhall (2005), this test measures anaerobic power rather than cardiorespiratory fitness, since participants must run at faster speeds, and muscular coordination, agility, pacing, and the type of floor surface can affect test validity.

Body Composition

Body composition, or body fatness, refers to the percentage of total body weight that is fat. All healthy persons deposit fat for energy storage, body temperature regulation, and shock absorption as well as to carry certain body nutrients (Corbin et al., 2002). Essential fat is estimated to be approximately 8 to 12% for females and 3 to 5% for males (Corbin et al., 2002). Desirable fatness for good health and fitness ranges from 10 to 20% in adult males and 15 to 25% in adult females (Powers & Dodd, 2003). Ideal fatness not only promotes good health but also facilitates physical and motor performance.

A person is considered overweight if he is 10 to 20% above his ideal weight, obese if he is 20 to 50% above his ideal weight, and severely obese if he is more than 50% above his ideal weight. One major problem, however, with using weight to determine overfatness, or obesity, is that weight alone may reveal little about body composition. Two people of the same height and weight may be vastly different in terms of percent body fat. Even among some persons appearing to be at or near ideal body weight, weight alone as an indicator of body fatness can be deceiving. A person may be of expected weight for age and gender, but her weight may be made up of too little muscle and too much fat. For health assessment purposes, weight measures should be interpreted with caution, and fat measures typically are more useful than weight measures.

Some researchers believe that deriving percent body fat measurements from children's skinfolds may not be valid, especially since the determination of body fat varies across age ranges during development. For example, while a 9-year-old girl with a skinfold thickness of 24 millimeters may be normal at the 25th percentile for that age group, an equal thickness in a 14-year-old girl may place her at the 50th percentile. In addition, formulas for estimating percent body fat have been derived primarily from measuring adults. Concern arises over the possibility that body density and fat content relationships may differ between adults and children. A child's skinfold measurement may indicate a poor result based on equations derived from adult norms when in fact the child's percent body fat is in a healthy range for his age and level of development.

Most methods for estimating body fat (such as air displacement, plethysmography, magnetic resonance, and hydrostatic weighing) are not applicable in field-based settings. In field-based settings, skinfolds typically provide the most valid and reliable means of estimating body fat, while measures of body mass index (BMI) and waist-to-hip ratio are also recommended.

Taking skinfold measurements in practical settings requires that the tester become skilled in using skinfold calipers. Each measurement must be taken at the exact site specified by the test. A skinfold measurement is taken by grasping tissue to be measured with the thumb and forefinger and gently drawing the tissue away from the subject's body. At a point adjacent to the thumb–forefinger grasp of the skinfold, the tester applies the caliper (figure 7.10, *a-b*), making sure

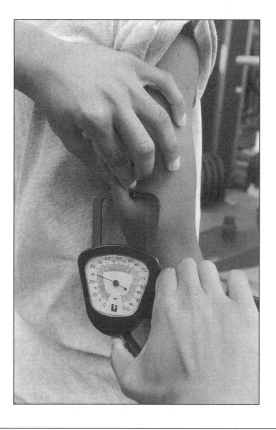
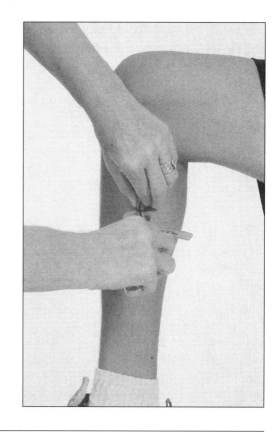

a

b

Figure 7.10 Measurement of skinfold fat: *(a)* triceps and *(b)* calf.

that *only* skin and adipose tissue (not muscle) is being measured. To ensure that muscle is not included in the measurement, the tester can ask the person to flex muscles directly beneath the skinfold measurement site. If the tester does not feel muscles tensing between the thumb–forefinger grasp, he may be assured that muscle will not be included in the measurement.

Body composition information for children and youth is included in most physical fitness batteries and is commonly shown as percentile rank norms rather than specific scores. Since variations in water and bone mineral content are apparent in children, specific equations have been developed for children (Lohman, 1982, 1986, 1987, 1992). In this procedure, the triceps, subscapular, and medial calf are recommended for three consecutive scores, while only the median score is recorded. The procedure is also used in the BPFT, along with BMI. Scoring is provided for the sum of the triceps and subscapular or triceps and calf skinfolds (table 7.2). Very little information is specific to persons with disabilities, although the recent edition of *Applied Body Composition Assessment* (Heyward & Wagner, 2004) provides some information on diabetes, respiratory, and neuromuscular disorders. Johnson, Bulbulian, Gruber, and Sundheim (1986) developed an equation for estimating body fat of 23 athletes with spinal injuries (paraplegia), while Kelly and Rimmer (1987) developed a predictive equation for adult men with mental retardation. In each case, the aim was to provide estimates of body fat specific to each population that could generalize to overall fitness.

Table 7.2   Percentage of Body Fat in Children

	Range	Skinfold measurement (mm)	Percentage of body fat
BOYS	*Triceps plus calf skinfolds*		
	Very low	0-5	0-6%
	Low	5-10	6-10%
	Optimal	10-25	10-20%
	Moderately high	25-32	20-25%
	High	32-40	25-30%
	Very high	40 or above	30% or higher
	Triceps plus subscapular skinfolds		
	Very low	0-5	0-6%
	Low	5-13	6-10%
	Optimal	13-22	10-20%
	Moderately high	22-29	20-25%
	High	29-39	25-30%
	Very high	39 or above	30% or higher
GIRLS	*Triceps plus calf skinfolds*		
	Very low	0-11	0-12%
	Low	11-17	12-15%
	Optimal	17-30	15-25%
	Moderately high	30-36	25-30%
	High	36-45	30-36%
	Very high	45 or above	36% or higher
	Triceps plus subscapular skinfolds		
	Very low	0-11	0-11%
	Low	11-15	11-15%
	Optimal	15-27	15-25%
	Moderately high	27-35	25-30%
	High	35-45	30-35.5%
	Very high	45 or above	35.5% or higher

Reprinted, by permission, from V.H. Heyward and L.M. Stolarczyk, 1996, *Applied body composition assessment* (Champaign, IL: Human Kinetics), 96; Data from T.G. Lohman, 1987, *Measuring body fat using skinfolds* (VHS) (Champaign, IL: Human Kinetics).

Katch and McArdle (1996) developed the following formula that incorporates reduction of percent body fat into an activity program designed to facilitate achievement of desirable weight.

$$\text{Desirable body weight} = \frac{\text{Lean body weight}}{1.00 - \%\text{ fat desired}}$$

Given: A 200-pound male teenager has 25% body fat. The goal is to achieve a body fat of 18%. A step-by-step computation to determine desirable body weight follows:

Step 1. Fat weight = 200 lb $\times$ 0.25 = 50 lb

Step 2. Lean body weight = 200 lb – 50 lb = 150 lb

Step 3. Desirable body weight = 150 lb/(1.00 – 0.18) = 150 lb/0.82 = 182.9 lb

Step 4. Desirable fat loss = present weight – desirable weight

= 200 lb – 182.9 lb

= 17.1 lb

Once the teenager loses approximately 17 pounds (assuming weight loss is, indeed, fat loss resulting from a combination of exercise and diet), he will have achieved his desirable body weight.

In absence of what constitutes a standard, Hubbard (1995) recommends using a body mass index based on the 85th percentile values for age and gender from Healthy People 2000 as an indication of overweight in adolescents. Hubbard defines *overweight* as a BMI greater than or equal to the following:

23.0	males 12-14 years	23.4	females 12-14 years
24.3	males 15-17 years	24.8	females 15-17 years
25.8	males 18-19 years	25.7	females 18-19 years

Body Composition Assessments

Measurement of body composition is difficult in children and persons with disabilities. Children's water and bone mineral content varies with developmental age, and disease can cause differences in fat-free body density (Lohman, 1992). Lohman reviewed several methods of estimating body composition in children, including the use of body mass index, anthropometry, body density, and bioelectric impedance. The following field-based measures of body mass index and skinfolds are included.

Body Mass Index

Body mass index is determined as follows:

$$\text{weight in kg/height in m}^2 = \text{BMI}$$

Higher values for this index indicate higher body fatness. Lohman (1989) gives it a fair rating and indicates that research on this measure found four correlations with skinfolds. BMI should be used only when other measures are unavailable or impractical.

Skinfolds

The work of Lohman and colleagues provides a more useful measure for evaluating percent body fat in children. Body composition standards by Lohman (1987) include the sites of the triceps, subscapular, and medial calf (see table 7.2). The sum of the triceps and medial calf are used in Fitnessgram (The Cooper Institute, 2004) and the BPFT. A recent text extends this work and covers biological influences such as age, ethnicity, gender, and body composition (Heymsfield, Lohman, Wang, & Going, 2005).

Two variations that have been used for persons with disabilities include an equation for adults with intellectual disabilities (Kelly & Rimmer, 1987) using anthropometric data to estimate percent body fat. The Kelly and Rimmer equation follows:

$$\text{Percent body fat} = 13.545 + 0.48691649 \text{ (waist circumference in cm)}$$
$$- 0.52662145 \text{ (forearm circumference in cm)}$$
$$- 0.15504013 \text{ (height in cm)} + 0.07707995 \text{ (weight in kg)}$$

Another equation developed by Johnson et al. (1986) for athletes with spinal injuries (paraplegia) uses circumference, diameter, and skinfold measurements to estimate percent body fat in the following five models:

Model I (anthropometric variables):

$$\text{Percent body fat} = 2.271 + 0.0754 \text{ (abdomen circumference in cm)}$$
$$- 0.305 \text{ (weight in kg)} + 0.567 \text{ (chest skinfold in mm)}$$
$$- 1.017 \text{ (chest diameter in cm)}$$

Model II (diameter and length in cm):

$$\text{Percent body fat} = -46.601 + 3.65 \text{ (bi-iliac)} + 7.75 \text{ (elbow)}$$
$$- 1.145 \text{ (upper-leg length)} - 1.004 \text{ (lower-leg length)}$$

Model III (circumferences in cm):

$$\text{Percent body fat} = -33.535 + 0.831 \text{ (abdomen)} - 0.587 \text{ (calf)}$$

Model IV (skinfolds in mm):

$$\text{Percent body fat} = 3.45 + 0.967 \text{ (chest)} + 0.392 \text{ (calf)}$$

Model V (abdomen circumference only):

$$\text{Percent body fat} = -31.804 + 0.617 \text{ (abdomen circumference)}$$

Power

Power, or explosive strength, is a combination of muscular strength and speed. It is demonstrated when muscles contract rapidly to overcome significant resistance. Power is called for in such skills as throwing, kicking, running (specifically accelerating), jumping, hopping, and leaping.

Case Study 3

Ms. Edwards is coaching a group of athletes with disabilities. How can she determine what events they are best suited for and whether her training program is successful?

Ms. Edwards should base her tests on components of the events she would like to see her class participate in. Muscular strength, speed, and power are common components of most sports skills. She can use a number of tests to measure strength in several muscle groups via bench presses or a manual muscle tester; measure flexibility with a sit-and-reach or modified Thomas test; and measure power with the vertical jump. With these assessments, Ms. Edwards can document strength, flexibility, and power to plan her training and periodically assess the progress of her athletes.

Several clinically based tests have been used to document explosive strength, including the Wingate peak power test (Bar-Or, 1983a, 1983b) and the Margaria-Kalamen leg power test (Margaria, Aghemo, & Rovelli, 1966; Mathews, 1978). The Wingate test uses the arms or legs to pedal an ergometer for 30 seconds at a constant resistance. Power output is recorded as a function of the number of pedal revolutions in 30 seconds (Bar-Or, 1983b). According to Bar-Or (1983a), this test can be used for persons with disabilities as well as children as young as 6 years of age.

The Margaria-Kalaman test requires running a series of steps (nine for adults and six for children). Power is based on the vertical distance, subject's body weight, and time to cover the designated distance (Bar-Or, 1983a). This test primarily assesses the lower extremities. It has not been used for persons with disabilities because it requires some skill to run the steps. The test should be given to individuals with no physical limitations that would reflect on their performance.

One dilemma encountered in using some power assessment items is that normative data either may be inadequate or unavailable. For example, medicine ball chest-pass norms are available, but only on a limited sample size of college men and women (Johnson & Nelson, 1986). The norms dilemma ceases to be a problem if the tester considers individual improvement. In this case, the person would become his own norm, and the score would indicate performance. Where norms are unavailable, the tester can generate local norms by testing an adequate number of subjects. Norms are almost nonexistent for persons with disabilities, so it is essential to document and record performance at yearly intervals.

Power Assessments

Power should be assessed in both the lower and upper extremities. In the lower extremities, the standing long jump and vertical jump are commonly used to assess power. For the upper body, the shot put (4 to 12 pounds [1.8 to 5.4 kilograms]) or medicine ball throw (6 to 9 pounds [2.7 to 4 kilograms]) can be used to record the distance thrown from a stationary position (McCloy & Young, 1954).

Lower-Extremity Power

Because the standing long jump and vertical jump require speed and strength for maximum performance, these measures are extremely helpful to document explosive strength, although the movements do also require coordination. Further, the Sargent vertical jump test (Sargent, 1921) has the added advantage of adjusting the jump height to account for body weight, presenting a relative measure of power.

Vertical jumping may provide a more valid measure of power than the long jump because the former requires less skill. The long jump clearly calls on power but also requires that the subject execute optimal forward body lean and foot placement in front of the body to jump the maximum possible distance.

The vertical jump (in terms of skill) may be less difficult to execute than the long jump, but it often cannot be scored with the same precision. Vertical jump scoring usually requires that the subject mark the wall immediately before jumping, then mark the wall again at the apex of the jump. Occasionally, height of the prejump chalk mark will be more valid than the apex mark. Although the tester can ensure that the prejump chalk mark is indicative of the person's highest reach, less control is evident when documenting where the chalk mark is made at the apex of the jump. Conceivably, a score can be invalid because the mark was made before or after the true apex had been reached. Furthermore, the tester can do little beyond visual or verbal prompting to ensure that the subject is reaching as high as possible when she marks the apex of her jump. One possible solution is to eliminate measurement dependent on reach. Alternatively, the tester may mark the wall to indicate the subject's standing height, then mark the wall at a point equivalent to the height of the person's head at the apex of the jump. This method is limited by the tester's ability to not only accurately judge where the apex mark should be placed but also to avoid the jumper. A wall-mounted vertical jump tester or long jump tester can be used. The Vertec is a vertical jump apparatus used by many college and professional teams to measure vertical jump by noting the specific vanes that move during the jump. Just Jump is another wireless device that measures the vertical jump to the nearest tenth of an inch.

Upper-Extremity Power

Upper-extremity power measures may be particularly appropriate among persons with significantly limited lower-extremity function. Although not originally designed for persons with disabilities, both the shot put and the medicine ball throw seem adaptable for students sitting in a wheelchair. Upper-extremity power can be measured unilaterally by putting a relatively heavy object such as a shot or bilaterally by imparting velocity to a medicine ball in chest-pass fashion. Depending on the person's ability, the weight or selection of the object may vary.

Should the shot-put item be administered, the subject should put the shot from a stationary position. This reduces the likelihood that lower-extremity movement, including skill needed to produce lower-extremity movement, will contaminate the upper-extremity power score.

The medicine ball chest pass can be administered with the person seated in a chair (the chair's legs are secured to the ground). Securing the chair ensures that it does not move during force application. Alternatively, the chair's back can be placed against a wall. Using both hands, the subject holds the medicine ball to the chest and then pushes or releases the ball as aggressively as possible. Upper-extremity power can be determined by measuring distance between the ball's release and landing points. Another version of the medicine ball chest pass is performed by sitting on the floor with the back against a wall and pushing the medicine ball with both hands.

A SAMPLING OF TEST BATTERIES

This section introduces a representative sample of fitness test batteries. Physical educators must show good judgment when selecting tests because some have been more carefully constructed than others. Teachers must not assume that a test—simply because it has been published and is in use—is valid, reliable, and objective. Some instruments do not reflect the population they were developed for or are outdated. We provide samples of tests that teachers can use to accurately assess children. In addition, previous sections have documented test items that can be used in adapted physical education.

Tests presented here are not necessarily being recommended. Rather, they are offered with comments and constructive criticisms for the potential user's consideration. Whether *any* test is selected for use must be determined by the test's technical adequacy, the tester's competence, the information desired, and the characteristics of the person to be tested.

Teachers should select items based on the information required to develop their program plans. Since many test batteries do not represent the variety of populations encountered in adapted physical education, it is recommended that physical educators select test items that are specific to the age and task requirements of their students. By doing so, teachers can assess children who need instruction to facilitate motor development, control body composition, promote flexibility, or develop strength and endurance needed in work-related settings.

AAHPERD Physical Best

The American Alliance for Health, Physical Education, Recreation and Dance (AAHPERD) recommends that Physical Best replace *all* previous tests. Similar in intent to the earlier AAHPERD Health-Related Fitness Test, Physical Best focuses primarily on health-related fitness. However, appendixes within the manual also provide instructions and norms for measuring selected motor fitness components. Physical Best health-related fitness items are appropriate for persons aged 5 to 18. Motor fitness items appearing in the appendixes are appropriate for persons 9 to 17.

Performance standards are provided for each health-related fitness test item by age and gender. For example, in the 1-mile run/walk for 6-year-old girls, the standard is 13 minutes. The person tested can be deemed either to have met or to have not met a single performance standard for gender and age. The test does not provide norms that permit the tester to determine, for example, that a person's time in the 1-mile (1.6-kilometer) run/walk places her in a percentile. Percentile norms, however, are available for motor fitness test items appearing in the manual's appendix.

Where percentile norms are not available, Physical Best test items are of somewhat limited value as tools for determining need for a child's placement outside the general class. Typically, qualification for special programs requires performance below a specified level on a norm-referenced test. For example, if the percentile is determined to be a program's entry criterion, a person scoring below the percentile would qualify for entry.

Physical Best and Fitnessgram

AAHPERD and the The Cooper Institute for Aerobics Research, now known as The Cooper Institute, joined forces to provide for the physical education assessment and programming needs of persons who have disabilities. The AAHPERD manual *Physical Best and Individuals With Disabilities,* published in 1995, utilizes the Prudential Fitnessgram (The Cooper Institute for Aerobics Research, 1992) health-related fitness test in partnership with Physical Best (Seaman, 1995). The manual offers guidelines for modifying Fitnessgram test items or selecting alternative items, as needed, to meet assessment needs of children with disabilities. The manual also includes curricula specific for persons with disabilities whose fitness needs may not be met in mainstream settings, as well as safety and measurement guidelines.

Alternative items for measuring aerobic capacity include submaximal assessments for some persons with respiratory and heart-related disabilities. Swimming, hand cycling, propelling a wheelchair, and walking are recommended as alternative items for persons with limited mobility.

Alternative body composition measures should take into consideration that certain disabilities may preclude taking skinfolds. In this case, body composition can be assessed on an individual basis, with the person becoming his own norm.

Alternative ways to test muscular strength, endurance, and flexibility include any valid test item that is within the child's capabilities. For example, when testing persons with motor limitations, the teacher can eliminate timing limits on test items or allow more trials for each criterion.

Since Fitnessgram items are incorporated into the assessment facet of the Physical Best Fitnessgram program, the assessment part of this package may not be useful for placement purposes. Generally, criteria for placement in a modified program require a specific score (e.g., two standard deviations below the mean) on a norm-referenced test. Information concerning publication of Fitnessgram (Seaman, 1995) and the Prudential Fitnessgram (The Cooper Institute for Aerobics Research, 1992) acknowledges this limitation. The recommendation is that test scores for persons with disabilities may be used for comparison purposes, wherein each person becomes his or her own norm on key cutoff points, such as the 50th and 75th percentiles, to make decisions concerning placement.

Brockport Physical Fitness Test (BPFT)

The Brockport Physical Fitness Test (BPFT) criterion-referenced test of health-related fitness is for persons aged 10 to 17 with mental retardation, cerebral palsy, spinal cord injury, and visual impairment, as well as for individuals without disabilities. Twenty-seven test items were drawn from AAHPERD Physical Best and Fitnessgram to provide the tester flexibility in personalizing the test for various children (Winnick & Short, 1999). Norms are not applicable for persons with multiple or progressive disabilities, but are offered for persons who do not have disabilities, for comparison purposes. Although Winnick and Short allude to establishing validity based on concurrent, construct, and logical validity, the test was not developed and validated on a normative sample. In this context, the test is useful for individualizing assessment for a variety of disabilities but is not an all-encompassing measure of fitness.

Kansas Adapted/Special Physical Education Test

One test specifically targeted for children in adapted physical education is the Kansas Adapted/Special Physical Education Test. This test is a noncategorical assessment of persons with disabilities who qualify for adapted physical education (Johnson & Lavay, 1988). Test items, which include sit-ups, sit-and-reach, isometric push-ups, bench presses, and aerobic movement, were field tested on 200 children who qualified for adapted physical education in Kansas. The test has been used numerous times in clinical and school-based settings with children as young as 5 years of age.

The strength of these test items is that they are so adaptable to a variety of populations in an adapted setting. Group means on test items are available in other sources (Eichstaedt & Lavay, 1992). This test may be applicable to school-based settings for documenting performance and developing program plans.

YMCA Fitness Testing and Assessment Manual

The YMCA was the pioneer of fitness testing, and this fourth edition (Golding, 2000) is an excellent revision of previous work. The YMCA's fitness assessment protocol was designed primarily for adults, providing norms for men and women in the age ranges of 18 to 25, 26 to 35, 36 to 45, 46 to 55, 56 to 65, and 66 and above. The YMCA has been a consistent leader in fitness testing, and since tests are usually done at a local YMCA, a minimal amount of equipment is needed. Generalizations and adaptations have been used for a variety of individuals. Because of the long history of the YMCA in developing fitness assessments, these tests should be considered for adapted physical education.

What You Need to Know ▶▶▶

Key Terms

1RM	flexibility	muscular strength and endurance
body composition	functional fitness	
body mass index	health-related fitness	performance
cardiorespiratory endurance	isometric strength	physical fitness
dynamic strength	motor fitness	power

Key Concepts

1. You should be able to differentiate between tests for physical fitness and functional capacity that are adaptable for students with disabilities. If specific tests are not available, what assessments would be appropriate?

2. You should be able to describe the effects on physical functioning that may be present with a disability; likewise, you should be able to determine if decreased functioning is due to inactivity or overprotection.

3. You should be familiar with field-based and laboratory fitness assessments as well as special considerations for testing individuals with disabilities.

4. You should be able to use fitness testing information to develop an intervention plan or conditioning program.

Review Questions

1. What factors characterize the development of muscular strength, muscular endurance, and aerobic functioning in children? How would a disability affect this development?

2. You are preparing some Special Olympics athletes for competition in throwing and running events. What assessments would you use to develop and monitor their training programs?

3. A 6-year-old child has some difficulty with standing from a sitting position, descending stairs, and rising from the floor. What components of fitness would you assess to develop your program plan?

4. How does body composition affect fitness and movement parameters in children with Down syndrome, visual impairments, or spina bifida?

5. For children with disabilities to exert a maximal effort during testing, what motivational or prompting strategies would you use?

Chapter **8**

Assessing Posture and Gait

A s children mature in the developmental process, they develop the ability to move within the environment. After learning to crawl and creep, children develop the ability to stand and then walk. Several factors that are specific to movement—and to any dysfunction within its physical development—should be included in the assessment process.

In this context, we address the basic components of posture and gait as they relate to movement development. The purpose of this chapter is to identify posture problems that require assessment, review specific posture tests, and discuss the transition from standing posture to movement by addressing components and problems associated with gait and selected gait-analysis techniques.

POSTURE

Knowledge of appropriate posture and of structural deviations that affect standing is essential for understanding movement problems. For many persons with disabilities, posture and gait abnormalities are the direct result of their condition or deterioration in functional ability. It is essential to identify specific posture or gait abnormalities before selecting an intervention program. For children with developmental disabilities, these problems become apparent early in motor development during walking, while climbing stairs, or in movement patterns.

Posture can be defined as the manner in which the body aligns itself against gravity. Posture is influenced by the skeletal system, ligaments, muscles, fatigue, and self-concept. Correct posture is achieved when all segments of the body are properly aligned over a base of support, with minimum stress applied to each joint. Body positions that compromise the body's base of support and increase stress on joints precipitate faulty posture (Magee, 2002).

Without proper maintenance of postural muscles and the use of corrective techniques, the deficiency may deteriorate, possibly become debilitating, and either interfere with physical performance capabilities or become a structural deviation. Some functional causes of faulty posture include lack of muscular development, muscular imbalance, muscle contracture, pain, obesity, muscle spasms, respiratory disorders, and loss of sensory input or proprioception.

Posture encompasses more than maintaining a static position, since movement requires the body to constantly assume and change positions. Muscles that have sufficient strength and joints that are flexible will accommodate changes in position and adapt readily to movement stresses. For the dysfunctional muscle, the ability to maintain an upright position may be affected by muscle weakness and the body's inability to accommodate stress (Magee, 2002).

The sitting position of back against the seat, feet on the floor, and thighs and back supported by the seat permits people to maintain a relaxed position while the chair provides body support. Additionally, arm rests positioned at elbow height support the arms and relax the postural muscles. Faulty sitting posture results in improper body alignment, slumping of the back and shoulders, and concentration of the majority of weight on one side of the body. Nonambulatory persons are especially susceptible to sitting postural faults and may develop complications such as pressure sores, scoliosis, and respiratory dysfunctions. The overall lack of muscular development and stability restricts appropriate physical development and, in turn, stresses joints that maintain the proper sitting posture needed to perform functional daily living tasks.

Standing posture is characterized by an erect position with an elevated head and chest, posterior-tilted pelvis, slightly curved abdomen and lower back, slightly flexed knees, and parallel feet spaced a comfortable distance apart to allow for an even weight distribution. Orthopedic impairments may apply inappropriate stress on the muscles and joints as well as affect standing posture if proper alignment or structural components are altered. If muscle development is not promoted via an intervention, the person may demonstrate posture problems including slumped shoulders, a head tilt, a protruding abdomen, spinal deviations or curves, and improper foot placement (table 8.1). The lack of feedback in sensory disorders often affects a person's ability to maintain an appropriate postural alignment.

Individual Differences in Posture

When analyzing proper posture, adapted physical educators should note individual differences associated with motor development, body type, and disability. Infants and children in the primary grades may exhibit a wide base of support, slightly bowed legs, and a slightly protruding abdomen, all of which are typical until sufficient strength is developed. A curvature of the spine at this developmental age does not necessarily constitute a postural defect. However, the same occurrence in adults would indicate a marked deficit or muscle weakness that may require corrective measures.

Persons with specific body types and builds are also apt to assume various postures. For example, body types may be classified as mesomorphic (muscular), endomorphic (round), or ectomorphic (slender), or any combination of the three. The upper torso may be the predominant characteristic of one body-type

Table 8.1   Common Posture Problems

Good posture	Body segment	Poor posture
Head in balance	Head	Chin out
Erect head position		Head tilted or rotated to side
Arms at sides, palms facing the body	Upper back	Stiff arms, palms rotated
Shoulders level and symmetrical		Shoulders rounded or one shoulder higher
Scapulae flat against the rib cage		Scapulae pulled back or far apart; scapulae prominent, standing out from the rib cage ("winged scapulae")
Trunk erect	Trunk	Depressed "hollow-chest" position
Back in good alignment		Ribs more prominent on one side
		Lower ribs protruding
		Trunk inclined to rear
Abdomen flat	Abdomen	Abdomen protrudes or sags
Pelvis and thighs in a straight line	Lower back	Lordosis, or forward curvature of the spine
Normal curve (neck and lower back: forward curve; upper back and spine: backward curve)		Pelvis tilts forward
		Kyphosis, or round upper back
		Increased forward curve in neck, round upper back, and forward head
		Scoliosis, or lateral curve of the spine (one side: C curve; both sides: S curve)
Hips level	Hips	One hip higher (lateral pelvic tilt)
Spine straight		Hips rotated forward, spine slightly or markedly curved
Legs straight	Knees and legs	Knees touch when feet apart (genu valgum)
		Knees apart when feet touch (genu varum)
		Knees curve actively backward
		Knees bend forward
		Patellae face slightly inward or outward
Standing feet straight ahead	Feet	Low arch ("flat-footed")
Walking feet parallel		Weight on the inner side of the foot (pronation)
Running feet parallel or toeing-in		Weight on the outer side of the foot (supination)
		Toeing-out
		Toeing-in ("pigeon-toed")

classification, while the lower extremities may characterize another specific body type. The mix of body-type classifications may lead to improper posture development (e.g., a muscular chest and back coupled with a slender abdomen and lower limbs may appear as a rounded upper back). Likewise, disabilities such as spinal injuries or amputations affect the amount of available muscle mass or alter body mechanics, often leading to faulty postures.

Causes of Postural Deviations

There is no single cause of posture deficits. Postural deviations can be either functional or structural. A functional condition may be overcome through corrective exercises or kinesthetic awareness training of proper positions. Structural deviations occur because of abnormalities or deformities of the skeletal system resulting from disease or injury. Common structural deviations include leg-length differences, spinal anomalies, scoliosis, kyphosis, and lordosis. Because of the severity of structural defects, most are treated by doctors with a combination of braces, casts, surgery, and prosthetic devices. The assessment of posture and subsequent instructional programming should be interrelated to avoid potential problems and minimize effects of faulty posture on physical functioning.

Specific disabilities may cause a lack of proper feedback among persons with sensory impairments; fatigue among individuals who use a wheelchair; and additional complications in walking postures, such as when shifting weight or regaining balance, among persons with a prosthetic device. As a group, persons with disabilities have a greater incidence of postural defects than do the general population because muscular function and sensory feedback are essential for appropriate posture (Horvat, Eichstaedt, Kalakian, & Croce, 2003). For example, lack of sensory information may contribute to poor posture or head tilts since the available sensory feedback is not used to maintain or reinforce appropriate posture. A person with an amputation, spinal injury, or neurological disorder may place undue pressure on his postural structure while sitting and may need to accommodate for balance changes to reestablish the center of gravity that was altered by injury or disability. Sitting upright is essential for performing functional skills, and upright posture relies on the trunk muscles for spinal stability. A deviation such as kyphosis compromises achieving the upright sitting position (Miedaner, 1990). Likewise, insufficient strength in the trunk muscles, often seen in persons with muscular dystrophy, spinal deviations, lower-back problems, and mechanical movement inefficiencies, may affect the ability to maintain upright posture.

ASSESSING POSTURE

In most cases, standing posture is assessed by means of a plumb line or by common instruments such as the New York State Posture Test (figure 8.1) or the San Diego State University Adapted Physical Education Posture Evaluation (figure 8.2). We recommend these instruments because of their history of extensive use and because they are cost and time efficient. In each assessment, the teacher observes a child in a variety of positions. The New York State Posture Test uses 13 sets and levels of posture. Three sets of pictures demonstrate various levels of posture: one sequence is the appropriate posture, the second is fair, and the third is poor posture. The tester observes the child and selects the level that best represents the student's posture, assigning the score for that posture at the appropriate grade level. If the teacher decides that posture affects movement ability or requires compensations, specific information must be obtained concerning the deficiency.

POSTURE RATING CHART

Grade | 4 | 5 | 6 | 7 | 8 | 9 | 10 | 11 | 12 |

Rater's initials

Date of test

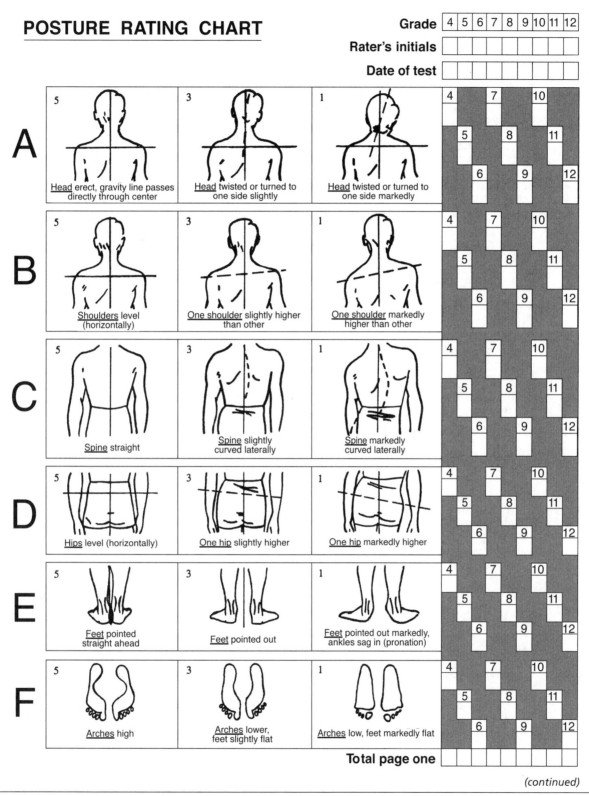

Total page one

(continued)

Figure 8.1 New York State Posture Test.

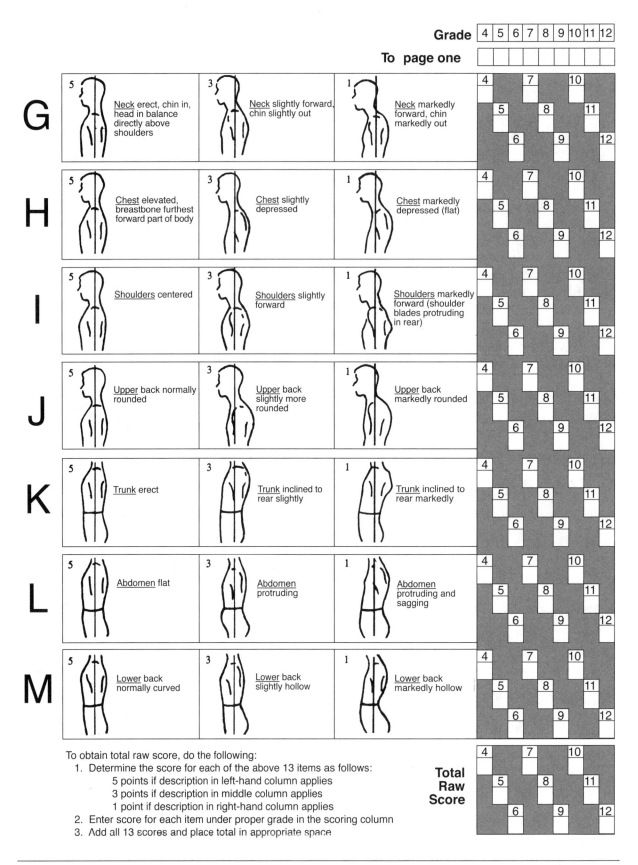

Figure 8.1 *(continued)*

San Diego State University
Adapted Physical Education Posture Evaluation

A. STRENGTH

    1. Abdominal: modified curl-ups

    SCORING: Record the number of curl-ups performed in 1 minute.

B. FLEXIBILITY

    1. Chest and shoulders. Assume hook-lying position. Keeping low back pressed to the floor (assistant should check by placing hand between lumbar area and floor), extend arms overhead and press back of arms and hands to the floor. Elbows must remain locked at all times.

    SCORING: *WNL: total contact of hands and forearms with floor

    **LOM: contact of hands only with floor or cannot make contact without arching low back

    2. Spine and hip extensor: sit-and-reach

    SCORING: Record the number of centimeters reached by the fingertips.

    3. Right hip flexors. Assume supine lying position with both knees bent over the end of a table. Pull bent left knee tight into the chest, keeping the right leg bent over the end of the table (Thomas test).

    4. Left hip flexors. Same as above but with positions of the legs reversed.

    SCORING: WNL: if thigh remains flat on the table

    LOM: if thigh lifts upward; estimate angle between leg and the table

    Note: If thigh rotates outward or inward, rotators are tight. Star and report on the back of posture sheet.

---

*Within normal limits   **Limitation of motion

C. ORTHOPEDIC EVALUATION

    1. Foot examination. Note pes planus (eversion), pes cavus (inversion), Achilles flare, hallux valgus, overlapping toes, corns, calluses, hammer toes.

    SCORING: Record degree of fluctuation. If greater than 1/4 inch, indicates pes planus.

    2. Scoliosis check: procedures for spinal screening

    FIRST: Ask if there is a history of scoliosis in the family.

    SECOND: Look at the students' backs while they are standing. Ask yourself the following:

        1. Is the head centered?

        2. Are the shoulders the same level?

        3. Are the tips of the scapulae the same level?

        4. Are the arms the same distance from the body?

        5. Are the trunk contours the same? Lateral deviation of spinous processes?

        6. Are the hips level?

        7. Are the popliteal creases level?

        8. Are both knees straight?

The above are pieces of a puzzle. A positive finding in any of the above may be a normal variant or may indicate scoliosis. The next check is perhaps the most important.

(continued)

Figure 8.2 San Diego State University Adapted Physical Education Posture Evaluation.

Adapted with permission of San Diego State University.

THIRD: The individual bends forward with hands together, head down as if diving into a pool. View the student from the back. Ask yourself the following:

1. Is one side of the thoracic or lumbar spine higher than the other?

FOURTH: The student bends forward as above, but you view the individual from the front. Ask yourself the following:

1. Is one side of the thoracic or lumbar spine higher than the other?

FIFTH: Take a quick look at the side view of the individual as a check for kyphosis. Ask yourself the following:

1. Is the curve even or does it peak?

NOW you make the decision for referral. The primary reason for referring a student is a rib hump, which is usually accompanied by asymmetry of some type in the back.

1. Anterior view. Use a plumb line drawn from a point equidistant from the medial malleoli and extending vertically, bisecting the body.
   a. Head twist (lateral flexion combined with rotation to the opposite side): torticollis
   b. Shoulder level: right or left drop of acromion process
   c. Linea alba: right or left shift
   d. Anterior spines (hip): right or left drop
   e. Legs
2. Internal or external rotation at the hip
3. Tibial torsion: patellae face inward when feet are together
4. Knock knees (genu valgum)
5. Lateral view. Use vertical lines and estimate degree of deviation based on the following fixed check points: beginning with a point 1 1/2 inches anterior to the lateral malleolus and proceeding upward to the center of the knee (behind patella), center of the hip (trochanter), center of the shoulder (acromion process), and through the earlobe (tragus).
   a. Body lean: forward or backward
   b. Head: forward or backward
   c. Shoulders: forward or backward
   d. Kyphosis (thoracic curve): use yardstick to check for perpendicular alignment to the floor
   e. Lordosis (lumbar curve): measure the distance in centimeters to a vertical line (use yardstick) drawn between the thoracic and sacral apices.
   f. Ptosis: abdominal protuberance; abdomen should not extend beyond a line extending down from the sternum
   g. Back knees (genu recurvatum); relaxed knees (flexed)
6. Posterior view
   a. Head tilt: right or left drop
   b. Winged scapula: right or left
   c. Thoracic: right or left shift
   d. Lumbar: right or left shift
   e. Posterior spine: right or left drop
   f. Bow legs (genu varum)

Figure 8.2 *(continued)*

g. Pronated or supinated ankles: draw a perpendicular line from the ASIS of the hip to the floor. The line should pass through the center of the knee and between the first and second metatarsals.

h. Short leg: note evenness of popliteal creases

D. DYNAMIC POSTURE

1. Walking. Observe walking front, side, and back view. Feet should be pointing straight ahead. The weight of the body should be taken on the heel first, then transferred to the outer border of the foot, then to the ball and finally pushing off the great toe. The body weight shifts smoothly and rhythmically. Arms swing freely and in alternation with the legs. Note any peculiarities such as pronating ankles, inward or outward rotation of the hip, improper weight transfer, scissoring of knees, excessive trunk movements, stiffness, and so on.

Figure 8.2   *(continued)*

Postural assessments should also detect conditions that can interfere with performing activities of daily living or work-related skills (e.g., deviations of the spine or a weak lower back). Problems that result from structural, sensory, mechanical, or neurological dysfunctions may inhibit the ability to perform functional tasks over a period of time. For example, upright and walking posture, with or without a prosthetic device, may be distorted after an amputation because of shifts in body weight, loss of balance, or loss of sensory feedback. Structurally, if the base of support and center of gravity are altered, movement and postural adjustment may be required to maintain an appropriate gait or sit upright in a wheelchair. Likewise, in recent spinal injuries, loss of function and subsequent time needed for various muscles to assume functions of nonwalking muscle groups contribute to difficulties in maintaining a sitting posture.

In addition, loss of sensory function may contribute to postural tilts or lead to inadequate sensory feedback. In acquired injuries, sensory function and "motor memory" may not be available to assume a posture or perform a specific movement. Likewise, in incomplete spinal injuries and hemiplegia, the maintenance of motor patterns and muscle weakness may result from sensory deficits (Bobath, 1990). A resultant loss of posture may be directly related to the lack of sensory information that signals foot placement, tripping, or dragging the feet. In other situations, individuals may not be able to recognize or locate sensory information, such as touch or pressure, from slight to complete agnosia. Since kinesthetic information does not provide appropriate feedback, and the movement of the limb feels awkward or distorted, the person encounters difficulty maintaining stability and moving the limb appropriately.

Muscle tone associated with posture also affects posture maintenance. Normal movements such as walking or running are supported by accompanying changes in posture and movement. In contrast, abnormal tone does not utilize the automatic adjustments in posture and movement needed for the tasks of walking or running. This effect can be seen in persons with cerebral palsy, where spastic movements produce varying distributions and degrees of strength that interfere with purposeful movement.

The spastic muscle may provide excessive resistance or excessive assistance to movement (Bobath, 1990). These complications make it essential to observe changes in tone and movement response and relate them to changes in posture. For example, leaning to one side is normally associated with the contraction of the head and neck muscles on the other side. If the normal adaptation to this change in position is disrupted (i.e., the postural reaction mechanism is absent), the result may be a fall.

Bobath (1990) recommends passively placing individuals in a variety of positions (adduction, abduction, internal rotation, external rotation, flexion, extension, supination, and pronation). As the examiner moves the limbs to various positions, the effects on posture and movement should be noted. For the practitioner, this can be a helpful screening device to note changes in posture occurring during movement. For example, in normal postures, adjustments are made as corresponding muscles adapt to specific movements. In abnormal postures, adjustment is not apparent. In addition, resistance may be encountered in some body segments such as the elbow, shoulder, hip, knee, or ankle. Directional movements, especially in spasticity, may provide uncontrolled assistance, as in a sudden pull or push. Moderate to slight spasticity may provide assistance at the end of the movement, while in flaccid movements no active adjustments are evident (Bobath, 1990). Abnormal postural reflex activity results in the inability to perform active movements. For the teacher, this may indicate that an inability to perform a movement is specific to the lack of response to postural changes.

In other cases, the sitting postures of children with motor impairments may be directly related to trunk strength and the position assumed. For example, Miedaner (1990) describes straight sitting as pelvis rotated forward, weight over the ischial tuberosities, back straight, and lumbar spine moved toward lordosis; anterior sitting as trunk straight, weight anterior to the ischial tuberosities; and posterior sitting as spinal kyphosis, pelvis rotated back and posterior to the ischial tuberosities. Using the modified Schober Measurement of Spinal Extension (American Academy of Orthopedic Surgeons, 1975), Miedaner compared sitting positions on a floor, bench, and Ther-A Chair and reported that sitting positions with anterior sitting postures increased trunk extension. This finding is noteworthy because the ability to maintain a postural position dramatically affects the level of functional ability. Since the trunk muscles are essential for postural control in a seated position, strengthening these muscles and maintaining an appropriate position will allow functional capabilities, such as pulmonary function and position changes, to fulfill daily living needs.

Case Study 1

A postural screening shows that Kimberly has lumbar lordosis. She also has a tendency to slouch. Her parents have contacted the physical education teacher about possible problems and recommendations for intervention.

It is important to assess causative factors that may be causing Kimberly's problems. First, the teacher should determine if Kimberly has insufficient flexibility in the back and hamstrings, which may contribute to her lordosis. She may also have a muscle imbalance, contraction, or weakness resulting from another condition. Likewise, the teacher should evaluate Kimberly's abdominal strength to look at opposing muscle groups that may exacerbate her lordosis. Her slouching may result from being taller than her peers, a growth spurt, onset of puberty, or muscle weakness. Depending on his assessment, the teacher can begin to remediate specific problems. In this case, the New York State Posture Test or the San Diego State University Adapted Physical Education Posture Evaluation would be recommended to determine Kimberly's problem.

Standing posture can also be affected by lower-extremity strength. For older people and those with disabilities, postural adjustments are compromised by a lack of muscular strength that may result in falls (Shumway-Cook & Woollacott, 2001). To facilitate adequate stability and posture, physical activity should be encouraged to eliminate patterns of inactivity that may contribute to reduced physical functioning and poor postural stability.

Further, to promote activities of daily living or work performance, identifying postural difficulties may help determine what is detracting from functional performance. For instance, in case study 1, if Kimberly's lack of auditory sensory feedback interferes with her sitting posture while working at a computer, manual or visual prompts can cue the proper sitting position. Likewise, if functioning is impeded by the inability to adjust body segments, the assessment of posture and muscle tone should be helpful in determining areas of weakness that can be remediated. Included in table 8.1 are the common problems associated with posture. The teacher should use this information with a standard static posture assessment such as the New York State Posture Test or the San Diego State University Adapted Physical Education Posture Evaluation to generate an accurate assessment of posture that can be used to develop instructional programs. Kimberly's lordosis may be caused by weak abdominal muscles. By incorporating exercises such as abdominal crunches during physical education or at home, this problem can be remediated.

GAIT ANALYSIS

Developmentally, posture is the parameter that affects transition from standing to movements such as walking or running. Although posture may be adequate for a person to stand, it may vary undesirably in walking or running if the person does not have adequate maturity, balance, or strength to maintain an upright posture during these activities. According to Clark and Whitall (1989), forces that are created in running may stress the postural system's ability to maintain an upright position. Since running and stair climbing use the same pattern of intra-limb coordination as creeping and walking, maintaining postures during these movements requires an increase in force production that commonly presents difficulties for young children and persons with disabilities.

Because of poor development and postural instability, children with disabilities have difficulty making transitions between basic locomotor patterns and dealing with the increase in force production. The transition from being nonambulatory to moving requires adequate balance and stability before the coordinative pattern of walking becomes apparent (Thelen, Ulrich, & Jensen, 1989). A child who has difficulty developing these patterns has difficulty rotating or adjusting to changes in the environment, such as variations in terrain. If the child does not develop a combination of strength and stability, she will not achieve independent walking or movement. Disorders that affect the ability to coordinate movement patterns, such as cerebral palsy, change basic movements. For example, the normal order of hip movements in walking is flexion, abduction, and external rotation. In children with spastic cerebral palsy, movements are flexion, adduction, and internal rotation (Sugden & Keogh, 1990).

Movement difficulties may result from some underlying neurological or muscular component that should be assessed to adequately portray the person's developmental needs. The observation that a child cannot run should be more thoroughly investigated to determine the specific components that may be interfering with or delaying development of the appropriate movement pattern. Likewise, if a child has difficulty ascending or descending stairs, a characteristic of muscular dystrophy, gait and underlying components such as strength and balance should be assessed to preserve function.

In clinical settings, a variety of gait-analysis techniques can be used to evaluate muscle functions and correlate them with gait. Most comprehensive gait assessments are conducted with electromyographs for muscle function and with force plates to record forces and torques on body segments. Although this information is beneficial, most field-based assessments rely on observational data and videotapes of gaits to detect abnormalities. These latter techniques should be sufficient for the teacher to detect problem areas in strength and posture that affect ambulation and development patterns. More important, the information generated can be incorporated in the program or instructional plan.

ASSESSING GAIT

Functional gait patterns are observed extensively in clinical settings. Vaughan, Davis, and O'Connor (1992a, 1992b) used an application of gait analysis with a computerized software package developed in conjunction with Human Kinetics. Although the framework is designed for biomechanical analysis, the framework of this program provides basic kinematics and muscle responses that can be used to functionally assess gait parameters. Observational assessments such as those used at the Los Amigos Research and Education Institute (LAREI, 2001) direct attention to a specific body segment at a point during a gait cycle. For example, the tester may observe heel striking at that specific point in the cycle to determine if normal or abnormal movements are occurring during walking.

Scoring may vary from a system of present, inconsistent, borderline, occurs throughout, absent, limited, or exaggerated gait deviations to the Rancho Los Amigos system of assessing movements of body segments in the gait cycle: ankle, foot, knee, hip, pelvis, and trunk (LAREI, 2001). The Rancho Los Amigos assessment consists of a full-body gait analysis through weight acceptance (WA), single-leg support (SLS), and single-leg advancement (SLA). This assessment, developed by Dr. Jacquelin Perry at Rancho Los Amigos National Rehabilitation Center, is the foremost instrument for observational gait analysis.

For the practitioner, observation of the movement pattern is the most useful and functional way to detect gait abnormalities. To conduct a gait analysis in a field-based instructional or recreational setting, it is recommended that the tester become familiar with normal gait, normal gait terminology, the normal gait cycle, and abnormal gait before applying the analysis to detect gait abnormalities.

Because observational gait analysis is subjective and requires quick decisions, the subject's patterns should be videotaped to provide a complete analysis of the process. The taping procedure also aids in determining reliability within the observational assessment.

Normal Gait and Gait Terminology

To adequately assess deviations in gait patterns, an understanding of gait terminology (table 8.2) and the normal pattern is necessary (Magee, 2002; Norkin, 2001). Developmentally, changes in gait patterns are achieved as early as 2 years

Table 8.2   Gait Terminology

Term	Description
Gait cycle	Time interval or sequence of motions between two contacts of the same foot
Stride	One complete gait cycle
Step	Beginning of sequence by one limb until beginning of sequence with the contralateral limb
Stance phase	Foot is on the ground bearing weight, allowing lower leg to support body and advancement of the body over the supporting limb; makes up 60% of gait cycle and consists of 5 subphases: 1. Initial contact (heel strike) 2. Loading response (foot flat) 3. Midstance (single-leg stance) 4. Terminal stance (heel-off) 5. Preswing (toe-off)
Swing phase	Foot is moving forward and not bearing weight, allowing toes to clear floor and adjusting the leg as well as advancing the swing leg forward; makes up 40% of gait cycle and consists of 3 subphases: 1. Initial swing (acceleration) 2. Midswing 3. Terminal swing (deceleration)
Double-leg stance	Phase when parts of both feet are on the ground, making up 25% of gait cycle
Single-leg stance	Phase when one leg is on the ground, occurring twice during gait cycle and making up approximately 30% of gait cycle
Base width	Distance between opposite feet (usually 2 to 4 in. [5 to 10 cm]); varies with poor balance, loss of sensation and proprioception
Step length	Distance between successive contact points in opposite feet; varies with age, height, fatigue, pain, and disease
Stride length	Linear distance between successive points of contact of the same foot (gait cycle); approximately 28 to 31 in. (71 to 79 cm)
Pelvic shift	Side to side (lateral) movement of pelvis necessary to align weight over stance leg
Pelvic rotation	Rotation of pelvis to lessen angle of femur with the floor to help regulate subject's walking speed and decrease center of gravity
Cadence	Number of steps per minute from heel strike to toe-off; approximately 90 to 120 per minute

for an advanced pattern. Pelvic rotation is usually evident at 13.8 months, knee flexion at midsupport at 16.3 months, base of support at 17 months, and heel and forefoot strike at 18.5 months (Payne & Isaacs, 2005).

Normal Gait Cycle

In a normal gait cycle, the swing and stance phases can be noted (LAREI, 2001). In the swing phase, the initial swing is the first subphase. Flexion of the hip and knee allow for initial acceleration and stabilization of the trunk in single support. The ankle will plantar flex, while the dorsiflexors help the foot clear the supporting surface. At midswing the hip continues to flex and medially rotate while the knee flexes. The body is aligned in a single support phase with the pelvis and trunk. Maximum knee flexion is evident as the leg moves forward, ending the acceleration phase and beginning deceleration. The terminal swing is the last phase as the leg decelerates in preparation for a heel strike. Hip flexion and rotation continue while the knee is fully extended. The trunk and pelvis maintain the support position, and the ankle is dorsiflexed and the forefoot supinated before heel strike. The hamstrings are also contracting to aid in the deceleration.

The stance phase begins with initial contact, or heel strike. Hip flexion is 30°, with the knees slightly flexed and the ankle in a neutral position. The pelvis is level, and the heel contacts the supporting surface. In the loading response as the sole of the foot contacts the floor, the weight is transported to the limbs. The foot is pronated to adapt to various surfaces and contacts the floor while the ankle is plantar flexed approximately 15°. Hips are flexed and laterally rotate while the knee flexes approximately 15°. Trunk alignment is in a neutral position with the stance leg, while the pelvis drops slightly and rotates medially on the swing leg.

The midstance phase begins when the contralateral limb leaves the ground and ends when the body is directly over the supporting limb, aligning the body over the trunk and pelvis with a neutral rotation. The hip assumes the greatest force with extension to a neutral position. The knee also flexes, and the ankle goes from plantar flexion to 10° dorsiflexion; the forefoot is pronated and the hindfoot inverted.

The terminal stance (heel-off) is from the midstance to point of contact with the contralateral extremity. The trunk is erect, and the hip moves from lateral to medial rotation. The knee is extended, and the ankle is in plantar flexion (with heel-off) before contact of the opposite foot. In the preswing phase, the initial contact of the contralateral extremity is before the toe-off of the reference extremity. The pelvis is level and laterally rotated, and the trunk is aligned over the lower extremities. The knee is flexed 35°, and plantar flexion of the ankle is approximately 20° to toe-off.

Abnormal Gait

To accurately assess difficulties with gait and the accompanying movement problems, it is necessary to observe improper elements of gait to determine specific causes and dysfunctions. Included in table 8.3 are several examples of gait abnormalities commonly seen in school and clinical settings (Magee, 2002; Norkin, 2001; Soderberg, 1986). Although this is not a complete list of gait abnormalities, these examples should be helpful in formulating information that is needed to understand movement problems and develop the instructional program.

Detecting Gait Abnormalities

Gait is assessed by observing the specific joint or body segments during the gait cycle. Table 8.4, which uses information from table 8.2 (Gait Terminology) and table 8.3 (Common Gait Abnormalities), is a screening instrument based on observation of a child's gait at the Pediatric Exercise and Motor Development

Table 8.3 Common Gait Abnormalities

Gait abnormality	Phase	Possible cause	Characteristics	Assessment
Ataxic	Initial contact	Cerebellum Ataxia and lack of motor control	Poor balance, broad base, exaggerated stagger to movements	Static balance Romberg Test for standing posture
		Weakness of dorsiflexor, lack of lower-limb proprioception	Foot slap; watches feet while walking; irregular, jerky gait	Walking line or beam, foot placement
Gluteus medius (Trendelenburg gait)	Stance	Weakness of gluteus medius	Excessive lateral lean over hip to compensate for muscle weakness, bilateral weakness resulting in waddling gait	Evaluate muscle strength or pain in hip
Gluteus maximus	Stance	Weakness of gluteus maximus	Lurching or leaning trunk posteriorly, hyperextension at hip	Evaluate muscle strength and pelvic position
Hemiplegic gait	Swing	Weak hip flexors, lack of motor control	Circumduction or lateral movement of entire lower extremity, with adduction and internal rotation; affected upper limb may be carried across trunk for stability	Assess strength of hip flexors and extensors, range of motion in hip, knee flexion, and ankle dorsiflexion
Scissors gait	Swing	Spasticity	Lack of motor control of hip adductor causes knees to move to midline; legs are moved forward by swinging hips	Assess foot placement and control of swinging leg
Foot drop or toe drag	Swing	Weakness of dorsiflexor and toe extensor, spasticity in plantar flexors, lack of hip or knee flexion	Weak dorsiflexion of foot does not allow toes to clear the surface; loss of control of dorsiflexors causes higher knee lift to compensate for toe drops, resulting in foot slap	Assess strength and range of motion in ankle, hip, and knee
Circumduction	Swing	Weak hip flexors, spasticity	Lateral movement of affected leg to move leg forward; consists of abduction, external rotation, adduction, and internal rotation	Assess range of motion and strength of hip and knee flexors, ankle dorsiflexors

Clinic at the University of Georgia. For the teacher, a simple method to screen potential problem areas is to observe the student's gait at all body segments and note any problems in each phase of the cycle.

The Rancho Los Amigos Observational Gait Analysis, a more formalized assessment, is shown in figure 8.3. In this example, a problem-solving approach helps

Table 8.4　Example of Observational Analysis of Gait

Body segment	Observation	Direction	Phase	Body side	Comments
Trunk	Rotation, circumduction	Lateral movement	Swing	Right	Arm adduction and flexion at elbow and wrist, forearm rotated medially
Pelvis	Rotation, circumduction	Lateral movement	Swing	Right	
Hip	Rotation, circumduction	Adduction	Swing	Right	Leg swings outward in a circle (circumduction)
Knee	Reduced flexion	Adduction	Swing	Right	
Ankle	Ankle dorsiflexion	Adduction	Swing	Right	
Feet	Toe drag	Adduction	Swing	Right	Inadequate hip flexion

Cause and remediation: neurological dysfunction; assess range of motion and strength in lower extremities.

identify significant deviations during the gait cycle that can be used to develop an intervention program. For example, after using the gait assessment in figure 8.3, a problem-solving approach can be applied to determine specific instructional needs. The steps in this process are shown in figure 8.4.

Case Study 2

Evan is 6 years old and is starting kindergarten. His gait appears unstable, and he often falls during activity. After observing him on the playground, the teacher notices his step length is very short while his step width is broad, with the feet toeing out and arms held out at the side for balance.

By 6 to 7 years of age, gait characteristics should be close to the mature adult pattern. Walking velocity and step length should both increase, and stability should be sufficient to support the body. Muscle structure and activation should also be appropriate for a mature gait pattern. If Evan has no diagnosis, an assessment of his balance and overall strength should be documented to see if they affect his gait. It is also possible that he has a visual or neurological impairment.

Specific posture limitations and accompanying gait problems should be documented, and the relevant characteristics that contribute to the movement problem should be determined. The resulting program planning should specifically address the problem (i.e., balance or strength deficiency) and incorporate it into the program plan. Follow-up assessment and observation can then be utilized to document the effectiveness of the intervention or teaching program.

Figure 8.3 Gait assessment.

Adapted from The Pathokinesiology Service and the Physical Therapy Department, *Observational Gait Analysis Handbook,* Los Amigos Research and Education Institute, Inc., Rancho Los Amigos National Rehabiliation Center, Downey, CA, 2001, page 56.

Reference Limb: L [X] R [ ]

☐ Major Deviation
▓ Minor Deviation

		WA		SLS		SLA			
		IC	LR	MSt	TSt	PSw	ISw	MSw	TSw
Trunk	Lean: B/F								
	Lateral Lean: R/L								
	Rotates: B/F								
Pelvis	Hikes								
	Tilt: P/A								
	Lacks Forward Rotation								
	Lacks Backward Rotation								
	Excess Forward Rotation								
	Excess Backward Rotation								
	Ipsilateral Drop								
	Contralateral Drop								
Hip	Flexion: Limited								
	Excess							✓	
	Past Retract								✓
	Rotation: IR/ER								
	AD/ABduction: AD/AB								
Knee	Flexion: Limited		✓						
	Excess	✓							✓
	Wobbles								
	Hyperextends								
	Extension Thrust								
	Varus/Valgus: Vr/Vl								
	Excess Contralateral Flex								
Ankle	Forefoot Contact	✓							
	Foot Flat Contact								
	Foot Slap								
	Excess Plantar Flexion	✓					✓	✓	✓
	Excess Dorsiflexion								
	Inversion/Eversion: Iv/Ev								
	Heel Off								
	No Heel Off								
	Drag								
	Contralateral Vaulting								
Toes	Up								
	Inadequate Extension								
	Clawed/Hammered: Cl/Ha								

Major Problems:

(WA) Weight Acceptance
- *forefoot contact*
- *excess knee flexion (IC)*
- *limited knee flexion (LR)*

(SLS) Single Limb Support

(SLA) Swing Limb Advancement
- *excess knee flexion*
- *excess plantar flexion*
- *post retract*

Excessive UE Weight Bearing ☐

Name _____

Patient # _____

① tibia & fibula fx

Diagnosis

153

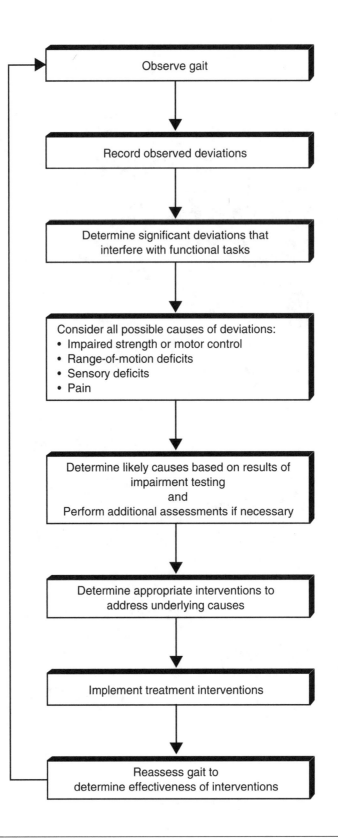

Figure 8.4 Problem-solving approach.

Adapted from The Pathokinesiology Service and the Physical Therapy Department, *Observational Gait Analysis Handbook*, Los Amigos Research and Education Institute, Inc., Rancho Los Amigos National Rehabiliation Center, Downey, CA, 2001, page 64.

▌ $\mathcal{W}$ hat You Need to Know ►►►

Key Terms

abduction	functional deviations	scoliosis
adduction	gait cycle	spasticity
body types	internal rotation	spinal anomalies
circumduction	kyphosis	stance phase
external rotation	lordosis	structural deviations
flexion	posture	swing phase
foot drop	scissors gait	

Key Concepts

1. You should be able to use assessment information regarding posture and gait to develop exercise interventions and program plans.

2. You should understand how deviations in functioning affect posture and gait.

3. You should be able to observe a gait pattern and determine possible causes of gait abnormalities.

Review Questions

1. What disabilities will affect posture?

2. Observe children of various ages and compare their posture and walking gait. What differences do you detect?

3. Discuss how muscle imbalances, contractures, muscle spasms, or loss of sensory input affects posture.

4. Observe several people and describe their gait characteristics

5. Describe the possible causes of gait abnormalities and the phase in which they occur. Then describe potential interventions.

Chapter 9

Assessing Behavior and Social Competence

Behaviors, social skills, and how well a child plays with equipment are important yet often undermeasured concepts in adapted physical education. Yet, many referrals for adapted physical education are for behavior or social interaction problems rather than physical or motor problems. It is often said that physical education can improve self-concept, but how a child feels about himself or herself in relation to physical education is rarely measured. Finally, many teachers talk about the importance of helping children without disabilities gain a positive, empathetic, caring attitude toward peers with disabilities. The purpose of this chapter is to review common assessment tools and practices that can be used to measure children's behaviors, social skills, self-concept, play, and attitudes. Each section begins with a short case study relating a real-life situation of a child with a disability.

ASSESSING CHILDREN WITH CHALLENGING BEHAVIORS

Children who present difficult behaviors are often the most challenging students for both general and adapted physical educators. Difficult behaviors can include passive-aggressive behaviors (refusing to participate), verbal outbursts, running away, destroying equipment, and even physical violence toward peers and staff. Before the student's IEP team can determine an appropriate behavior program for a child with challenging behaviors, the team needs to determine the types of behaviors being displayed, the intensity of the behaviors, and possible causes of the behaviors.

Case Study 1

Rachel, a 9-year-old fourth grader with Down syndrome at Woodfield Elementary School, is known to her teachers and her peers as a "mean little girl." No one knows why Rachel is so mean to other children, but everyone knows to avoid Rachel whenever possible (even though her peers have been encouraged to interact and play with her). Rachel's "mean-ness" is displayed through physical aggression. She has been known to bite, hit, scratch, pinch, kick, and push other children for no apparent reason. This has been going on ever since Rachel was moved from a self-contained special education class to a general education fourth-grade class. Rachel's teacher (and Rachel's classmates) want to know how often Rachel displays these aggressive behaviors, why she is displaying these aggressive behaviors, and what to do to help her develop more appropriate behaviors.

The ability to effectively meet social and community expectations for personal independence, physical needs, and interpersonal relationships expected for one's age and cultural group is termed *adaptive behavior* (Brown & Snell, 2000). Behaviors that interfere with everyday activities are called *maladaptive behaviors,* or more often, *problem behaviors.* Maladaptive behavior is behavior that is undesirable, that is socially unacceptable, or that interferes with the acquisition of desired skills or knowledge (Bruininks, Woodcock, Weatherman, & Hill, 1996). Problems in acquiring adaptive skills may occur at any age—in developing and mastering basic maturational skills (e.g., the ability to walk or perform self-help skills), in learning academic skills and concepts (e.g., basic reading, writing, and math), or in making social and vocational adjustments (e.g., getting along with others and developing basic job skills).

Maladaptive behavior ultimately limits independence. Independence, the ability to do things on one's own without getting into trouble, is also critical for success at school, at home, and in the community. Independence means not only being able to perform a task but also knowing *when* to do it and having the willingness to do so. When children exhibit behavior problems that affect independence, it leads to restrictions, extra supervision, additional assistance with behaving more appropriately, and possibly a more segregated placement (Bruininks et al., 1996).

With regard to physical education, adaptive behavior includes following directions, getting along with peers, using equipment appropriately, putting forth an appropriate amount of effort, and generally behaving appropriately for the setting (e.g., not running away or getting into fights). Good adaptive behavior and a lack of behavior problems in physical education allow the child to be more independent (does not need a teacher assistant), be more successful, and be accepted more readily by the general physical education teacher and by peers.

In behavioral assessments, the first step is defining the targeted behavior to determine the extent of occurrence of the behavior before treatment. The assessment of behavior depends on accurate observation and precise measurement. Therefore, it is important that the examiner clearly and objectively define the behaviors to be assessed and then accurately observe and record these defined behaviors (Janney & Snell, 2000). For example, saying a child is "always getting in trouble" is vague and not measurable. Even a statement such as "Emily is aggressive toward her peers" is too vague to target for intervention. *Aggressive* could mean that she hits, bites, yells, or displays other forms of aggression. A better definition might be that "Emily touches and pushes other children 2 to 3 times while waiting in line to drink water and 4 to 5 times when sitting in a group waiting for instructions."

It is also important to examine antecedents (things that happened just before the behavior occurred that may cause the behavior) as well as consequences (things that happened immediately after the behavior occurred that may reinforce the behavior). For example, being paired with a particular peer may upset a child and cause an inappropriate behavior (screaming when the child sees that peer coming toward him), while chasing after a child who runs away may reinforce that behavior (running away becomes a game for the child) (see the section on functional behavioral assessment in this chapter for more details on measuring antecedents and consequences).

Traditional behavioral assessments usually focus on two areas: adaptive behaviors and behavior problems. Assessing adaptive behaviors involves information such as a child's ability to perform certain adaptive behaviors (e.g., dressing, getting from one place to another, staying on task), how often he performs an adaptive behavior, and how well he performs an adaptive behavior. Assessing behavior problems includes types of maladaptive behaviors, frequency of such behaviors, and intensity of such behaviors. For example, a question on the Scales of Independent Behavior–Revised (SIB-R) (Bruininks et al., 1996) asks whether or not the child is hurtful to others (e.g., biting, kicking, pinching, pulling hair, scratching, or striking). The scale includes a place for the examiner to note the frequency *(never* to *one or more times per hour)* as well as the perceived severity of the problem *(not serious, not a problem* to *extremely serious, a critical problem).* Thus, the examiner is able to obtain an idea of the child's present abilities, strengths, and deficits with regard to adaptive behaviors and problem behaviors. This information can then be translated into behavioral goals such as "demonstrates the ability to wait turn when playing small-group game in physical education" or "maintains appropriate personal space when playing games and interacting with peers in physical education."

Information from this type of assessment can also help the general physical education teacher determine if a behavior is significant enough (i.e., occurs fairly frequently and at a serious level) to warrant additional support—such as a teacher assistant or adapted physical educator—or perhaps removal from general physical education into a self-contained setting. Other areas that are measured in behavioral tests include the following (Kazdin, 2001):

- *Frequency:* number of behaviors during a designated time period
- *Response rate:* number of responses divided by the amount of time in an interval
- *Intervals:* behaviors during a specified time rather than by discrete responses that have a beginning and end point
- *Time sampling:* observations conducted for brief periods at different times rather than during a single block of time
- *Duration:* amount of time the response is observed (effective for measuring continuous rather than discrete behaviors)
- *Latency:* duration measure that observes the time lapse between the cue and the response

- *Categorization:* classifying responses according to their occurrence (correct or incorrect, appropriate or inappropriate)
- *Group:* number of individuals who perform a specific behavior or response as opposed to individual responses

Behavioral Tests

This section reviews four different adaptive behavior assessment scales. The first is a teacher-developed checklist specifically designed for physical education: the University of Virginia Adapted Physical Education Program (UVA-APE) Initial Observation and Referral Form. This is followed by a review of three well-known, commercially available adaptive behavior scales: the Scales of Independent Behavior–Revised (SIB-R), the Vineland Adaptive Behavior Scales (VABS), and the AAMR Adaptive Behavior Scale–School (ABS-S:2). Each test measures everyday living skills—skills that are related to, but distinct from, academic ability and intelligence. These commercially available tests provide results that can be described qualitatively or as age equivalents, percentile ranks, or standard scores.

Note that adaptive behavior measures have been criticized over the years. First, adaptive behavior can be difficult to evaluate because the concept of adaptive behavior is vague. For example, although self-help skills are relatively easy to measure, demonstration of age-appropriate social and emotional behaviors can be difficult to quantitatively assess. Second, adaptive behavior scales do not usually focus on the child's ability to adapt to changes in the environment and to problem-solve when something unexpected arises. Finally, adaptive behavior measures focus on what the child can and cannot do rather than on what might be causing the particular behaviors (Brown & Snell, 2000). Despite these concerns, adaptive behavior measures are still popular.

An alternative way to assess behaviors of children with disabilities is to conduct a functional analysis to determine what might be causing the behaviors. This tactic is part of the positive behavioral support approach to working with children with behavioral problems (Janney & Snell, 2000). The advantage of this approach compared with simply noting the child's adaptive behaviors and behavior problems is it gives an idea of why the child is displaying the inappropriate behaviors. If the physical education teacher can determine why a child behaves the way she does, then the teacher will have a better chance of finding a strategy to prevent the child from exhibiting the behavior while at the same time teaching the child more appropriate behaviors. Since there are no specific functional behavioral assessment tools, key questions used in the functional assessment process are presented.

UVA–APE Initial Observation and Referral Form

As noted earlier, many children with disabilities are referred to adapted physical education because of problems in general physical education. It is important that both adapted and general physical educators have a quick way of determining if a child's behaviors are significant enough to warrant further testing, extra support, or perhaps adapted physical education services. The UVA-APE Initial Observation and Referral Form (figure 9.1) is a quick, simple-to-use screening tool designed to help general and adapted physical educators determine the significance of a child's behavioral problems in physical education. The form is divided into five main categories: transition to and from physical education, responding to the teacher, relating to peers and equipment, effort and self-acceptance, and cognitive abilities. Each of these categories has four to six

University of Virginia Adapted Physical Education Initial Observation and Referral Form

Part II–Behaviors, Cognitive Abilities, and Social Skills in Physical Education

Child's name: _____ Evaluator: _____

School: _____ Date: _____

Use this form when first observing a child with a disability who has been referred for adapted physical education. Rate each item based on how the child compares with other children in his or her physical education class.

	Adequate	Needs improvement	Significantly inadequate	Not observed
Transition to and from physical education				
Enters without interruption	☐	☐	☐	☐
Sits in assigned area	☐	☐	☐	☐
Stops playing with equipment when asked	☐	☐	☐	☐
Lines up to leave when asked	☐	☐	☐	☐
Responding to teacher				
Remains quiet when teacher is talking	☐	☐	☐	☐
Follows directions in a timely manner: warm-up	☐	☐	☐	☐
Follows directions in a timely manner: skill focus	☐	☐	☐	☐
Follows directions in a timely manner: games	☐	☐	☐	☐
Accepts feedback from teacher	☐	☐	☐	☐
Uses positive or appropriate language	☐	☐	☐	☐
Relating to peers and equipment				
Works cooperatively with a partner when asked (e.g., shares, takes turns)	☐	☐	☐	☐
Works cooperatively as a member of a group when asked	☐	☐	☐	☐
Uses positive or appropriate comments with peers	☐	☐	☐	☐
Seeks social interactions with peers	☐	☐	☐	☐
Displays sportsmanship by avoiding conflict with others	☐	☐	☐	☐
Uses equipment appropriately	☐	☐	☐	☐
Effort and self-acceptance				
Quickly begins the activity once instructed	☐	☐	☐	☐
Continues to participate independently throughout activity	☐	☐	☐	☐
Adapts to new tasks and changes	☐	☐	☐	☐
Strives to succeed and is motivated to learn	☐	☐	☐	☐
Accepts his or her own skill whether successful or improving	☐	☐	☐	☐
Cognitive abilities				
Understands nonverbal directions	☐	☐	☐	☐
Understands verbal directions	☐	☐	☐	☐
Processes multistep cues	☐	☐	☐	☐
Attends to instructions	☐	☐	☐	☐

Comments regarding behaviors, social abilities, or cognitive abilities: _____

_____

Figure 9.1 University of Virginia Adapted Physical Education Program Initial Observation and Referral Form, Part II–Behaviors, Cognitive Abilities, and Social Skills in Physical Education.

From the University of Virginia *Adapted Physical Education Initial Observation and Referral Form,* courtesy of M.E. Block.

different behaviors that are important for success in general physical education. Each behavior is observed and then scored on a three-point scale: adequate, needs improvement, and significantly inadequate. There is also a place to note when a behavior was not observed. The general or adapted physical educator should observe the targeted child in general physical education on at least two different occasions. The teacher fills out the form by putting a mark by the behavior in one of the three scoring boxes or in the "not observed" box. Observations on the second day as well as any subsequent observations are used to fill in behaviors that were not observed on the first day and to confirm behaviors seen on the first day.

Analysis of the scale involves simply scanning the results of the form. If most of the items are scored at the "needs improvement" level, then the recommendation to the IEP team might be peer tutor or teacher assistant support as well as training the general physical educator on ways to modify instruction, motivate the child, and deal with behavior problems. If most of the items are scored at the "significantly inadequate" level, then the recommendation might be a teacher assistant part of the time and adapted physical education part of the time within general physical education, or perhaps pull-out adapted physical education. For example, Jorge has general physical education two times per week. If he scored "significantly inadequate," then he could be accompanied by the teacher assistant to general physical education once a week and also see the adapted physical education specialist once a week. His program would continue to focus on motor and fitness goals but also include additional goals that focus on behaviors. The adapted physical educator would be in charge of training the teacher assistant and the general physical educator as well as peers without disabilities.

There have been no reports of validity or reliability on this observation and referral form. It is designed as a quick screening tool, and results can be used for programming as well as to recommend more formal behavioral assessment. For example, this tool has been used to find out if a child can follow simple directions, stay on task, and generally display appropriate behaviors, either without support or with a peer tutor, to determine if the child needs a teacher assistant to be successful in general physical education.

Scales of Independent Behavior—Revised (SIB-R)

Scales of Independent Behavior–Revised (SIB-R), a revision of the 1984 Scales of Independent Behavior, is a comprehensive norm-referenced assessment of adaptive and maladaptive behavior. The scales assess 14 areas of adaptive behavior and 8 areas of problem behavior. The test is appropriate for a wide age range of children and adults, from infancy through older adulthood (80-plus years). Test administration is estimated at 15 to 20 minutes for the short form and 45 to 60 minutes for the full scale (Bruininks et al., 1996).

The SIB-R's 259 adaptive behavior items comprise 14 subscales grouped into four clusters: motor skills (gross motor, fine motor), social interaction and communication skills (social interaction, language comprehension, language expression), personal living skills (eating and meal preparation, toileting, dressing, personal self-care, domestic skills), and community living skills (time and punctuality, money and value, home and community, orientation). Each SIB-R adaptive behavior item is a statement of a task (e.g., washes, rinses, and dries hair). The examiner rates the individual being assessed on each task, using a scale from 0 to 3.

0 = never or rarely performs the task (even if asked)

1 = does the task but not well, or about 25% of the time (may need to be asked)

2 = does the task fairly well, or about 75% of the time (may need to be asked)

3 = does the task very well, always or almost always (without being asked)

The SIB-R is somewhat unique in that instead of using a checklist, the examiner assesses a child against a set of eight categories of behavior in open-ended questions. In addition, the examiner assesses both the frequency and the severity of behaviors. The result is a short test with a reliability of approximately 80% (Bruininks et al., 1996). The eight categories of problem behavior follow:

- *Hurtful to self:* behavior that causes injury to a person's own body
- *Hurtful to others:* behavior that causes physical pain to other people or to animals
- *Destructive to property:* behaviors such as deliberately breaking, defacing, or destroying things
- *Disruptive behavior:* behavior that interferes with the activities of others
- *Unusual or repetitive habits:* behavior that involves excessive repetition of unusual actions
- *Socially offensive behavior:* behavior that is offensive to other people
- *Withdrawal or inattentive behavior:* behavior that reflects the person's difficulty associating with other people or maintaining attention
- *Uncooperative behavior:* behavior that reflects difficulty following rules or working with other people

Each category in the SIB-R includes 6 to 12 typical examples of problem behavior. The respondent indicates whether the subject exhibits a given category of behavior, and if applicable, reports the single behavior that is the *biggest problem* in this category. The examiner rates the behavior according to frequency of occurrence and severity, then documents how the problem behavior is usually managed by other people when it occurs. How others generally respond to the problem behavior is of considerable value in assessing the dynamics of that behavior and the appropriateness of its consequence in the subject's environment (Bruininks et al., 1996).

These four dimensions (specific problem behaviors, frequency of occurrence, severity, and usual management response by others) represent the primary basis for evaluating the effects of problem behavior on the student, his peers, and his environment. This information is necessary for developing individual plans, as well as for planning service intensity such as student–teacher ratios.

The SIB-R yields a total score, as well as normed numeric scores that vary by age, for problem behaviors in three areas (internalized, externalized, and asocial). Scores range from +10 (good) to –74 (extremely serious), with an average of 0 and a standard deviation of 10 (Bruininks et al., 1996). The SIB-R also assesses the quality of performance and the person's motivation. That is, even though someone may be able to perform a task, she may not do so independently, either because she does not realize it is necessary to do so or because she refuses to (a behavior problem). From infant to adult levels, the SIB-R yields highly accurate adaptive behavior scores that include age equivalents, percentile ranks, and standard scores (Bruininks et al., 1996).

Vineland Adaptive Behavior Scales (VABS)

The Vineland Adaptive Behavior Scales (VABS) (1984) is a revision of the Vineland Social Maturity Scale first published in 1935. The VABS measures social competence of children with and without disabilities from birth through 19 years (the classroom edition is designed for children aged 3 through 12). The classroom edition consists of 224 items that are completed by the child's IEP team (or lead teacher). The interview edition, which is filled out by the child's parents or caregiver, comes in two forms: the survey form contains 297 items, while the expanded form includes 577 items. In both the classroom and interview editions, items are rated on a 3-point Likert scale (0 = never performs activity; 1 = sometimes performs activity; 2 = usually or habitually performs activity). The VABS measures adaptive behavior in four domains—communication, daily living skills, socialization, and motor skills (up to age 6 for children without disabilities)—and maladaptive behavior. The classroom edition takes approximately 20 minutes to complete, the survey form of the interview edition takes 20 to 60 minutes to complete, and the expanded form of the interview edition takes 60 to 90 minutes to complete.

The VABS has a mean score of 100 and a standard deviation of 15 for the four domains and the maladaptive behavior composite score (these results match typical IQ testing means and standard deviations). Unfortunately, the actual means and standard deviations vary from age group to age group (Silverstein, 1986). The VABS was normed on more than 2,900 children for the classroom edition and more than 3,000 children for the interview edition. The scales have strong reliability, ranging from 62 to 78% on interrater reliability, 81 to 86% on test–retest reliability, and 83 to 90% on internal consistency. Validity (content, concurrent, and construct) is claimed to be moderate to strong (Sattler, 1989). The adapted physical education specialist might find that the special education teacher uses this test to get an accurate measurement of a child's present adaptive behaviors in various settings, including physical education, and the special education teacher may ask the APE specialist to complete part of the form with reference to the child's behaviors in physical education.

AAMR Adaptive Behavior Scale—School (ABS–S:2)

The AAMR Adaptive Behavior Scale–School (ABS-S:2), which was revised in 1993 from an earlier version, is a popular norm- and criterion-referenced test that measures both adaptive and maladaptive behaviors. Divided into two parts, the test's first part measures adaptive behaviors in nine behavioral domains: independent functioning, physical development, economic activity, language development, numbers and time, prevocational and vocational activity, self-direction, responsibility, and socialization. The second part measures social maladjustment and is divided into seven behavioral domains (related to personality and behavior disorders): social behavior, conformity, trustworthiness, stereotyped and hyperactive behavior, self-abusive behavior, social engagement, and disturbing interpersonal behavior.

The age range for the ABS-S:2 is 3 to 18 years, and testing time is estimated at 15 to 30 minutes. Information is obtained via a standardized interview format conducted by a trained examiner. Some items are measured on a Likert scale, ranging from 0 (behavior not present) to 3 (behavior present in highest form). An example is how well a person functions when visiting a fast-food restaurant. Other items require a yes or no (1 or 0) response. Examples of these items include taking food off others' plates, eating too fast or too slow, and swallowing food without chewing.

The ABS-S:2 was standardized on more than 2,000 children with disabilities and 1,000 children without disabilities from 31 states. Percentiles, age equivalents, and standard scores can be produced from the data. As was the case with the VABS, adaptive behavior quotients can be derived that have a mean of 100 and a standard deviation of 15 to match typical IQ tests. Data can also be easily translated for use with an IEP. For example, a teacher can identify a child's deficits in adaptive behavior as well as the presence of maladaptive behavior. She can then create objectives that focus on areas needing attention and instruction (Lambert, Nihira, & Leland, 1993). The test is reported to have high reliability and validity. Also similar to the Vineland, the APE specialist might find that special education teachers in the district use this test to get an accurate measurement of a child's present adaptive behaviors and behavior problems in various settings, including physical education, and the special education teacher may ask the APE specialist to complete part of the form with reference to the child's behaviors in physical education.

Functional Behavioral Assessment

As noted earlier, functional behavioral assessment is a process in which the IEP team attempts to determine why a child displays a particular behavior. The purpose of the assessment is to understand the underlying cause of the behavior in hopes of planning a program that can prevent it. The focus of a functional behavioral assessment (and the subsequent positive behavioral support program) is on creating positive ways to help the child develop more appropriate adaptive behavior and become more independent.

There is no array of functional behavior assessment tools on the market. Rather, there are specific questions that any functional behavioral assessment tool should include. The questions listed in figure 9.2 are modified from worksheets created by Janney and Snell (2000). The functional behavioral assessment begins with a clear description of the child's targeted behavior written in an objective way, including the type of behavior (destructive, disruptive, or distracting) as well as the frequency, intensity, and duration of the behavior. For example, a child who is aggressive toward peers in physical education (further defined as hitting, pushing, and scratching) is demonstrating destructive behavior. The IEP team would note how often the child (Joey) is disruptive and the intensity of this disruptive behavior. The team might observe that Joey is aggressive on average three times per 30-minute physical education class, and the aggressiveness is at a moderate level (pushing and grabbing at peers, but not to the point where the peers get hurt).

The second step in the assessment process is a functional analysis of the cause of the behavior. In other words, what triggers the behavior? This is also known as examining the antecedents, or what happened just before the behavior occurred.

Functional Behavior Assessment

Student: _____ Date: _____

School: _____ DOB: _____

1. **Define the student's problem behaviors:**
   Is the behavior destructive ☐   disruptive ☐   distracting ☐

2. **Describe the behavior** in detail (frequency, intensity, duration).

3. What seems to **trigger** the behavior?
   - Who is present when the problem behavior occurs?
   - What is going on when the problem behavior occurs?
   - When does the problem behavior happen?
   - Where does the problem behavior occur?

4. **What happens to the student** immediately after he or she engages in the problem behavior (consequences)?

5. **What does the child get or avoid** by behaving this way (tangible items, escape or avoid, attention, self-entertainment)?

6. **Hypothesis statement:** "When (antecedent) happens in (specific setting), he or she does (problem behavior) in order to (perceived function)."

7. What are some **strengths and likes** of the student?

8. What are some ways to **prevent** the problem behavior?

9. What **alternative behaviors** can be **taught** and used in place of the problem behavior?

10. Describe ways to **respond** to the problem behavior when it occurs.

Figure 9.2 Functional behavior assessment.

Modified from the *Albemarle County Schools Functional Behavior Assessment Form*, Form 80.01. Reprinted by permission of M.F. Block.

The analysis includes questions and observations of who is present when the behavior occurs, what is going on when the behavior occurs, and finally where the behavior occurs. The focus at this point in the assessment is determining if something in the child's setting (person, place, activity, or time) is causing the behavior. Continuing with the previous example, the team observes Joey in physical education and notes that aggressive behaviors seem to focus on two specific peers (who). The child shows these aggressive behaviors only when the general physical educator has the children grouped together to give instructions (when the behavior occurs, what is happening, and where it happens). Further observation reveals that aggressiveness can be expected nearly 100% of the time when the teacher asks the children to sit and wait while she sets up equipment or when instructions take several minutes.

The next step involves observing what happens to the student after he engages in the problem behavior (consequences). The team is watching for anything that occurs immediately after the child displays the behavior that might be reinforcing or maintaining the behavior. For example, Joey might get a lot of attention from his peers as well as from the general physical education teacher when he starts to push other children. He can be seen smiling and continuing the behavior while peers try to stop the behavior. He does not stop the behavior until the teacher comes over and places him in time-out.

The fourth step in the functional assessment process is determining the reason for the behavior, or what the child gets or avoids when he or she displays the behavior. In other words, what is the purpose of the behavior? Functional purposes of problem behaviors include getting attention, escape, getting something tangible, self-regulation, and play or entertainment (Janney & Snell, 2000). In our example, Joey might be displaying aggressive behavior to escape the activity (he seems to keep up the behavior until the teacher comes and puts him in time-out). Or he might be displaying the behavior to get attention (he seems to enjoy having peers try to stop him). Getting attention might make sense because the behavior occurs during "down time" when no one is attending to Joey and he is bored.

This leads to the next step of the process, creating a hypothesis statement that includes when (antecedent), where (specific setting), what (problem behavior), and why (perceived function). For Joey, the hypothesis statement might read: When the physical education class is sitting and waiting for the teacher to set up equipment, or when the teacher is giving a great deal of instruction and the children have to sit and wait, Joey is aggressive toward peers (hits, pushes, scratches) in order to gain their attention. With a strong hypothesis statement, the team can then continue with the assessment process to determine the child's strengths and likes (to see if there is a powerful reinforcer the child might like to work for), ways to prevent the behavior (e.g., allow this child to start at a station or do an activity with a peer when a lot of wait time is anticipated), alternative behaviors to be taught in place of the maladaptive behavior (e.g., holding hands with a peer while the teacher gives instruction), and how the team might respond to the behavior in a positive way if the behavior does occur. (See Janney and Snell [2000] for more details on the entire positive behavioral support process.)

SOCIAL COMPETENCE

Displaying appropriate social competence is important for a child with disabilities to be successful in general physical education (or for that matter, in school, at work, or in the community). Children who cannot get along with peers, who cannot deal with basic interactions, who do not understand basic safety as well as rules of games, and who cannot cope with criticism or situations such as losing will have a problem in most general physical education settings.

Case Study 2

Malcolm is a wonderfully energetic and physically skilled 7-year-old second grader in Mr. Johnson's fifth-period physical education class. In fact, Malcolm's motor skills and fitness put him at the top of the class compared with his peers. Unfortunately, his behaviors often get him into trouble in physical education. Malcolm's problems often begin as soon as he enters the gym. Mr. Johnson expects Malcolm and his classmates to enter the gymnasium quietly and sit in a "good" space away from peers and any equipment that might be set up. Malcolm often enters the gymnasium and runs to whatever equipment has been set up, whether it is a ball or jump rope or even cones marking boundaries. Then he begins to play with the equipment until Mr. Johnson reminds him that he is supposed to sit and wait for instructions. But this is only the beginning of Malcolm's problems. He often will sit too close to his peers and begin conversations with them when all the students are supposed to be listening to the teacher. When Mr. Johnson asks questions to the class, Malcolm often blurts out answers without raising his hand. When the class is engaged in a fitness activity, skill activity, or game, he is often loud and physically aggressive with his peers, bumping and pushing them or running by them very fast to scare them. Mr. Johnson knows that Malcolm has a behavior problem, and he would like to document as clearly as possible his concerns so both he and Malcolm can get the help they need. What types of assessment tools measure and detect children who display behavior problems in physical education?

Social competence includes many subareas such as basic classroom skills (e.g., listening to the teacher, doing your best), basic interaction skills (e.g., making eye contact, using the right voice, turn-taking when talking), getting-along skills (e.g., using polite words, sharing, following rules), making-friends skills (e.g., good grooming, smiling), and coping skills (responding appropriately when someone says "no," responding appropriately when expressing anger) (Snell & Janney, 2000; Walker et al., 1988). Social skills and expectations differ for preschool children compared with elementary children compared with middle and high school children. Sharing toys may be important in preschool, while participating appropriately in a conversation is more important in high school. Nevertheless, all social skills are interrelated and reveal the ability of a child with disabilities to get along with peers and demonstrate socially acceptable behaviors.

A child who lacks basic social skills has problems with social acceptance. He may be known as the "weird kid" or be the student the general physical educator will notice. But without assessing the array of behaviors that fall under the umbrella term *social competence,* it is difficult for the general physical educator to determine exactly what social competencies the student is lacking. Also, assessing social skills allows the teacher to determine the child's present strengths and weaknesses with regard to social competence, identify goals for social competence, and determine if the child is making progress toward these social goals. Three social skills tests are reviewed in this section: one formal test, the Walker-McConnell Scale, and two informal screening tests, the University of Virginia Adapted Physical Education Program (UVA-APE) Social Skills Inventory and the Matrix to Target Social Skills Deficits.

Walker–McConnell Scale (WMS)

The Walker-McConnell Scale of Social Competence and School Adjustment (WMS) rates children's social behaviors. It focuses on behaviors that are relatively easily observed during the school day, many of which occur in a physical education setting (e.g., accepts constructive feedback, sensitive to needs of others, uses free time appropriately). There are two versions of the WMS: one for elementary-aged children (K–6) and one for adolescents (grades 7 to 12). The elementary version consists of three subscales (teacher-preferred social behavior, peer-preferred social behavior, and school adjustment) totaling 43 items. The scale relies on teacher ratings of how frequently (never, sometimes, frequently) a child exhibits a particular social behavior. The 43 items of the elementary scale typically require no more than 10 minutes to complete for each student. The adolescent version contains four subscales (self-control, peer relations, school adjustment, and empathy) totaling 53 items. The adolescent scale also relies on teacher ratings of how frequently (never, sometimes, frequently) a child exhibits a particular social behavior, and the entire scale typically takes no more than 10 minutes to complete per student (Walker & McConnell, 1995). The scale can be used as a pretest to determine present level of social competence and ongoing progress toward development of specific social skills. Both the elementary and adolescent versions of the WMS have excellent validity and reliability, and the scales are widely used in schools across the United States.

The adapted physical education specialist might find that special education teachers in a district use the WMS to measure social competence, and they may ask the APE specialist to participate in the administration of this test in the physical education setting. Information from this test will also cue the APE specialist as to the specific social competencies and problems a particular child may have in various settings during the school day, including physical education. This information could then be used to create an intervention program to help the child improve his or her social skills and competencies.

UVA–APE Social Skills Inventory

The University of Virginia Adapted Physical Education (UVA-APE) Social Skills Inventory is a simple criterion-referenced tool designed to measure the social competence of children with disabilities. The inventory is divided into 10 subcategories, with descriptions of appropriate social behaviors listed under each category (figure 9.3). Categories include such social competence areas as accepting authority (e.g., complying with requests of adults, knowing and following classroom rules, following rules in the absence of a teacher), gaining attention (e.g., raising hand, waiting quietly for recognition, asking peer for help), making conversation (e.g., paying attention in a conversation, talking to others in appropriate tone of voice, waiting for pause in conversation before speaking), and care of property (e.g., taking care of personal property, asking permission to use another's property, sharing personal property). These categories were determined by practicing APE specialists in Albemarle County, Virginia, to be the most important social categories for success in general physical education. The inventory has not been tested for validity or reliability, but practicing general and adapted physical educators find it useful for determining the basic social competencies of children with disabilities in physical education.

University of Virginia Adapted Physical Education Social Skills Inventory

Child's name: _____ Evaluator: _____

School: _____ Date: _____

Use this form when first observing a child with a disability who has been referred for adapted physical education. Rate each item based on how the child compares with other children in his or her physical education class.

Interpersonal Relations

	Adequate 3	Needs improvement 2	Significantly inadequate 1	Not observed 0
Accepting authority				
Complies with request of adult in position of authority	☐	☐	☐	☐
Complies with request of peer in position of authority	☐	☐	☐	☐
Knows and follows classroom rules	☐	☐	☐	☐
Follows classroom rules in the absence of the teacher	☐	☐	☐	☐
Questions rules that may be unjust	☐	☐	☐	☐
Coping with conflict				
Responds to teasing or name calling by ignoring, changing the subject, or some other constructive means	☐	☐	☐	☐
Responds to physical assault by leaving the situation, calling for help, or some other constructive means	☐	☐	☐	☐
Walks away from peer when angry to avoid hitting	☐	☐	☐	☐
Expresses anger with nonaggressive words rather than physical actions or aggressive words	☐	☐	☐	☐
Constructively handles criticism or punishment perceived as undeserved	☐	☐	☐	☐
Gaining attention				
Gains teacher's attention in class by raising hand	☐	☐	☐	☐
Waits quietly for recognition before speaking out in class	☐	☐	☐	☐
Uses "please" and "thank you" when making requests of others	☐	☐	☐	☐
Approaches teacher and asks appropriately for help, explanations, instructions, and so on	☐	☐	☐	☐
Asks a peer for help	☐	☐	☐	☐
Greeting others				
Looks others in the eye when greeting them	☐	☐	☐	☐
States name when asked	☐	☐	☐	☐
Smiles when encountering a friend or acquaintance	☐	☐	☐	☐
Greets adults and peers by name	☐	☐	☐	☐
Responds to an introduction by shaking hands and saying, "How do you do?"	☐	☐	☐	☐
Introduces self to another person	☐	☐	☐	☐
Introduces two people to each other	☐	☐	☐	☐

(continued)

Figure 9.3 University of Virginia Adapted Physical Education Program Social Skills Inventory.

Adapted from T.M. Stephens, A.C. Hartman, and V.H. Lucas, 1982, *Teaching children basic skills: A curriculum handbook,* 2nd ed. (Columbus, OH: Bell & Howell Company). Reprinted with permission of M.E. Block.

	Adequate 3	Needs improvement 2	Significantly inadequate 1	Not observed 0
Helping others				
Helps teacher when asked	☐	☐	☐	☐
Helps peer when asked	☐	☐	☐	☐
Gives simple directions to a peer	☐	☐	☐	☐
Offers help to teacher	☐	☐	☐	☐
Offers help to a classmate	☐	☐	☐	☐
Comes to defense of peer in trouble	☐	☐	☐	☐
Expresses sympathy to peer about problems or difficulties	☐	☐	☐	☐
Making conversation				
Pays attention in a conversation to the person speaking	☐	☐	☐	☐
Talks to others in a tone of voice appropriate to the situation	☐	☐	☐	☐
Waits for pauses in a conversation before speaking	☐	☐	☐	☐
Makes relevant remarks in a conversation with peers	☐	☐	☐	☐
Makes relevant remarks in a conversation with adults	☐	☐	☐	☐
Ignores interruptions of others in a conversation	☐	☐	☐	☐
Initiates conversation with peers in an informal situation	☐	☐	☐	☐
Initiates conversation with adults in an informal situation	☐	☐	☐	☐
Organized play				
Follows rules when playing a game	☐	☐	☐	☐
Takes turns when playing a game	☐	☐	☐	☐
Displays effort in a competitive game	☐	☐	☐	☐
Accepts defeat and congratulates the winner in a competitive game	☐	☐	☐	☐
Positive attitude toward others				
Makes positive statements about qualities and accomplishments of others	☐	☐	☐	☐
Compliments another person	☐	☐	☐	☐
Displays tolerance for persons with characteristics different from his or her own	☐	☐	☐	☐
Informal play				
Asks another student to play on the playground	☐	☐	☐	☐
Asks to be included in a playground activity in progress	☐	☐	☐	☐
Shares toys and equipment in a play situation	☐	☐	☐	☐
Gives in to reasonable wishes of the group in a play situation	☐	☐	☐	☐
Suggests an activity for the group on the playground	☐	☐	☐	☐
Care of property				
Distinguishes own property from the property of others	☐	☐	☐	☐
Lends possessions to others when asked	☐	☐	☐	☐
Uses and returns others' property without damaging it	☐	☐	☐	☐
Asks permission to use another's property	☐	☐	☐	☐

Comments: _____

_____

_____

Figure 9.3 *(continued)*

To administer the inventory, the teacher observes the student in a general physical education setting in situations that require the demonstration of social competence. This may take several observations and some staging of social situations to view all the various social competencies on the inventory. For each behavior observed, the child is scored on a 3-point Likert scale (adequate, needs improvement, and significantly inadequate). Children who receive a "significantly inadequate" rating on 50% or more of the behaviors on the overall checklist, or children who receive a "significantly inadequate" rating on all the items in two or more subcategories, clearly have social competency inadequacies that require intervention (even significantly inadequate ratings on a handful of social behaviors may be worth noting and planning intervention for). Social behaviors that are inadequate can be targeted for instruction, and follow-up assessments can be administered to chart improvement.

Matrix to Target Social Skills Deficits

The Matrix to Target Social Skills Deficits is similar to the UVA-APE Social Skills Inventory. Key social skills that are appropriate for a particular age group are listed down one column, and a 1 (unskilled) to 5 (very skilled) Likert scale is listed across the top of the matrix (figure 9.4). The physical educator observes the child in a social setting (such as physical education) and rates each behavior. A student who receives a rating of 3 or less on 75% of the skills will benefit from training on all skills in the curriculum. Students who score low in some areas would benefit from spot training on specific social deficiencies. Note that the matrix can be used with a class of students. If 70% of the class earns a rating of

Matrix Observation of Social Skills

Social skills	Unskilled 1	2	Moderately skilled 3	4	Very skilled 5
Listening	☐	☐	☐	☐	☐
Greeting others	☐	☐	☐	☐	☐
Joining in	☐	☐	☐	☐	☐
Complimenting	☐	☐	☐	☐	☐
Expressing anger	☐	☐	☐	☐	☐
Keeping friends	☐	☐	☐	☐	☐
Doing quality work	☐	☐	☐	☐	☐
Following rules	☐	☐	☐	☐	☐
Using self-control	☐	☐	☐	☐	☐
Offering assistance	☐	☐	☐	☐	☐
Disagreeing with others	☐	☐	☐	☐	☐
Being organized	☐	☐	☐	☐	☐
Having conversations	☐	☐	☐	☐	☐

Figure 9.4   Matrix observation of social skills.

Adapted from H.M. Walker, G. Colvin, and E. Ramsey, 1995, *Antisocial behavior in school: Strategies and best practices* (Pacific Grove, CA: Brooks/Cole).

3 or less on a skill, then the entire class would benefit from spot training on that skill (Walker, Colvin, & Ramsey, 1995). We recommend the UVA-APE Social Skills Inventory over the Matrix to Target Social Skills Deficits because the UVA-APE inventory is more relevant to the physical education setting.

SELF-CONCEPT

Positive self-concept is critical in order for children with disabilities to stay motivated to try their best in school, including physical education. If a child is not successful in physical education, there is a good chance she will not feel good about herself. There are many specific terms associated with self-concept. *Self-esteem* is defined as a general positive self-regard, self-worth, or overall good feeling about oneself. Self-esteem is most directly related to self-concept. Children who have a strong self-esteem feel good about themselves and are not troubled by sadness, loneliness, or depression. Self-esteem is believed to be a global concept that is different from perceived competence and self-perception. *Perceived competence* and *self-perception* refer to how competent one feels in particular activities or pursuits (Harter, 1988). Typical domains associated with perceived competence include school, sports, work, close friendships, social acceptance, romantic appeal, physical appearance, and behavioral conduct.

For adapted physical education, it might be important to determine how some children feel about themselves globally (self-worth or self-esteem) as well as how they feel specifically about certain characteristics (e.g., appearance, athletic ability, social acceptance). This is particularly true for adolescents with physical or sensory disabilities who may begin to think they are not as capable or as worthy as their nondisabled peers. For this reason, adapted physical educators may want to seek out instruments that measure self-esteem and perceived competence. Two scales in particular seem to be most appropriate for adapted physical education: Harter's Self-Perception Profile for Adolescents (SPPA) and Ulrich's Pictorial Scale of Perceived Physical Competence (PSPPC).

Case Study 3

Chandra is a 13-year-old eighth grader at Eastern Middle School. She was born with a severe hearing impairment that cannot be corrected with hearing aids or surgery. She is fluent in sign language and has an interpreter for all her classes. She can read lips a little when she is one-on-one with someone, and she can speak, but her speech is difficult to understand. Chandra has always gone to general education classes, including general physical education. She does receive special speech services, and she goes to a resource room for about an hour a day for academic help, but she is basically on age level academically. Physical education has never been a problem for Chandra because she has relatively typical motor skills and physical fitness, so she has never received any special physical education services. Chandra has had the same physical education teacher, Ms. Avery, for all 3 years she has been at Eastern Middle School. Ms. Avery has never considered Chandra a behavior problem or someone she has any concerns about. However, she has noticed that Chandra has gradually become less enthusiastic and less involved in physical education activities. Chandra dresses and participates, but Ms. Avery considers Chandra's effort less than what she sees from the other eighth graders. The teacher has also begun to notice that Chandra stays on the periphery in games rather than trying to get involved. Finally, this year Ms. Avery has noticed that Chandra often chooses her interpreter as her partner rather than seeking out a peer.

Harter's Self-Perception Profile for Adolescents (SPPA)

Susan Harter from the University of Denver has created several different scales designed to measure self-perception in children and adults. The scales that are most appropriate for adapted physical education are her Self-Perception Profile for Children and her Self-Perception Profile for Adolescents. Both scales are designed to assess children's self-perceptions in several different domains. The childhood scale measures self-perceptions in global self-worth as well as in five domains: scholastic competence, social acceptance, athletic competence, physical appearance, and behavioral conduct. The adolescent scale covers these six areas plus friendship, romantic appeal, and job competence.

The SPPA utilizes a structured alternative-response format. Children are given two descriptions and asked to choose which description they are most like. Then within the description they choose, they select "really true for me" or "sort of true for me" (figure 9.5). Harter suggests that this type of format increases the

Select Items from Harter's Self-Perception Profile for Adolescents

Really true for me	Sort of true for me				Sort of true for me	Really true for me
_____	_____	Some teenagers are often disappointed with themselves	but	other teenagers are pretty happy with themselves.	_____	_____
_____	_____	Some teenagers don't like the way they are leading their lives	but	other teenagers do like the way they are leading their lives.	_____	_____
_____	_____	Some teenagers are happy with themselves most of the time	but	other teenagers are often unhappy with themselves.	_____	_____

Select item from the importance scale

_____	_____	Some young people think that being good at school isn't important	but	other young people think that being good at school is important.	_____	_____

Items from the athletic competence domain

_____	_____	Some teenagers do very well in sports	but	other teenagers don't think they are very good when it comes to sports.	_____	_____
_____	_____	Some teenagers think they could do well at just about any new athletic activity	but	other teenagers are afraid they might not do well at a new athletic activity.	_____	_____
_____	_____	Some teenagers think they are better than others their age in sports	but	other teenagers don't think they can play as well.	_____	_____
_____	_____	Some teenagers don't do well at new outdoor games	but	other teenagers are good at games right away.	_____	_____
_____	_____	Some teenagers do not think they are very athletic	but	other teenagers think they are very athletic.	_____	_____

Figure 9.5 Select items from Harter's Self-Perception Profile for Adolescents.

From S. Harter, 1988, *Manual for the self-perception profile for children* (Denver, CO: Author).

likelihood that children will respond based on how they truly feel rather than in a way they think is desirable or expected. The profile also includes an importance scale, which asks children to rate whether or not something is important to them. The format for the importance scale is the same as for the Self-Perception Profile (i.e., structured alternative-response format). Harter's Self-Perception Profile for Children and Self-Perception Profile for Adolescents have both been widely used in sport psychology research. Both instruments have very good reliability (both internal consistency and test–retest reliability) as well as validity supported through factor analysis.

Of interest to physical educators is the subscale in figure 9.5 that measures perceived athletic competence (competence in sports and games). Results from the five items in this subscale provide a sense of how a child feels about her athletic abilities and to a lesser degree her abilities in physical education. This information could be used for children with physical or sensory disabilities or mild cognitive disabilities to get a general sense of how they feel about their physical athletic competence. The adapted physical educator could also create other items more directly related to physical education. The following are examples of statements using Harter's structured alternative-response format that adapted physical educators can use for students with disabilities to get a more accurate idea of their self-perception and self-confidence in physical education:

- Some children enjoy physical education, but other children do not enjoy physical education.
- Some children do well in most physical education activities, but other children do not do well in most physical education activities.
- Some children enjoy physical fitness activities, but other children do not enjoy physical fitness activities.
- Some children enjoy working with a partner in physical education, but other children do not enjoy working with a partner.
- Some children enjoy playing group games in physical education, but other children do not enjoy playing group games.
- Some children wish games could be modified more so that everyone could be successful, but other children like playing the games following the regulation rules.
- Some children get a little embarrassed when they cannot do a skill in physical education, but other children don't really care if they have trouble doing a skill.

Ulrich's Pictorial Scale of Perceived Physical Competence (PSPPC)

Ulrich and Collier (1990) adapted Harter's Pictorial Scale of Perceived Competence and Social Acceptance for use with children with mild intellectual disabilities. The adapted scale became known as Ulrich's Pictorial Scale of Perceived Physical Competence (PSPPC). The PSPPC was designed to assess the self-perceptions of motor skills competence among elementary-aged children and children with mild mental retardation. Since this is a pictorial scale, it is ideal for children who cannot read, such as young elementary students and students with mild intellectual disabilities and learning disabilities (Ulrich & Collier, 1990). Subjects are shown a series of two contrasting pictures of children performing gross motor skills such as throwing or jumping (see list that follows). One picture shows a child who is "pretty good" at the skill, and the other picture shows a child who is "not very good" at the skill. Children are then asked to point to the picture of the child they feel most like and to indicate if they feel "a lot" like the child they chose or "a little" like the child they chose. Thus, the scale is a 4-point scale, with a 1 indicating a child selected the picture of the child who is not very good at a skill and then stated he feels "a lot" like that child. A score of 4 indicates a child selected the picture of the child who is very good at a skill and then stated he feels "a lot" like that child (figure 9.6).

As noted already, the PSPPC was modified from Harter's original pictorial scale. Modifications focused on adding fundamental gross motor skills commonly seen in elementary physical education programs as well as items recommended by adapted physical educators (hopping was eliminated, and many sports skills were added). Ulrich and Collier's final scale consists of the following fundamental gross motor skills:

Swinging	Climbing on a jungle gym	Skipping
Running	Bouncing a ball	Jumping rope
Jumping	Kicking	Throwing
Catching		

The final scale also includes the following sport-specific skills:

Baseball:	batting a baseball	throwing a baseball	catching a baseball
Basketball:	dribbling a basketball	shooting a basketball	passing a basketball
Soccer:	dribbling a soccer ball	kicking a soccer ball	soccer throw-in

The PSPPC was analyzed and validated in a study by Ulrich and Collier (1990) using children with mild intellectual disabilities. Results found the PSPPC to have good internal consistency (82% total-scale Cronbach alpha reliability) and good test–retest reliability (77% for the overall mean score but somewhat lower on select individual items [26% on the skip and 63% on the dribble]). There are no norms, and validity was not cited in the Ulrich and Collier study. Care should be taken to make sure children completely understand the pictures as well as the skill being demonstrated in each picture. To better understand why a child responds the way she does, it is recommended that the examiner ask the following additional questions: Have you ever done this skill? When? A lot or a little? Who taught you? Do you like doing the skill? Is it fun?

PLAY BEHAVIORS

Play is a critical part of early childhood development. Play allows children to have fun, use their imaginations, and appropriately occupy their free time. In addition, social play (playing with or around others) allows children to learn from peers; to take turns and cooperate with peers; and to learn different, appropriate ways to play with toys and peers (hyperdictionary, 2004). Learning to play appropriately also prevents children with disabilities from being socially rejected and avoided

This boy is pretty good at jumping.

Are you:

Pretty good   or   Really good at jumping

This boy is not very good at jumping.

Are you:

Not very good   or   Sort of good at jumping

This girl can run pretty fast.

Are you:

Pretty fast or Really fast

This girl can't run very fast.

Are you:

Not very fast   or   Sort of fast

Figure 9.6   Select items from Ulrich's Pictorial Scale of Perceived Physical Competence.

From D.A. Ulrich and D.H. Collier, 1990, "Perceived physical competence in children with mental retardation: Modification of a pictorial scale," *Adapted Physical Activity Quarterly* 7: 338-354.

by their peers without disabilities (Sherrill, 2004). Unfortunately, many children with autism as well as some children with mental retardation do not have developmentally appropriate play skills. These children may not spontaneously play with toys or objects that are attractive to their peers, they may not seek to play with other children, or they may not play appropriately when they do engage in play with toys or peers. Additionally, these children may react to play settings in ways that are different from what is expected of children their age (Powers, 2000; Reid, O'Conner, & Lloyd, 2003). For example, when other children are excited about sharing balls in a tossing and dodging game, a child with autism may just pick up one ball, hold it tight to his chest, and then run to the corner of the gym. Similarly, when other children are laughing and having fun with a parachute, a child with autism might be holding his ears and crying.

Case Study 4

Terry is a 7-year-old second grader who enjoys cartoons, McDonald's Chicken McNuggets, playing with toy soldiers, and tossing and chasing a small yarn ball. Terry also has autism, and he rarely shares his favorite things with his family or peers. This is particularly noticeable in physical education, where Terry often wanders the perimeter of the gymnasium, tossing and picking up his yarn ball. He does have a teacher assistant who tries to coax him to participate with his peers, but she has not been very successful. One of Terry's global goals (a goal that all IEP team members are working toward) is to move from isolated play to more interactive play. The team has some ideas on how to help Terry become more sociable in his play, but how can they measure progress toward more appropriate play?

One important goal of programming for children with autism and similar developmental disabilities is to teach them how to play more appropriately. The child's present level of play behavior should be assessed, as well as her progress toward demonstrating more appropriate play behavior throughout the program. Sherrill (2004) notes that assessment should include observations of a child's spontaneous play and interactions with objects and people in her environment. Sherrill suggests the following questions to ask when observing these children in play: "Do they initiate contact with people and objects, and is their contact appropriate? How long do they sustain contact? Do they demonstrate preferences for some objects and people?" (p. 499). With such baseline information, the IEP team can design a developmentally appropriate intervention plan and appropriate objectives. Additionally, the team should conduct ongoing observations to determine a child's progress toward more appropriate play behaviors. There are no formal play behavior assessments that are appropriate for physical education. The following is an example of a teacher-developed assessment specifically designed for physical education settings.

Sherrill—UVA–APE Social Play Behavior Inventory

Sherrill (2004) created a simple-to-use social play behavior inventory to measure a child's current play behaviors as well as ongoing improvement in play. This social play behavior inventory was slightly modified by the University of Virginia Adapted Physical Education Program (UVA-APE) to include four behavior levels: always, most of the time, sometimes, and rarely or never (figure 9.7). These levels allow

Sherrill–University of Virginia Adapted Physical Education Social Play Behavior Inventory

Child's name: _____ Evaluator: _____

School: _____ Date: _____

Use this form when first observing a child with a disability who has been referred for adapted physical education. Rate each item based on how the child compares with other children in his or her physical education class.

	Always 4	Most of the time 3	Sometimes 2	Rarely or never 1
Autistic/Unoccupied				
Shows no spontaneous play	☐	☐	☐	☐
Makes no response	☐	☐	☐	☐
Shows no object or person preference	☐	☐	☐	☐
Makes stereotyped or repetitive movements	☐	☐	☐	☐
Pounds, shakes, or mouths objects without purpose	☐	☐	☐	☐
Self-stimulates	☐	☐	☐	☐
Wanders about aimlessly	☐	☐	☐	☐
Self-mutilates	☐	☐	☐	☐
Solitary/Exploratory				
Reacts to stimuli (approaches or avoids)	☐	☐	☐	☐
Reacts to persons or objects	☐	☐	☐	☐
Understands object permanence (peek-a-boo, hide and seek)	☐	☐	☐	☐
Explores body parts	☐	☐	☐	☐
Explores objects or toys	☐	☐	☐	☐
Shows object preference	☐	☐	☐	☐
Shows person preference	☐	☐	☐	☐
Parallel				
Establishes play space near others	☐	☐	☐	☐
Shows awareness of others but doesn't interact	☐	☐	☐	☐
Plays independently with own things	☐	☐	☐	☐
Plays on same playground apparatus as others	☐	☐	☐	☐
Follows leader in imitation games and obstacle course	☐	☐	☐	☐
Associative/Interactive				
Initiates contact or play with others	☐	☐	☐	☐
Talks, signs, or gestures to others	☐	☐	☐	☐
Imitates others	☐	☐	☐	☐
Rolls or hands toy or ball to another without being asked	☐	☐	☐	☐
Retrieves objects for another without being asked	☐	☐	☐	☐
Offers to share objects or toys	☐	☐	☐	☐
Engages in make-believe play with others	☐	☐	☐	☐
Takes turns talking and listening	☐	☐	☐	☐

(continued)

Figure 9.7 Sherrill–University of Virginia Adapted Physical Education Program Social Play Behavior Inventory.

From C. Sherrill, 2004, *Adapted physical activity, recreation, and sport*, 6th ed. (New York: McGraw-Hill), 500. Used with permission of The McGraw-Hill Companies.

	Always 4	Most of the time 3	Sometimes 2	Rarely or never 1
Cooperative				
Participates in small-group games	☐	☐	☐	☐
Sustains play in group of 3 or more for 5 minutes	☐	☐	☐	☐
Follows simple game rules	☐	☐	☐	☐
Understands stop and go	☐	☐	☐	☐
Understands safety zone, boundary line, base	☐	☐	☐	☐
Understands "It" and "not It"	☐	☐	☐	☐
Understands game formations (circle, line, file, scattered)	☐	☐	☐	☐
Plays games demanding one role (fleeing)	☐	☐	☐	☐
Switches roles to achieve game goals: hide or seek, chase or flee, tag or dodge	☐	☐	☐	☐

Figure 9.7   *(continued)*

the examiner to determine "how much" a child shows a particular play behavior and allows for a more sensitive measurement of progress. The inventory is divided into five developmental levels of play starting with autistic or unoccupied play (shows no spontaneous play, makes no response to stimuli, play is stereotypical or repetitive) and ending with cooperative play (participates in small-group games; sustains play in a group; follows simple game rules; understands safety zones, boundaries, and rules).

To use the inventory, the examiner watches a child in settings that provide opportunities to play with (1) age-appropriate toys, (2) one or two children in both unstructured play and structured partner activities, and (3) a large group of children in a structured game. The examiner then marks the box with the description that best describes the child's behavior. To gain reliability, it makes sense to observe the child multiple times in each of the three scenarios. For example, the examiner might organize a session in which balls are provided to all children in the class. Minimal instructions are provided, and the teacher simply observes the child to see how he plays with the ball. Then other toys and equipment can be given to the children such as beanbags, hula hoops, yarn balls, jump ropes, or cones to see how the child plays with these toys. Similarly, several different opportunities to observe the child playing with a peer and playing in a group game should be arranged to get a true measure of the child's current social play behaviors.

ATTITUDES

Children without disabilities do not automatically include children who are disabled in their social play activities, including the social play of physical education, recreation, and sport activities. Nondisabled children who have positive feelings toward peers with disabilities are more likely to accept and include them in their social play activities. On the other hand, children who hold negative feelings toward peers with disabilities will be less likely to want to include these children in their social play activities. Clearly, how children without disabilities "feel" toward children with disabilities plays an important part in the successful inclusion of students with disabilities in general physical education and recreation.

Case Study 5

William is a 16-year-old sophomore at Washington High School. He and his friends are the "in crowd" at school. They are all athletes and very popular, and pretty much every day you can find William and his friends hanging out during breaks between classes with cheerleaders and other popular girls. Unfortunately, pretty much every day you can also find William and his friends teasing and picking on children who are not in the "in crowd." The most intense teasing is saved for Johnny and Tim, two boys with mild mental retardation. William and his friends can be seen tripping and pushing these two boys in the hallway. And during physical education, they make fun of Johnny and Tim, make sure no one picks them to be on their team, and push and trip and intimidate the two boys whenever possible. Early in the semester, the teasing and physical antics were pretty minimal, so Ms. Delgado, the general physical educator, let it go. But recently William and his friends have been more overt in their negative behaviors, and Ms. Delgado is ready to put a stop to it. However, she does not want to simply punish William and his friends. First, she wants to find out why they behave the way they do. Then she would like to try a disability awareness intervention to see if this improves their attitudes and behaviors toward the two boys. What is a good way for Ms. Delgado to measure the present attitudes of William and his friends and then measure whether or not the intervention she implements has been effective?

This "feeling" is captured in the concept of attitudes. Attitudes specify one's preference to either avoid or approach someone or something (Tripp & Sherrill, 2004). Furthermore, attitudes are believed to be directly connected to intentions, and in turn intentions are believed to be directly related to behaviors (Ajzen & Fishbein, 1980).

For example, Jan doesn't like roller coasters (attitude), so she plans to avoid roller coasters (intention). When faced with a chance to ride a roller coaster, she will not ride the roller coaster (behavior). With regard to children with disabilities, how a child without disabilities feels toward a peer with a disability (attitude) reflects her intentions to play with a child with a disability, which in turn reflects whether or not she will actually play with the child with a disability when given the opportunity.

With regard to assessment, physical educators need to measure how nondisabled children feel about including children with disabilities in their physical education class. By measuring attitudes, the general physical educator will have a good idea of the behaviors to expect of the children without disabilities toward peers with disabilities (behaviors such as picking a child with disabilities to be their partner or to play on their team, helping a peer with disabilities learn a skill, or accepting modifications to games and equipment to make the activity more fair for the child with disabilities). Attitude assessments conducted early in the school year can then leave time for the general physical educator to do some disability awareness and acceptance activities. Such activities may change some children's negative attitudes toward children with disabilities and prevent new negative behaviors and resentment from emerging (e.g., "Why does he have to be on my team?" and "Why does she get to shoot at a lower basket?") (Block, 2000). Assessment of attitudes can also be conducted after the disability awareness training session and occasionally throughout the year to make sure nondisabled children still have positive attitudes toward peers with disabilities. Three of the more widely used attitude inventories are presented in this section.

Children's Attitudes Toward Integrated Physical Education—Revised Inventory

The Children's Attitudes Toward Integrated Physical Education–Revised (CAIPE-R) is a simple-to-administer attitude inventory specifically designed for physical education (Block, 1995). The purpose of the CAIPE-R is to determine attitudes of children without disabilities toward including peers with disabilities in physical education as well as toward modifications to sports typically played in general physical education. The inventory begins with a description of a child with a disability, usually a child similar to the student to be included in the specific physical education class. In other words, if a child who has cerebral palsy and uses a wheelchair is going to join a fifth-period general physical education class, then the description of the child on the CAIPE-R should be a child who uses a wheelchair and who has similar movement abilities to a child with cerebral palsy. After the students read (or have read to them) the description of the targeted child, they respond to 12 to 14 statements using a 4-point Likert scale (a yes answer equals 4 points, a no equals 1 point) (figure 9.8). The first 7 statements on the CAIPE-R focus on generally including a child with disabilities in physical education. The last 5 to 7 questions focus on whether or not the students would accept specific modifications to a sport played in physical education (such as basketball, volleyball, or soccer). For example, modifications for basketball might include shooting at a shorter basket, not allowing anyone to steal the ball, allowing a free pass, and not calling traveling or double dribbling.

The CAIPE-R is analyzed by totaling each subscale (general physical education and sport-specific modifications) and dividing by the number of statements to get a score of 1 to 4. Scores of 1 or 2 indicate negative attitudes, while scores of 3 or 4 indicate positive attitudes. Each item on the CAIPE-R can also be analyzed to determine if the majority of children in the class disagree with a specific part about inclusion or a specific modification. If the students feel negative about a particular statement, then the teacher can lead a discussion to determine why so many students feel that way. For example, let's say a majority of students disagree with the following statement: "If the ball were hit to Mike, the batter could run only as far as second base." The teacher can explain her rationale for the modification, find out why the class does not like this modification, and then suggest a new modification that is satisfactory to everyone.

Siperstein's Adjective Checklist

Siperstein's Adjective Checklist is a quick, simple tool designed to measure children's attitudes toward peers with disabilities. The premise of the adjective checklist is that children will choose adjectives (e.g., *clever, crazy, healthy, weak*) that describe how they feel about a peer with a disability (this could be a real peer in the class or an imaginary child with a disability). According to the theory, children who have negative feelings toward a child with a disability will choose adjectives that have negative connotations (e.g., *weak, sloppy, dumb)*, while children with positive feelings will choose adjectives that have positive connotations (e.g., *happy, clever, cheerful)*. To administer the checklist, the examiner places the name of a particular student (e.g., Sarah) or a description of a disability (e.g., child with mental retardation) on the blank line at the top of the checklist. Students circle all the words they would use to describe that person or that disability (children are directed to circle as many or as few adjectives as they wish). Figure 9.9 shows the adjectives on Siperstein's Adjective Checklist.

Children's Attitudes Toward Integrated Physical Education–Revised

Part I: General inclusion	Yes	Probably yes	Probably no	No
1. It would be okay having Mike in my physical education class.	☐	☐	☐	☐
2. Because Mike cannot play sports very well, he would slow the game down for everyone.	☐	☐	☐	☐
3. If we were playing a team sport such as basketball, it would be okay having Mike on my team.	☐	☐	☐	☐
4. Physical education would be fun if Mike were in my class.	☐	☐	☐	☐
5. If Mike were in my physical education class, I would talk to him and be his friend.	☐	☐	☐	☐
6. If Mike were in my physical education class, I would like to help him practice and play the games.	☐	☐	☐	☐
7. During practice, it would be okay to allow Mike to use special equipment such as a lower basket in basketball or a batting tee in softball.	☐	☐	☐	☐

Part II: Sport-specific modifications	Yes	Probably yes	Probably no	No
What rule changes during physical education do you think would be okay if a child like Mike were playing softball?				
1. Mike could hit a ball placed on a batting tee.	☐	☐	☐	☐
2. Someone could tell Mike where to run when he hits the ball.	☐	☐	☐	☐
3. The distance between home and first base could be shorter for Mike.	☐	☐	☐	☐
4. Someone could help Mike when he plays in the field.	☐	☐	☐	☐
5. If the ball were hit to Mike, the batter could run only as far as second base.	☐	☐	☐	☐

Figure 9.8   Children's Attitudes Toward Integrated Physical Education–Revised (CAIPE-R) inventory.

Adapted, by permission, from M.E. Block, 1995, "Development and validation of the Children's Attitudes toward Integrated Physical Education–Revised (CAIPE-R), *Adapted Physical Activity Quarterly* 12: 60-77.

Factor analysis conducted on data from 2,200 children revealed three factors for the Adjective Checklist. Factor 1 (labeled *P* for positive factor) represents a bright, socially able classmate (e.g., *smart, friendly, nice);* factor 2 (labeled *N* for negative factor) represents a dull, socially inept classmate (e.g., *dumb, careless, greedy);* and factor 3 (labeled *E* for empathetic factor) represents empathetic responses toward the targeted child or feelings inferred to be held by the targeted child (e.g., *lonely, unhappy, ashamed).* Scores on the Adjective Checklist show whether or not a student believes the targeted child manifests traits underlying each of the three factors. Each student's score is calculated as a proportion of adjectives

Siperstein's Adjective Checklist

If you had to describe _____ to your classmates, what kind of words would you use? Below is a list of words to help you. CIRCLE the words you would use. You can use as many or as few words as you want. Here is the list:

Healthy	Clever	Crazy	Honest	Lonely	Proud
Bored	Friendly	Glad	Dishonest	Mean	Kind
Slow	Alert	Greedy	Ashamed	Pretty	Weak
Helpful	Sad	Stupid	Smart	Ugly	Bright
Sloppy	Okay	Cheerful	Neat	Cruel	
Dumb	Careful	Careless	Unhappy	Happy	

Figure 9.9 Siperstein's Adjective Checklist.

From G.N. Siperstein, 1980, *Instruments for measuring children's attitudes toward the handicapped.* Unpublished manuscript. Center for Human Services. University of Massachusetts, Boston.

selected by the total number of adjectives in each factor (17 for the P factor, 10 for the N factor, and 7 for the E factor). Results become three separate scores, each representing a ratio ranging from 0 to 1.0. Scores approaching 1.0 (e.g., 0.6 or higher) indicate a high score on that factor (Siperstein, 1980). For example, a student who chooses 7 out of 10 items on the N factor would have an N factor score of 0.7, suggesting she holds negative feelings toward the targeted child.

As was the case with the CAIPE-R, results of the Adjective Checklist should be examined and then discussed with the class. If several children describe a peer who has intellectual disabilities with adjectives such as *weak, dumb, stupid,* and *ugly,* the teacher should talk about why so many children feel that way about this child. Then perhaps an intervention should be considered, such as showing videos of Special Olympics athletes or bringing in someone with intellectual disabilities who does not meet the stereotype held by many of the students (Sherrill, 2004).

Siperstein's Friendship Activity Scale

Siperstein believed that measuring a child's intentions to play and interact with a peer with a disability would be a strong indicator of the child's actual behaviors. Because observing a child's actual play and interaction behaviors is difficult, Siperstein created the Friendship Activity Scale to measure friendship intentions (Siperstein, Bak, & O'Keefe, 1988). The original Activity Preference Scale was made up of 30 activity statements that children responded to with yes, no, or not sure. A yes response received a point score of 3, not sure received 2, and no received 1, yielding a possible range of scores from 30 to 90. The original scale was administered twice, first when the object of the scale was a friend and once when the object was the targeted child.

The revised scale is a shortened version of the original, with 15 activity statements judged on a 4-point Likert scale (yes, probably yes, probably no, no). Scores are weighted from 4 (yes) to 1 (no), representing a range of scores from 15 to 60 (figure 9.10). The revised scale need only be administered once, with the focus on only the targeted child with disabilities. Internal consistency (Cronbach alpha coefficient) of the revised scale is 90% (*N* = 696 children). Again,

Siperstein's Revised Activity Preference Scale

Monitor Instructions

[Read aloud to class] Make believe that Amy or Ben is moving into your neighborhood and will be coming into your class. What types of activities would you like to do with her or him? Below is a list of activities to help you decide. If you would like to do an activity with Amy or Ben, circle *Yes*. If you would probably do an activity with Amy or Ben, circle *Probably yes*. If you would probably not do an activity with Amy or Ben, circle *Probably no*. If you would not do an activity with Amy or Ben, circle *No*.

Remember, the answer to each question depends on you, and your answers will probably be different from other kids' answers. When you are all done, you'll probably have some yeses, some probably yeses, some probably nos, and some nos, or your answers could all be one thing. Does anyone have any questions [look around and wait for questions]?

Answer Sheet

Student's code: _____

If you would like to do an activity with Amy or Ben, circle *Yes*. If you would probably do an activity with Amy or Ben, circle *Probably yes*. If you would probably not do an activity with Amy or Ben, circle *Probably no*. If you would not do an activity with Amy or Ben, circle *No*.

1. Invite her or him to your house?	Yes	Probably yes	Probably no	No
2. Sit next to each other in class?	Yes	Probably yes	Probably no	No
3. Go sledding or ice skating together?	Yes	Probably yes	Probably no	No
4. Work on a class project together?	Yes	Probably yes	Probably no	No
5. Play games outside together after school?	Yes	Probably yes	Probably no	No
6. Eat lunch together in school?	Yes	Probably yes	Probably no	No
7. Listen to music at home together?	Yes	Probably yes	Probably no	No
8. Play together during recess or snack time?	Yes	Probably yes	Probably no	No
9. Play games inside your house together?	Yes	Probably yes	Probably no	No
10. Do errands for the teacher together?	Yes	Probably yes	Probably no	No
11. Go bicycle riding together?	Yes	Probably yes	Probably no	No
12. Play games in class together?	Yes	Probably yes	Probably no	No
13. Go on a picnic or swimming together?	Yes	Probably yes	Probably no	No
14. Play on the same team in gym?	Yes	Probably yes	Probably no	No
15. Go to the movies together?	Yes	Probably yes	Probably no	No

Thank you! You are finished!

Figure 9.10   Siperstein's Revised Activity Preference Scale.

From G.N. Siperstein, 1980, *Instruments for measuring children's attitudes toward the handicapped.* Unpublished manuscript. Center for Human Services. University of Massachusetts, Boston.

results should be examined and then discussed with the class. For example, if several students note that they would not like to play games outside together with the targeted child after school or during recess, the teacher can ask why so many children feel this way. Information from these discussions can then be used to change behaviors of the child with the disability (e.g., children said they do not like to play with this child because he is too aggressive) or change the attitude and behavior of children without disabilities (e.g., ask these students how they would feel if no one played with them during recess or after school).

What You Need to Know ▸▸▸

Key Terms

adaptive behavior	functional analysis	positive behavioral support
antecedent	maladaptive behavior	self-concept
attitudes	perceived competence	self-esteem
behavior	play behavior	social competence
consequence		

Key Concepts

1. You should know the difference between adaptive and maladaptive behavior, why it is important to measure adaptive behavior, and different ways to measure adaptive behavior in children with disabilities.

2. You should be able to contrast the traditional versus the functional way to assess behavior problems. You should be able to administer a functionally based behavioral assessment for children with disabilities.

3. You should understand the concept of social competence and why it is important to assess social competence. You should be familiar with key testing protocols used to assess social competence in children with disabilities.

4. You should understand the concepts of self-concept, self-esteem, and perceived competence and why they are important. You should be familiar with key testing protocols used to assess self-concept and perceived competence in children with disabilities.

5. You should understand the concept of play and why it is important to assess play behaviors. You should be familiar with key testing protocols used to assess play in children with disabilities.

6. You should understand the terminology related to attitudes and why it is important to assess attitudes. You should be familiar with key testing protocols used to measure attitudes of children without disabilities toward peers with disabilities.

Review Questions

1. Rachel in case study 1 displays several maladaptive behaviors. How would you determine the extent of her behaviors (frequency, duration) and why these behaviors occur? Once you have more information about Rachel's behaviors, how would you create a positive behavior plan for her that would prevent her from displaying these behaviors and teach her to respond more appropriately?

2. Malcolm in case study 2 clearly displays unique behavior problems that can best be categorized as social problems. How could you determine the specific social problems Malcolm displays? What type of remedial program would you implement for Malcolm to teach him how to behave more appropriately in social situations?

3. Chandra in case study 3 appears to be having problems with how she feels about herself, or her self-esteem. How would you measure her self-esteem? What modifications to your program would you create to improve Chandra's self-esteem? How would you change how you interact with Chandra to improve her self-esteem?

4. Terry in case study 4 clearly has trouble with play behaviors. How would you measure Terry's specific developmental play level? Once assessed, how would you create a program that would improve his play behaviors?

5. William and his friends in case study 5 seem to have some problems with how they feel about their peers with disabilities. How could you measure their attitudes toward their peers with disabilities? How could you apply this information to create a disability awareness program to change their attitudes?

Translating Assessment Into Action: A Team Approach

nformation gathered about a person's performance, motor proficiency, or level of physical fitness can provide a description of overall functional ability. These data are of little use, however, unless they are interpreted correctly. The general purpose of assessment is not to provide a diagnosis but to generate useful information for planning and implementing appropriate programs that are functional and achievable. The challenge confronting the programming team is translating the data gathered from the assessment process into action. This includes guidelines for preparing and interpreting the assessment data, assigning roles to members of the programming team, writing long-term goals and short-term objectives, making decisions about instructional activities, and monitoring the instructional plan.

Case Study ①

Mr. Fletcher, an adapted physical education specialist, has just reviewed his caseload for the year. It includes children with a wide range of disabilities, including cognitive impairments, sensory disorders, and neurological impairments. What steps should Mr. Fletcher take to begin the process of planning programs for these children?

Mr. Fletcher should follow the six phases of ecological assessment espoused by Block (2000) to determine the following:

- Who qualifies for adapted physical education
- What to teach
- How to teach
- Where to teach
- Who will teach
- How well the skills are learned

PREPARATION AND INTERPRETATION OF ASSESSMENT INFORMATION

If a comprehensive assessment of functional capabilities has been completed, the tester will be faced with data in varying forms. An informal test of behavior may yield data consisting of summaries of observational tallies. A standardized test will yield raw scores, percentiles, and stanines, while a developmental profile may result in developmental ages. A summation of all available data is required in order to draw conclusions. In addition, ongoing information from parents, therapists, teachers, and doctors must be utilized to ensure understanding of individual needs and functional capabilities. Mr. Fletcher, the adapted physical education teacher in case study 1, will need to gather all the assessment information available for the children in his caseload. However, before he can use the data for program planning and instruction, he must prepare the data for interpretation.

Preparing the Data

Whether the assessment results are presented verbally or in written form, a systematic picture of the person's characteristics should be determined. Included in this information are the following assessment components:

- *Demographic data.* Include the full name, birthdate, grade placement, address, telephone number, classroom teacher, parent, and case manager (primary special education teacher, if appropriate).
- *Referral data.* Include the name of the person who initiated the referral, the referral date, and the reason for referral.
- *Background data.* May include information from doctors, therapists, parents, and others regarding physical education and sociocultural background and status.
- *Observational data noted during assessment.* Notes and comments about the child's behavior during the assessment sessions should be recorded.
- *Test data.* All assessment data should be tallied and summarized in raw scores to prepare for further analysis and interpretation.
- *Functional data.* Raw scores and observations should be specific to the task or functional skill. If muscular strength is required in the neck and abdominal area to ensure head control and use of a computer for transition into the community, the data should be documented to promote functional development.

The evaluator should thoroughly review the completed response forms to ensure that the data have been recorded properly. At this point, the evaluator should choose only relevant data specific to program planning and avoid any data that may violate individual privacy (e.g., achievement scores, family socioeconomic status).

Several methods expedite the process of summarizing test data into strengths and needs in a concise form that facilitates both communication and decision making. Informal and formal assessment data of the highest quality should first be summarized as raw scores. Note, however, that raw scores by themselves are of extremely limited value. If a formal standardized test has been administered, raw scores should be converted to allow comparisons with scores achieved by others in the standardization population. Raw scores may also be converted to derived scores such as age-equivalent scores, grade-equivalent scores, percentiles, standard scores, and stanines. Generally, a tester can convert raw scores to other scores by using tables provided in the test manual. Derived scores include the following:

- *Age-equivalent scores.* Raw scores are translated into the average chronological age (CA) at which the students in the standardization population achieved a particular raw score. For example, Kathy, whose CA is 8.3, achieved an age-equivalent score of 5.60 on locomotor performance on the TGMD-2. Kathy's motor performance on this test was like that of children aged 5 years 6 months, revealing a problem area for a child aged 8.

- *Grade-equivalent scores.* Raw scores are translated into the average grade at which children in the standardization population achieved a particular raw score. For example, Markus, who is at the beginning of third grade, achieved a grade-equivalent score of 1.5 (based on a raw score of 6) on an abdominal strength subtest. This means that the average grade-equivalent score in the standardization group that received a raw score of 6 on the subtest was grade 1.5, indicating grade one and five-tenths.

- *Percentiles.* Most standardized tests provide tables for the conversion of raw scores to percentile ranks. A percentile rank indicates the percentage of students in the standardization group that received the same raw score or a lower raw score. For example, if Lisa, age 8, achieved a raw score of 14 in running speed and agility, the corresponding percentile rank in the test norms might be the 35th percentile. This means that a raw score of 14 is equal to or higher than the scores achieved by 35% of the standardization group. Lisa obtained a score higher than 35 out of every 100 children in a representative sample of 8-year-olds. Percentile ranks are commonly used in IEP team meetings for reporting test results because they are fairly easy to calculate and interpret.

- *Standard scores.* In standardized tests, raw scores are usually converted to standard scores before further conversions or percentiles and stanines are made. Standard scores provide a scale of scores that can be used for comparisons of all children to whom the test was administered. The mean and the standard deviation are used to calculate standard scores, which are usually presented in the norm tables of the test manual. The mean *(M)* of a set of scores is the arithmetic average, and it is usually presented in motor test manuals for children of different ages. The standard deviation *(SD)* of a set of scores describes the variability of the scores. For example, Todd, when compared with his age peers, achieved a standard score of 40 on a motor ability test. Since the mean standard score on this test is 50 and the standard deviation is 10, Todd's score indicates that his performance was one standard deviation below the mean of the norm group for his age.

- *Stanines.* Some standardized tests allow the tester to convert raw scores to stanines. Stanines are simply ranges of standard scores. They have become increasingly popular in public schools for interpreting and describing formal test results. There are nine stanines, or "standard nines." One advantage of using stanine scores is that collapsing the full range of standard scores into nine categories helps guard against overinterpretation of test data, particularly when differences between children's scores are slight. The conversion of raw scores into stanines is usually provided in tables in the test manual.

Derived scores such as percentiles, standard scores, and stanines provide a means of comparing one person's raw scores with a "normal distribution" of raw scores. The standardization sample reported in the test manual has raw scores that are distributed normally in a bell-shaped curve.

When a formal standardized test has been administered and raw scores converted to derived scores, a child's test scores may be plotted on a profile. A test profile provides a visual presentation of a child's test performance and can be useful when interpreting test results to parents and other team members. In addition, teachers can use the information to develop the instruction plan.

Case Study 2

Katya seemed to be having problems in her physical education class, so her teacher recommended that she be assessed with the Bruininks-Oseretsky Test of Motor Proficiency (BOT-2). She scored poorly on all the gross motor items, including running speed and agility, balance, strength, and bilateral coordination. With this information, teachers, team members, and parents can quickly determine strengths and weaknesses in order to develop a program plan that is specific to Katya's needs. Likewise, the profile can be used in conjunction with other assessments to aid in the decision-making process.

Katya will require a program based on her level of functioning. Because she scored lower on all gross motor items, goals should be developed to

- increase running speed and agility,
- develop static and dynamic balance,
- increase muscular strength and endurance, and
- enhance bilateral coordination.

Summarizing Informal Test Data

When interviews, observational checklists, and criterion-referenced assessment methods are used, the form of the test data is frequently more qualitative than quantitative. Such methods compare a child with a criterion rather than with scores of age peers. Although informal assessment methods have the advantage of being immediately applicable to the understanding and resolution of relevant problems and functional skills, the results must be easy to interpret. Some informal measures do include criteria for motor performance, but some criteria are subjectively established, while other criteria may come from an analysis of the skill or task.

To assist in summarizing informal test information, we recommend that results be depicted in relation to program goals and instructional objectives. For example, if a certain level of physical fitness is consistent with school and program guidelines, the summary of test information should include whether a specific level of functioning (criterion) has been achieved. If not, objectives that meet program goals can be developed and presented in a summary profile or graph (figure 10.1). The levels of mastery for age or grade level may also be recorded, while a clear description of strengths and needs should be readily apparent in an examination of the graph or profile. Since many teachers or clinical personnel have assessment data in varying forms, a summary should be compiled on the child's strengths and needs.

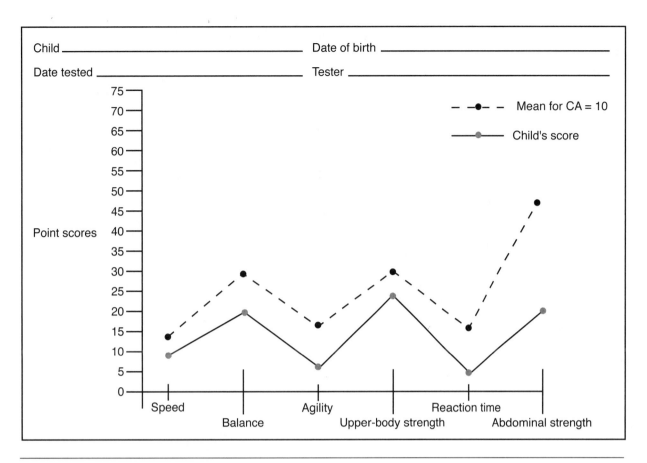

Child _____ Date of birth _____

Date tested _____ Tester _____

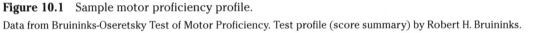

Figure 10.1   Sample motor proficiency profile.

Data from Bruininks-Oseretsky Test of Motor Proficiency. Test profile (score summary) by Robert H. Bruininks.

Figure 10.2 presents a summary of assessment information from four different assessment instruments. In addition, the appendixes contain several written reports of assessment data. In each case, the information contributed allows the educational programming team to develop a greater understanding of individual needs and functioning. This information can be used to determine the general goals of the individualized education plan as well as to communicate results and functional capabilities of children to their parents.

Interpreting Test Results

Once the information from the tests has been collected and summarized, the results should be interpreted to suggest program options and implementation strategies based on individual needs. At this point, overall functional capabilities in a variety of areas should be determined to provide the current level of performance in each specific area (e.g., arm strength, static balance, cognition, social interaction). The noted strengths and weaknesses will help in evaluating the child's needs as well as in determining any factors that affect performance and overall physical functioning.

When analyzing the results of data assessment, the evaluator should look for patterns, trends, or flags that can pinpoint potential problem areas. If reliable and valid assessment techniques have been used, consistencies or inconsistencies

Profile of Instructional Needs From Assessment Data

Child: _____

Age: _____ Classification: _____

	Formalized test	History or developmental profile	Observation or checklist	Criterion-referenced test
Muscular strength and endurance	Persistence of grasping reflex Average in strength for 1RM and 10RM	Prolonged labor or delivery		
Flexibility	Sit-and-reach scores			
General coordination and perception	Below average on jumping, hopping, object control	Delay in visual-perceptual development	Problems with eye–hand coordination	Immature pattern on object control skills
Cardiorespiratory endurance	Poor in walking test			
Social interaction	At solitary play level in play-based assessment			Withdrawn Absences from class Stands in background: quits
Cognitive skills			Difficulty following game strategies	
Mobility		Delay reaching developmental landmarks		

Recommendations for intervention and placement: _____

_____

_____

_____

Figure 10.2 Comprehensive summary of areas of instructional need.

should be noted and checked. For example, if one test revealed deficits in balance but another assessment demonstrated "average" performance, the inconsistencies should be examined. Another check of reliability and validity may reveal the source of the inconsistencies.

Carefully administered tests and assessment methods disclose consistent areas of other strengths and needs. In case study 2, if one test reveals deficits in upper-limb coordination while observation of performance reveals problems with throwing and catching skills, the tester can be reasonably confident that these areas represent skill discrepancies. When examining test results for interrelationships, it may also be apparent that balance deficits coincide with problems in gross agility. Difficulties in locomotor patterns may coexist with problems caused by inadequate strength or primitive reflexes, as seen in the figure 10.1 profile. A continual analysis of test data and input from other team members can be used to note patterns, trends, and inconsistencies among the data before recommendations are made for program planning and instruction.

The evaluator must also study any relationships between potential problem areas and effects of disabilities. For example, a person with muscular dystrophy will most likely demonstrate deficits in strength, endurance, and locomotor skills to varying degrees, depending on the progress of the disease and age of onset. Progressive deterioration of strength or, hopefully, maintenance of functional strength is expected. In contrast, lack of strength and motor control in persons with cerebral palsy may respond to intervention or erode into the inability to coordinate movements. Likewise, knowledge about learning problems, social interaction, or cognitive style can assist in the selection of appropriate instructional strategies based on individual needs.

Next, the tester must explore the degree to which disabilities may influence performance and overall physical functioning. The tester should possess a thorough understanding of the individual's strengths and difficulties as well as the current environment. Several factors should be considered:

- Severity of performance deficits
- Areas of special education need
- Goals for motor skills and fitness
- Expectations for physical functioning outside the school, along with skills required for transition

Severity of Performance Deficits

The severity of the performance deficits should be noted and compared by age or grade expectations. Standardized tests provide percentile ranks, stanines, and standard scores to facilitate interpretation. One or more standard deviations below the mean; stanine scores of 1, 2, or 3; and percentile ranks of below 16 may all indicate below average performance. Scores closer to the mean (e.g., less than one standard deviation from the mean) indicate potential problems but to a milder degree. These deficits are not severe and may respond to interventions to achieve peer-group expectations. Children with discrepancies more than two standard deviations from the mean in age-group expectations usually require placement in adapted physical education or supplementary services to meet their educational goals.

Placements and needs are not always directly linked to numerical ranks. People with functional losses may not fall at a certain rank or level yet require adequate assessments of their capabilities to offset potential problems that interfere with overall functioning.

When informal assessments are being interpreted, decisions about the severity of discrepancies are more complex. When a person's performance has been measured against a criterion and does not meet expectations, it is essential to analyze the severity of the discrepancy, the individual performance, and the criterion. For example, evaluating performance on a balancing task may be limited by sensory impairment, neurological dysfunction, or poor strength development. Questions such as the following should be asked to determine the balance variations in the assessment process:

- What level of balance should be expected given the age, grade level, and disability, and is balance functional?
- Does the child possess a sufficient level of strength to complete the task?
- What complicating factors, such as visual impairment and ataxia, are present that affect this task?

In this context, the child's needs can be addressed for placement (what is appropriate) and services (what is needed) and the program (instructional activities) related to the level of functioning.

Areas of Special Education Need

While analyzing the results of the assessment, the tester should note areas that require intervention. A person with numerous deficits will require more specific interventions than will a person with difficulties in one area. For example, Jenna has below average physical fitness. Her program may not be as intensive as the one designed for Sam, who has poor fitness as well as difficulties with general coordination, movement control, and communication. Although Jenna may need special assistance to improve fitness levels, programming can be implemented within the general class, at home, or in some combination. In contrast, Sam may require an extensive program at school in conjunction with the teacher, therapist (speech and physical), and adapted physical educator. Depending on the severity of the difficulties, the intervention may occur through an adapted specialized class as a training supplement, as therapy, or as a home-based program. The proposed interventions to meet the child's needs are implemented after analyzing the severity and scope of his problem areas, as well as the availability of program services.

Goals for Motor Skills and Fitness

The motor skills and fitness levels needed for successful performance in any given setting should also be carefully considered in conjunction with the objectives of the program. For example, an eighth-grade class curriculum is based on prerequisite skills for volleyball and soccer, but assessment reveals that a child with a disability exhibits serious difficulties in those prerequisite skills. The tester can be reasonably confident in predicting that the child will struggle with those skills in the general class, necessitating an individualized program to provide special instruction in prerequisite skill areas. In contrast, for a student with a lower-limb disability, it may be more appropriate to target fitness skills that allow the child to function in the school environment or participate in community recreational activities that are consistent with goals for the school.

Expectations for Physical Functioning

Another consideration when interpreting assessment results is the expectations of children for physical functioning in environments outside the school. Expectations for infants and young children include ambulation, appropriate play skills, and functioning in leisure and family settings. Older persons require preparation for transition from school to home settings and community-based recreational programs, along with training for work-related and vocational skills (Croce & Horvat, 1992; Zetts, Horvat, & Langone, 1995; Seagraves, Horvat, Franklin, & Jones, 2004). Recognized levels of physical functioning that are appropriate for program goals include the following:

- *Physical functioning level I:* nonambulatory; simple upper-body skills such as reach, grasp; trunk control; head control
- *Physical functioning level II:* rudimentary locomotion such as creep, crawl, cruise, stand; basic object manipulation such as grasp, release, throw,

push, pull; basic body awareness; motor skills for personal care such as feeding, toileting, dressing; righting reflexes

- *Physical functioning level III:* functional pattern of fundamental motor skills such as walk, run, vertical jump, up and down stairs, overhand throw, underhand throw; low to average levels of physical fitness; basic body awareness and body management; participation in playground activities

- *Physical functioning level IV:* mature patterns in some fundamental skills of locomotion and object control; good static and dynamic balance; average levels of fitness; may participate in intramural activities or sports or community recreational, vocational, or family activities

TEAM DECISION MAKING

In individualized education plan (IEP) or individualized transition plan (ITP) meetings, a team of parents and professionals cooperate to make the best possible programmatic decisions based on the assessment results. Teachers, including adapted physical educators, offer valuable contributions to IEP and ITP planning and should attempt to attend all meetings or at least provide written summaries of the physical and leisure capabilities of persons with disabilities.

Program-Planning Meetings

The purpose of a program-planning meeting is to discuss the results of assessment procedures to determine eligibility and special services and to design an appropriate education or services plan. To meet state regulations, an IEP meeting must usually take place within 30 calendar days of a determination that a student has a disability and is in need of special services. A completed IEP must be in place before the services are to be delivered and must be implemented as soon as possible after the meeting. After the initial meeting, subsequent IEP meetings are held annually to reexamine and revise the program.

Case Manager

When a child is first referred for special education assessment, a case manager is assigned to facilitate ongoing communication with other team members regarding the status of due process procedures. Usually, the case manager is someone specially trained in the area of the child's primary disability. An adapted physical education teacher will generally be the case manager only for those students whose primary disabilities are physical impairments that interfere solely with physical education. The case manager is responsible for notifying all team members of the following:

- Time and place of the meeting
- Names of other team members
- Due date for completed assessments
- Information needed for parents
- Written parental permission for assessment and implementation of the program plan

Communication During Program–Planning Meetings

If professionals are prepared and knowledgeable about assessment results, the key to productive decision making is effective communication among team members. Effective communication requires sharing and discussing the assessment data to portray an adequate picture of the student. The development of an appropriate instruction program is the intent of the program-planning conference. This goal cannot be accomplished without communication and collaborative efforts among team members (without regard to roles or issues of responsibility), whether the program is ultimately implemented in the school, home, or community setting.

Reviewing Rights

Often overlooked in the development of the IEP are the specific due process rights of parents. Although federal mandates guarantee parental rights in the education of children with disabilities, most states have more specific regulations outlining step-by-step due process procedures. At the beginning of each IEP conference, the case manager or a designated staff member should briefly explain and review the rights and due process system for the parents. This review is not intended to be a legal "reading of the rights" activity, but rather a reminder to everyone present that the parent or guardian has an equal partnership role in the decision-making process.

Sharing Results

Each team member who conducted an assessment must present his or her findings at the program-planning conference. Since a program-planning conference usually takes place in a limited time period, some general suggestions for efficient reporting follow.

• *General procedure used.* Briefly review the assessment procedure. If a standardized fitness test was administered, give a brief description of the reason fitness was measured and the instrument or method used. If no standardized tests were used, explain the uniqueness of the child's needs and why informal methods were selected instead.

• *Clarity.* Titles of subtests and terminology may sound like jargon to other team members or parents. When reporting test results, briefly explain the meaning of each term and provide examples to team members or parents.

• *Reporting ranges.* Instead of reporting specific scores, explain the results of an assessment descriptively. It is more useful to report that a child's balance skill level is below average for her age or at the 10th percentile than to say that she achieved a score of 17 on balance. In addition, information should be specific to functional skill development. For example, the low score on balance is one of the major reasons the child has difficulty walking up stairs. McLoughlin and Lewis (1981) proposed a five-level system for reporting assessment results.

1. Above average: more than two standard deviations above the mean
2. High average: from one to two standard deviations above the mean
3. Average: within one standard deviation above or below the mean
4. Low average: from one to two standard deviations below the mean
5. Below average: more than two standard deviations below the mean

When using this system, the reporter can simply indicate the desired scores, or age equivalents, along with the corresponding levels, if desired. Each statement of assessment results should reflect the child's current level of performance. As current skill status is explained, this five-level system can be used to report strengths as well as weaknesses. When motor performance in one area seems to be related to performance in another area, indicate the relationship.

• *Recommendations.* While reporting assessment results, it is advisable to postpone making recommendations until later in the conference. As results are summarized and explained, emphasize clearly the areas of strengths and difficulties. It is both professional and wise to listen to the reports of other team members, to ask relevant questions, and to answer the questions that others may have before making recommendations.

Listening to Team Members

Although the role of the adapted physical education teacher may appear to be one of reporting assessment results and making recommendations, listening to other team members is equally important. Parents can provide interesting insights into a child's functional and motor behavior, while personnel such as the school nurse may have worthwhile observations on effects of medication. Everyone present at the program-planning conference plays an important role in shaping the development process, and information gleaned from a variety of sources allows for informed programming decisions.

Writing the Program Plan

According to federal guidelines concerning the contents of the program plan, it is essential to include the following:

1. Statement of the child's present levels of educational performance
2. Statement of annual goals, including short-term objectives
3. Statement of the specific educational and related services to be provided to the child and the extent to which the child will be able to participate in general educational programming
4. Projected dates for initiation of services and anticipated duration of services
5. Appropriate objective criteria, evaluation procedures, and schedules for determining on at least an annual basis whether the objectives are being achieved

Current Level of Performance

A brief statement about the current level of performance should be developed to indicate general areas of need and functional capabilities. Usually, this statement is incorporated with information from other team members concerning the present state of the person's capabilities. This information is specific to developing the IEP as well as the ITP. The present level of performance summarizes the assessment data and provides recommendations that logically lead to long-term goals and short-term instructional objectives.

Annual Goals

Annual goals should represent recommendations for instruction within the instructional period or academic year and are clearly linked to the assessment report previously discussed. Since the goals are broad-based generalizations, they may vary according to individual capabilities, age, areas of need, input from parents, and expectations within the general instructional setting. Although goals may vary by person or setting where the instruction will occur (home, community), they should be based on results of the assessment data and current level of functioning.

Goals for Fitness

Physical fitness is a goal for all children, beginning with preschool and primary children, who require sufficient levels of strength and endurance to stand, move about, and ascend and descend stairs, as well as to perform some motor skills that require sufficient fitness, such as jumping. Fitness becomes a more crucial goal for intermediate and secondary grades, as children are required to perform activities for long periods of time and begin vocational skills training. It is essential that a child's functioning be clearly documented to determine if low levels of fitness are affecting his capabilities, or in the case of adolescents, what type of fitness is required for transition into community recreation or a work-performance situation (Seagraves et al., 2004). Examples of annual physical fitness goals include the following:

- David will improve abdominal strength.
- David will improve cardiovascular endurance by walking consistently for 30 minutes.
- David will increase his upper-body strength by 20%.
- David will improve overall flexibility.

Goals for Locomotor Skills

If it is determined that a component of fitness is lacking, appropriate goals can be initiated in that area. Some children may have motor skill development needs that should be addressed. For example, if delays in motor skills that interfere with play-based behaviors are evident from the assessment data, and subsequent parental observations substantiate that locomotor skills are delayed, goals may be written for improving locomotor skills (Horvat, Malone, & Deener, 1993). Sample annual goals for locomotor skills follow:

- Beth will demonstrate a mature creeping pattern for 8 to 10 feet (2.5 to 3 meters).
- Beth will walk unassisted and maintain balance for 10 steps.
- Beth will demonstrate opposition while walking.

Locomotion goals include creeping, crawling, walking, running, vertical jumping, horizontal jumping, hopping, galloping, skipping, sliding, and leaning. Specially designed locomotion goals may include propelling a wheelchair or walking with canes or other assistive devices. In addition, infants and toddlers delayed in achieving developmental milestones may require motor goals to develop appropriate play skills (Horvat, Malone, et al., 1993).

Goals for Object Control Skills

The ability to manipulate objects is important from preschool through secondary grades. Infants manipulate and exchange objects to receive sensory information, and objects serve as sensory lures for infants to reach and initiate crawling movements (Horvat, Malone, et al., 1993). For older children, play, sports, and recreational activities require grasping, releasing, and controlling objects. Each of these activities is important in school, home, and community settings. In addition, many self-help skills require identical prerequisite skills for functional needs such as dressing. Sample annual goals for object control skills follow:

- Jason will demonstrate a mature overhand throw with distance (30 feet, or 9 meters) and accuracy (10-foot [3-meter] diameter target).
- Jason will grasp a 4-inch (10-centimeter) Nerf ball 9 or 10 times.
- Jason will move an object from one hand to the other 4 or 5 times.
- Jason will initiate movement to a ball and grasp the object 4 or 5 times.

Object control skill goals for preschool children for play and development may include pushing, pulling, reaching, exchanging, manipulating, grasping, releasing, and underhand rolling (Fewell, 1991; Linder, 1993). Elementary-level skills include overhand throwing, catching, kicking, batting, underhand striking, and ball bouncing. Object control skills at secondary levels include dribbling, shooting baskets, chest passing, one-hand catching, serving and volleying (tennis and volleyball), soccer kicking, and soccer dribbling as well as the golf swing, shuffleboard push, racquetball swing, and bowling swing. Other object control skills may include buttoning, zippering, tying, writing, and typing on a computer.

Goals for Body Management

Several motor ability and developmental profiles contain subtests that measure the components of body management, including balance and awareness of body parts, laterally and directionally. Balance helps infants and young children maintain an upright position, and at the preschool through secondary levels, students rely on balance for a range of activities, from jumping rope to skiing. Test items that evaluate balance must be generalized into meaningful instructional goals and activities, as in the following examples:

- LaToya will maintain a one-foot balance for 10 seconds.
- LaToya will balance on three parts of her body for 10 seconds.
- LaToya will walk heel to toe on a 2-inch (5 centimeter) tape line for six consecutive steps.
- LaToya will maintain a tripod position for 10 seconds.

Tests that address equilibrium, vestibular system function, or righting reflexes are in essence measuring various factors in the balance domain in either static or dynamic positions. Static balance involves maintaining balance while stationary, while dynamic balance involves maintaining it while moving.

Other body management goals focus on the areas of agility, spatial direction, body actions, body awareness, and spatial relations. Examples of body management goals include the following:

- Mario will identify basic body parts on request (body awareness).
- Mario will move on request according to the directions forward, backward, sideways, up, down, over, and under (spatial direction).
- Mario will demonstrate the actions of twisting, turning, bending, straightening, and reaching on request (body actions).
- Mario will participate in a large-group physical activity and maintain his own space while respecting the space of others. He will not bump into other children or objects as he moves across the playground (spatial relations).

Goals for Social Interaction

An often overlooked area in development is the social interaction that is necessary for successful participation in physical education and leisure settings. Although the social domain is not considered part of the instructional process as defined by federal mandates, social skills are critical to the overall developmental process. In the very basic stages of play development, lack of social interaction interferes with cooperation, communication, and appropriate interactions with peers (Bailey & Wolery, 1989; Horvat, Malone, et al., 1993). Children deprived of social interaction opportunities may also demonstrate deficits in physical and motor skill proficiency. Further, inappropriate social responses can interfere with instruction and affect learning (Malone & Stoneman, 1990). Unfortunately, most standardized physical education tests do not assess difficulties with social skills.

Social participation can be measured by recording observed social behaviors and interactions in a naturalistic play, home-based, or instructional setting. When social problems are clearly interfering with safe and successful participation in physical activity, annual social skill goals should be written into the IEP. Following are sample annual goals in the social domain:

- Jamal will cooperate with others by taking turns and sharing his toys.
- Jamal will play with one or two other children in a cooperative setting.
- Jamal will respect play equipment by using it properly and safely.
- Jamal will participate in group games and congratulate the opposing team when his team loses.
- Jamal will attend and follow directions in the activity setting.

Goals in the social domain may also interact directly with other annual goals, such as appropriate behaviors, and may be directly related to how much the student learns and develops. When appropriate, goals should be written to include behaviors that are general to home and recreational settings. For example, goals in the social domain such as taking turns, decreasing inappropriate behaviors, respecting the performance of others, using equipment properly, and attending and interacting properly are all applicable to instructional and home-based settings.

Other Annual Goals

Annual goals may be written for any problem area in the developmental domain and should be broad enough to address the individual needs category for which specific objectives are written. Since the IEP is in part a communication tool for the school and the child's parents, annual goals should be written clearly to address all input from team members.

Instructional Objectives and Criteria

Once the major areas of need for individualized intervention have been outlined, specific instructional objectives should be developed for each annual goal area. Short-term instructional objectives are statements of specific physical education skills to be developed to attain a particular annual goal. Here are three examples:

1. *Goal:* to develop a mature running pattern

   Objectives:

   a. Given 1 minute, a running course of at least 50 yards (46 meters), and the verbal cue, "Run until I say stop," the child will demonstrate running with arms in opposition to legs 90% of the time.

   b. Given 1 minute, a running course of at least 50 yards, and the verbal cue, "Run until I say stop," the child will demonstrate running with heel–toe placement 95% of the time.

2. *Goal:* to improve abdominal strength

   Objectives:

   a. Given 30 seconds, the child will demonstrate 20 curl-ups with knees bent and hands behind head.

   b. Given 20 seconds, the child will demonstrate continuous V kicks 1 inch (2.5 centimeters) from floor while balanced on seat and elbows.

3. *Goal:* to demonstrate a functional vertical jump

   Objective:

   a. Given a 3-foot (1-meter) square, the child will demonstrate 9 or 10 vertical jumps with feet together and a full arm swing, maintaining balance when landing.

To develop appropriate instructional objectives that are specific to annual goals, the following guidelines should be observed:

1. State the task or skill in behavioral terms, including positioning (e.g., 30 to 40° curl-ups with bent knees and hands clasped across the chest).

2. Describe the instructional cues, environmental boundaries, time limits, and equipment.

3. State the criteria for attainment or the standard against which the child will be measured (e.g., 9 of 10 trials).

Clarity will aid in communicating the objectives to parents, team members, and students, as well as in evaluating progress and achievement.

SERVICE DELIVERY

When assessment is completed and individual needs identified, the means of meeting the instructional activities must be decided. The program should be determined by individual needs in the least restrictive environment rather than designed to accommodate the available program facilities. The convenience of facilities, equipment, and programs too often dictate how services are delivered.

Least Restrictive Environment

A child's program should be delivered in the least restrictive environment to meet documented needs. Aufsesser (1991) developed a range of adapted physical education services, from traditional specialized classes to home- and community-based instruction. Recently, the focus on inclusion has seen variable placements in general and specialized settings (Block, 2000). Modifications of program plans, teaching aids, and consultations with other teachers and support services may fulfill the needs of many children for safe and successful instruction in school and community settings. For children with severe disabilities, individualized programs conducted on a one-on-one or small-group basis may be more appropriate as the least restrictive environment. The primary focus should be individual needs and expectations.

By using a functionally based curriculum, adapted physical educators can implement program plans to acquire age-group and developmental skills in preschool and the primary grades as well as in community and recreational settings. As children progress through the school years, the emphasis may change to daily living skills, transitional skills or work-related skills, and fitness or leisure development aimed primarily at community participation. At each level, teachers must be sensitive to every child's needs and evaluate individual capabilities based on goals for the situation.

What You Need to Know ▸▸▸

Key Terms

age-equivalent scores	percentiles	standard scores
current level of performance	performance deficits	stanines
grade-equivalent scores	raw scores	

Key Concepts

1. You should be able to describe the capabilities or deficiencies of a child from assessment data.

2. You should be able to draft a program plan including annual goals and short-term objectives for a child with a disability.

3. You should be able to summarize the functional capabilities of an individual from raw data.

4. You should be able to follow the six phases of assessment to determine (1) who qualifies for adapted physical education, (2) what to teach, (3) how to teach, (4) where to teach, (5) who will teach, and (6) how well the skills are learned.

Review Questions

1. Ron is the 17-year-old individual with Down syndrome from chapter 7 (see case study 1 on page 110). Describe how you will develop his transition plan.

2. Describe what should be included in determining the current level of performance.

3. Describe how you will determine annual goals and how they will be accomplished.

4. Develop a program plan from a practicum setting. Describe the level of performance, goals, teaching objectives, and the setting that is recommended. Provide a rationale for the assessments used in your report.

5. Included in the appendixes are several sample cases that provide results from test data and written program descriptions. Analyze the results and prepare a placement recommendation, long-term goals, short-term instructional objectives, and a sample program plan.

Sample Write-Up for Tests of Infant and Early Childhood Motor Development

ADAPTED PHYSICAL EDUCATION OBSERVATION AND EVALUATION

Name: Xena Golemis
DOB: 09/09/96
Evaluator: Martin E. Block, PhD

Date: 02/15/02
School: Beach Cove Elementary School

Background Information

Xena is a 5-1/2-year-old female who has met the Individuals with Disabilities Education Act (IDEA) and Surf County Public Schools eligibility criteria for "a child with multiple disabilities." As reported by Xena's mother as well as staff and specialists in Surf County Public Schools, Xena has mixed spastic/athetoid cerebral palsy with involvement in all four limbs (she cannot walk or use a wheelchair independently, but she is learning how to walk with a Pacer gait trainer); some level of unspecified cognitive impairment; significant speech and language deficits (starting to say single words on occasion such as "no"; can make requests known through verbal utterances and body language); medical problems including respiratory and eating problems as well as osteoporosis; and low vision (she has some vision loss, but it is unclear as to the exact degree).

Xena has received special education services through Surf County Public Schools since preschool. She attends kindergarten at Beach Cove Elementary School in Surf County, with support from a special education teacher, full-time one-on-one nurse, speech therapist, occupational therapist, and physical therapist. She receives physical education with her kindergarten classmates in general physical education once per week with the support of her nurse.

Xena's parents, special education staff, and general physical educator were concerned about Xena's physical education program, and they sought an independent evaluation of Xena's motor skills and an analysis of her physical education needs. This evaluation was conducted by Martin E. Block, PhD, director of the master's program in adapted physical education (see attached copy of Dr. Block's vitae for validation of his qualifications). His assessment focused on a developmental evaluation of Xena's motor skills, an analysis of her functional motor abilities using various mobility apparatuses, a discussion with Xena's physical education teacher and therapists, and a discussion with Xena's mother.

Xena was tested in the therapy room at Beach Cove Elementary School. Testing lasted approximately 1 hour. Testing was conducted by Dr. Block with assistance from Ms. Cast, Xena's occupational therapist; Ms. Alvarez, Xena's physical therapist; Ms. Smith, Xena's general physical education specialist; and Mr. Reneeson, Xena's nurse. Xena's mother was present during the assessment to provide feedback to the evaluation team and to assist and motivate Xena as needed. Testing included the Peabody Developmental Motor Scales; observation of Xena in her Creeper-Crawler, Pacer, and scooter; and discussion with Xena's mother. Xena's therapists, who have been working with her for several months, thought that Xena had a "good day" demonstrating her abilities, staying focused, and trying her best. Therefore, I believe the results from this assessment are a fair representation of Xena's motor skills.

Peabody Developmental Motor Scales

The Peabody Developmental Motor Scales 2 (PDMS-2) is a norm-referenced motor test that was standardized on a normally developing sample of children from birth to 84 months of age. The PDMS-2 was chosen for two reasons: to obtain a baseline developmental motor score for Xena and to guide a developmental, qualitative analysis of Xena's motor patterns and motor abilities. The test is divided into six parts: reflexes, stationary, locomotion, object manipulation, grasping, and visual-motor integration. The original PDMS (1983) and the new PDMS-2 (2000) are widely accepted developmental tests used by diagnosticians, occupational therapists, physical therapists, psychologists, early intervention specialists, and adapted physical education teachers (Folio & Fewell, 2000).

The PDMS-2 norms are based on scoring each item as 2, 1, or 0. The examiner must decide how to score an item based on his or her clinical judgment of the child's performance and the specific criteria provided for each item. The general criteria for scoring items are as follows:

2   The child performs the item according to the criteria specified for mastery.

1   The child's performance shows a clear resemblance to the item-mastery criteria but does not fully meet the criteria.

0   The child cannot or will not attempt the item, or the attempt does not show that the skill is emerging.

Xena was administered the PDMS-2 in the therapy room of Beach Cove Elementary School. The test was administered by Dr. Block and other members of the evaluation team. The results of the test are listed in table A.1.

Table A.1 PDMS-2 Test Results for Xena

Subpart	Raw score	Age equivalent (months)	Percentile rank for age
Reflexes	1	1	<1%
Stationary	2	1	<1%
Locomotion	9	2	<1%
Object manipulation	0	1	<1%
Grasping	12	3	<1%
Visual-motor integration	13	3	<1%

The following summarizes the results of testing.

- *Reflexes.* Reflex items focus on the presence or disappearance of early infant reflexes and the appearance of righting and protective responses. Xena still has a strong asymmetrical tonic neck reflex (ATNR), and she appears to have remnants of the symmetrical tonic neck reflex (STNR). She does not have any protective reactions or righting reactions, and she does not have the Landau response (when held in prone, raises head above horizontal plane, extends trunk, and attempts to extend legs). The presence of the ATNR along with the lack of righting or protective reactions is limiting Xena's ability to sit and stand independently.

- *Stationary.* Stationary items focus on trunk and head control when lying on the back and stomach and when sitting, as well as more advanced stationary skills such as balancing in standing. Xena was able to align her trunk when supported in sitting with a rounded back. However, she had very little head control in prone, supine, or sitting positions. She had almost a full head lag when pulled to sit, a very difficult time moving her head from side to side when on her stomach, and great difficulty keeping her head upright in supported sitting. She appears to have weak muscles in her neck that contribute to her lack of head control. Lack of head control makes it difficult for Xena to regard objects in her environment. Also, lack of head control coupled with the lack of righting and protective responses make it difficult for her to sit and stand independently.

- *Locomotion.* Locomotion items focus on early leg and arm movements; early locomotor movements such as crawling and creeping; and more advanced locomotor skills of walking, jumping, and galloping. Xena was able to thrust her legs when lying on her back, turn from side to back, thrust arms when lying on her back, and momentarily bear weight in standing. She also was close to rolling over, using her opposite arm to facilitate the roll. She was unable to prop herself up on forearms, bring arms to midline when in supine, perform a complete roll, scoot on her bottom, crawl forward on her stomach, or creep forward on her hands and knees. She also was unable to stand independently, but she was able to take some reciprocal steps in her Pacer.

- *Object manipulation.* Object manipulation items focus on catching, throwing, and kicking, with the lowest item as follows: "catches a tennis ball that is rolled to child while the child is sitting independently." Xena was unable to do any items in the object manipulation category.

- *Fine motor skills.* Fine motor items focus on grasping and releasing and the pattern the child uses to grasp objects. Xena displayed remnants of the grasp reflex, but she also was able to purposely hold and release objects with a palmar grip (using palm mostly, with fingers wrapped around object). She did not display higher levels of fingertip or pincer grasping.

- *Visual-motor integration.* Visual-motor integration items focus initially on tracking and grasping objects. Later, items focus on putting objects in and taking objects out of containers, building with blocks, cutting with scissors, stringing beads, and prewriting and drawing skills. Xena was able to track objects placed in her visual field by turning her head and by moving her eyes. She was able to regard her hands, and she attempted to reach for objects placed in her visual field. She did not display the ability to bring her hands to midline to grasp an object or to play with two objects at the same time. Her limitations in visual regard are no doubt due in large part to her ATNR.

Locomotion: Crawler and Pacer

Crawling

Xena was placed for several minutes in an adapted crawling device known as the Creeper-Crawler. She attempted to move her legs when secured in this device, but she was unable to generate any of her own forward momentum. With the assistance of her therapist (support provided by her feet to assist in pushing off), Xena was able to move forward a few inches. Xena tolerated the Creeper-Crawler for about 3 to 5 minutes; however, she was unable to display the head-up position in the device for any length of time. Both Xena's mother and therapist noted the head-down position that Xena preferred in the Creeper-Crawler, and this position seemed to promote drooling. Xena began to protest being in the Creeper-Crawler after about 3 minutes.

Walking

Xena was placed in an adapted gait trainer known as the Pacer for several minutes. This gait training device provided a lot of support for Xena in the upright position with her feet hanging down to the floor. Once secured in the Pacer, Xena was able to generate enough momentum to move backward approximately 3 to 5 inches. Her therapist and mother noted that she could move much farther (1 to 2 feet or more) backward in her Pacer than she demonstrated during testing. In addition, her mother and therapist noted that Xena could move several inches forward in the Pacer, but Xena was unable to demonstrate forward movement during testing. The Pacer seemed to be a good piece of equipment for Xena, promoting weight-bearing upright posture that would aid in postural muscle development. In addition, it appears that Xena might learn how to move the Pacer more functionally with direction and purpose in the future.

Conversation With Xena's Mother

I had a chance to have a brief conversation with Xena's mother, Jane, to find out what she would like from a physical education program. I asked her to focus on general motor goals for Xena as well as specific physical education goals and activities. In terms of general motor goals, Jane noted functional motor skills were the most important thing for her and her family now and in the future. She specifically noted that activities and goals from the Mobility Opportunities Via Education (MOVE) program were important, including sitting independently, weight bearing in standing, assisting in pivoting, using hands and arms to assist in dressing and feeding, and mobility. In terms of specific goals for physical education, she would like Xena to use and improve her ability to move in her gait trainer while other children are doing locomotor patterns. Jane would also like to see Xena out of her wheelchair for part of physical education to work on her stretching and strengthening activities. Finally, she would like Xena to continue receiving general physical education with the support of her nurse. She would like to see peers work and play with Xena more during these general physical education settings.

Summary and Recommendations

Xena is a 5-1/2-year-old female whose motor skills are significantly delayed compared with her peers. Functional motor abilities are limited because of persistence of primitive reflexes, lack of balance and protective reactions, minimal strength and postural control, and mixed spastic/athetoid cerebral palsy. Xena is an outgoing, engaging child who truly loves movement. In addition, her mother and her therapists have noted small but consistent motor gains in the last few years, and they all believe she will continue to make progress toward more functional and independent movement.

Xena receives physical education once a week in the general setting with support from her nurse. General physical education can be appropriate for Xena as long as the nurse and general physical educator make sure Xena works on IEP objectives rather than simply trying to do what her peers are doing. For example, in a dodging and fleeing game, Xena can practice moving in her Pacer, and during throwing and catching activities, Xena could practice grasping and releasing skills with small beanbags. Because of the significance of Xena's delays, I would recommend that Xena receive at least one additional day of adapted physical education in a one-on-one setting with her physical education teacher to focus on specific motor goals that might be more difficult to work on in a general physical education setting. In addition, the one-on-one session would give Ms. Smith, the general physical educator, more direct time with Xena (in general physical education, Ms. Smith has to work with all the children, not just Xena). This one-on-one session could include a few peer tutors to encourage social interactions and to motivate Xena.

It is also recommended that global motor goals be established that can be implemented by all members of the team, whether Xena is in general or adapted physical education, in physical or occupational therapy, in her classroom, or at home. As suggested by her mother, goals should focus on functional motor abilities (e.g., sitting and standing with a gradual reduction in support, walking in her Pacer with a gradual reduction in support, and functional use of hands and arms) and opportunities to interact with peers during motor sessions. Finally, the team should develop a home exercise program to give Xena more opportunities to improve her motor function.

Sample Write-Up for Tests of Fundamental Motor Patterns

ADAPTED PHYSICAL EDUCATION OBSERVATION AND EVALUATION

Name: Jesse Dore
DOB: 09/23/99
Evaluator: Christina Surf, APE

Date: 10/10/05
School: Rutherford Elementary School

Background Information

Jesse is a 6-year-old male student who is repeating kindergarten at Rutherford Elementary School. Jesse has participated in general physical education (GPE). He was referred for evaluation by Ms. Jones, who completed an initial request form with Jesse's parents. The request form addressed concerns about Jesse's motor skills, with the biggest concern being not alternating feet while going down stairs.

The following were used to evaluate Jesse's skills in physical education to determine if he requires APE: percentile ranking compared with age peers on the Test of Gross Motor Development 2, observation of Jesse in general physical education, and feedback from Jesse's GPE teacher. Ms. Curry, CAPE, APE specialist for Rutherford Elementary School, conducted the testing. All testing was conducted at Rutherford Elementary School during Jesse's GPE class, in the hallway by the gymnasium and in the gymnasium itself. Jesse was observed on 10/07/05 while he participated with his kindergarten class in the gym. He was very cooperative during all testing, and he seemed to try his best in all testing situations. Dr. Martin E. Block, PhD, associate professor at the Curry School of Education in the area of APE, was present during the TGMD-2 test to ensure the highest quality and accuracy of the test results. Therefore, these test results are a fair representation of Jesse's skills in physical education.

Test of Gross Motor Development

The Test of Gross Motor Development 2 (TGMD-2) is an individually administered norm- and criterion-referenced test that measures the gross motor functioning of children 3 to 10 years of age. The test measures 12 gross motor skills frequently taught to children in preschool and elementary school. The skills are grouped into two subtests: locomotion and object control. The locomotion subtest measures

213

the run, gallop, hop, leap, horizontal jump, and slide. The object control subtest measures the two-hand strike, stationary dribble, catch, kick, overhand throw, and underhand roll. Each of these motor skills has been broken down into 3 to 5 components. Skills are analyzed to determine if each component was present (1) or not present (0). Results are tallied across two trials and then totaled for locomotor and object control subtests. Each subtest score is compared with a normative sample for analysis.

Jesse scored at the 63rd percentile for locomotor skills (age equivalent of 6.9 years) and at the 50th percentile in object control skills (age equivalent of 7.0 years) compared with 6-year-olds in the norm sample. Jesse passed all the components of the run, gallop, leap, and horizontal jump, and he passed all but one component of the slide. He missed two out of five items on the hop (see table B.1 for detailed results). Jesse passed all the components of the strike, kick, and underhand roll. He missed one out of three on the catch, one out of four on the overhand throw, and two out of four on the stationary dribble (see table B.2 for detailed results). It should be noted that, with the exception of the underhand roll, ball skills tested on the TGMD-2 are not expected to be mastered, according to the Albemarle County elementary physical education curriculum, until second (stationary dribble), third (two-hand strike), fourth (overhand throw, catch), and fifth grades (kick), so it is not surprising that Jesse did not pass all the components of the catch, overhand throw, and stationary dribble. Most children Jesse's age have not mastered these object control skills. Jesse's movements seemed fluid and precise, and he demonstrated reasonably good rhythm in locomotor skills and reasonably good eye–hand coordination in object control skills. Jesse

Table B.1   Locomotor Skills: TGMD-2 Results*

		Trial		
		1	2	Score
Run	1. Arms in opposition to legs, elbows bent	1	1	2
	2. Brief period where both feet are off the ground	1	1	2
	3. Narrow foot placement, landing on heel or toe	1	1	2
	4. Nonsupport leg bent approximately 90°	1	1	2
Gallop	1. Arms bent and lifted to waist level	1	1	2
	2. A step forward with the lead foot followed by a step with the trailing foot to a position adjacent to or behind the lead foot	1	1	2
	3. Brief period where both feet are off the ground	1	1	2
	4. Maintains a rhythmic pattern for four consecutive gallops	1	1	2
	Locomotor skills subtest score			42
	Percentile rank			63
	Age equivalent			6.9 years

*Note: Only the first two locomotor subitems are shown. Test results for the remaining four subitems would be shown in an actual write-up. Totals are shown.

Table B.2   Object Control Skills: TGMD-2 Results*

		Trial		
		1	**2**	**Score**
Two-hand strike	1. Dominant hand grips bat above nondominant hand	1	1	2
	2. Nondominant side of body faces the tosser, feet parallel	1	1	2
	3. Rotates hips and shoulders during swing	1	1	2
	4. Transfers body weight to front foot	1	1	2
	5. Bat contacts ball	1	1	2
Stationary dribble	1. Contacts ball with one hand at about belt level	0	0	0
	2. Pushes ball with fingers (not slap)	1	1	2
	3. Ball contacts floor in front of or to the side of foot on the side of the hand being used	0	0	0
	4. Maintains control of ball for 4 consecutive bounces without having to move feet to retrieve it	1	1	2
	Object control skills subtest score			41
	Percentile rank			50
	Age equivalent			7.0 years

*Note: Only the first two locomotor subitems are shown. Test results for the remaining four subitems would be shown in an actual write-up. Totals are shown.

had the most difficulty with the stationary dribble. His stance made it easy for the ball to contact his foot and roll away from him in the middle of the dribble. During the catch, he would scoop the ball rather than catch it with two hands, therefore scoring a two out of three.

Observation in General Physical Education

Following Directions and Staying on Task

I observed Jesse in general physical education one time this fall. I also talked with Kathy Guilford, his GPE teacher. We both agreed that Jesse is able to follow directions given by the lead teacher in a large-group setting (as many as 25 children) without any redirections. However, when Jesse is doing warm-ups, he will not participate in any of the activities unless Ms. Guilford individually addresses him to do so. For example, the students went from stand-up stretches to floor exercises, and Jesse realized he was the only one still standing, so he quickly sat down on the floor, continuing to do nothing until Ms. Guilford told him to do his sit-ups. He then completed two sit-ups and went back to playing with the tape on the floor. Ms. Guilford had them play a floor maze game ("Pac-Man"), and Jesse completed every task the first time without needing any additional cues. I believe Jesse engages in activities that grab his attention, which has nothing to do with his motor ability.

Behaviors and Social Skills

Jesse has never displayed any inappropriate behaviors that would cause him to be considered a behavior problem by his peers or GPE teachers. I have seen him off task during warm-ups, but he is easily refocused to the task at hand, usually by the GPE teacher. I never observed him (or heard from the others who work with him more regularly) having any behavioral outbursts such as a tantrum, crying, or getting very angry. Jesse interacts appropriately with his peers; his personality truly comes out during every game played. Most of the physical education activities I observed were individual in nature, and the pace of the program did not lend itself to lots of social interactions by any of the children. On the other hand, Jesse is not opposed to holding a peer's hand, being a partner with a peer, being in a group, or playing a group game.

Conversation With Ms. Guilford

I also talked with Jesse's physical education teacher. She did not consider Jesse's motor or fitness skills to be delayed compared with his age peers. In addition, she did not consider Jesse to be a behavior problem. She did note that he veers off task very easily during individual activities, such as warm-ups or closing songs, but he promptly gets back on task upon her request. She further noted that Jesse was able to keep up with his peers in various conditioning, skill-building, and game activities. Ms. Guilford believes there is something different about Jesse, but it is definitely not motor or skill related, nor does it interfere with the education of his peers in his class.

Summary and Recommendations

Results from the TGMD-2, observation in general physical education, and conversation with Jesse's GPE teacher lead me to recommend that Jesse does not qualify for adapted physical education services at this time. Even though he is repeating kindergarten, he is functioning at age level on gross motor development and on skills required by Rutherford Elementary schoolchildren his age. He seems to follow directions very well in general physical education, he does not need anything to make his participation any more successful, and he does not exhibit any behaviors that would cause him to interfere with other children's learning. Although it was indicated in the initial request form that his balance is poor, his running is awkward, and he does not alternate feet going down stairs, I did not observe any of these things in his general physical education setting. The concerns addressed in the initial request form can be corrected within the activities that Ms. Guilford leads in her classes. Ms. Guilford includes numerous cross-lateral activities, which integrate both sides of the brain, ultimately improving Jesse's balance and running ability. I would recommend placement in general physical education without any special accommodations or adapted physical education services for the 2005-2006 school year.

In the event that the general physical education staff believe that Jesse is not making adequate progress or is causing a behavior problem, then the APE specialist can reevaluate the need for accommodations to general physical education.

Sample Write-Up for Tests of Motor Proficiency

ADAPTED PHYSICAL EDUCATION OBSERVATION AND EVALUATION

Name: Renee Gross
DOB: 08/23/95
Evaluator: Christina Surf, APE

Date: 10/10/05
School: Crooked Stick Elementary School

Background Information

Renee is a 10-year-old fourth grader at Crooked Stick Elementary School. Renee has participated in general physical education. She was referred for evaluation by her parents. The request form addressed concerns about Renee's specific motor ability, balance, and coordination problems that they believe are related to her learning disability.

Given Renee's parents' specific concerns, the Bruininks-Oseretsky Test of Motor Proficiency 2 (BOT-2) was administered to Renee. In addition, she was observed in general physical education over two class sessions. All testing was conducted by Martin Jones, adapted physical education specialist for the school district, at Crooked Stick Elementary School during Renee's physical education class, in the hallway by the gymnasium and in the gymnasium itself. Renee was very cooperative during all testing, and she seemed to try her best in all testing situations. Results are a fair representation of Renee's skills in physical education.

Bruininks-Oseretsky Test of Motor Proficiency

The BOT-2 is an individually administered norm-referenced test that assesses the motor functioning of children from 4 to 21 years of age. The complete battery—eight subtests made up of 53 separate items—provides composite scores in four motor areas (fine manual control, manual coordination, body coordination, and strength and agility) and one comprehensive measure of overall total motor proficiency, represented as the total motor composite. Administration of the complete battery for Renee took approximately 60 minutes. Results from each of the eight subtests and battery composites are presented in this report (see table C.1).

Results indicate that Renee did well on fine motor control items (fine motor precision and integration). In fact, Renee scored on age level or close to age level on both subtests in this category. With a percentile rank of 38, she scored better than 38% of children in fine motor control. Renee did display a slight delay in manual coordination items. In manual dexterity, her score was age equivalent to 8.0-8.2 years, and in upper-limb coordination, she scored age equivalent to 8.6-8.8 years. With a percentile rank of 8, 92% of children would score better than Renee on manual coordination items. Renee's greatest delays were on body coordination items (bilateral coordination and balance), where her percentile rank was 5, and strength and agility items (running speed/agility and strength), in which she had a percentile rank of 2. Strength (age equivalent of 4.6-4.7 years), balance (age equivalent of 5.2-5.3 years), and running speed and agility (age equivalent of 5.10-5.11 years) were clearly her weakest areas. Results from this test suggest that Renee is significantly delayed in the area of gross motor abilities.

Table C.1   Results From the Bruininks-Oseretsky Test of Motor Proficiency 2

	Total point score	Scale score	Standard score	Percentile rank	Age equivalent	Category
Subtest 1. Fine motor precision	39	16			10.0-10.2 years	Average
Subtest 2. Fine motor integration	37	13			8.9-8.11 years	Average
Fine manual control		**29**	**47**	**38**		**Average**
Subtest 3. Manual dexterity	26	10			8.0-8.2 years	Below average
Subtest 7. Upper-limb coordination	30	10			8.6-8.8 years	Below average
Manual coordination		**20**	**36**	**8**		**Below average**
Subtest 4. Bilateral coordination	19	8			6.9-6.11 years	Below average
Subtest 5. Balance	27	7			5.2-5.3 years	Below average
Body coordination		**15**	**33**	**5**		**Below average**
Subtest 6. Running speed and agility	24	8			5.10-5.11 years	Below average
Subtest 8. Strength	8	4			4.6-4.7 years	Well below average
Strength and agility		**12**	**30**	**2**		**Below average**
Total motor composite		**76**	**146**	**5**		**Below average**

Observation in General Physical Education

Renee was observed in two different general physical education sessions. At first glance, she was indistinguishable from her peers. In other words, she was not so delayed or impaired to cause her to appear significantly different from her peers. In fact, her GPE teacher was surprised that Renee was being observed and tested. He thought that she did well in most general physical education activities, was well behaved and happy, and seemed to try her best. I observed her in tagging and dodging games that were used for the warm-up. She was able to keep pace with her peers in that game, and I did not notice any limitations in functional speed, balance, or agility. I also observed her in activities that required catching and throwing with a partner. Again, although Renee's skills were not the strongest in class, her skills were not the weakest either. She demonstrated the general throwing and catching pattern, and she was accurate with her throws and successful with catching (in at least 75% of the trials I observed).

The second observation included a warm-up that focused more on strength (sit-ups, push-ups, mountain climbers). Again, while one of the weaker individuals in these strength activities, she was clearly not the weakest child. She seemed to try her best, and I did not see any signs of frustration in her struggle to complete 10 modified push-ups and 10 sit-ups. In a throwing and catching game that followed, Renee was as active and engaged in the activity as the other children in the class. Her throwing and catching patterns did deteriorate in the game setting versus the skill setting observed the previous day (but this was true for many of the children in the class).

Summary and Recommendations

Renee is a 10-year-old at Crooked Stick Elementary School. She was recommended for testing by her parents. Results from the Bruininks-Oseretsky Test of Motor Proficiency indicate that Renee is significantly behind her age peers in motor proficiency. Her strengths are in fine motor precision and fine motor integration, as well as upper-limb coordination. Her weakest areas are in strength, running speed and agility, and body coordination (balance and bilateral coordination). She was slightly delayed in manual coordination (manual dexterity and upper-limb coordination) and she did not show any significant delays in fine motor control (fine motor precision or integration). With regard to general physical education, Renee seems able to keep up with her peers in all activities. She seems well adjusted and enjoys general physical education activities. The weaknesses seen in the BOT-2 did not seem to present problems for her in general physical education.

Given that Renee did score at a level that would indicate a significant motor impairment, it is recommended that Renee receive adapted physical education services for 30 minutes per week. Since Renee does well in general physical education, this adapted session should take place at another time of the day, away from general physical education. This one-on-one or small-group session should focus on remediating some of the specific areas Renee had the most trouble with—strength and agility as well as body coordination.

Sample Write-Up for Tests of Sports Skills

ADAPTED PHYSICAL EDUCATION OBSERVATION AND EVALUATION

Name: Li Xiang   Date: 02/13/03
DOB: 01/23/91   School: East Middle School
Evaluator: Martin E. Block, PhD

Background Information

Li Xiang is a 12-year-old male who attends sixth grade at East Middle School in Albemarle County. He attended Lewis Elementary School in West County until third grade, and he was homeschooled for the past 2 years. Li has qualified for special education through Albemarle County as a child with a disability. He currently participates in general physical education (GPE). Li was referred for evaluation by his special education teacher, Ms. Sey, and his GPE teacher, Ms. Luck. Specifically, Ms. Luck had concerns about Li's refusal to participate in most GPE activities. In addition, Li's mother had concerns regarding his motor skills.

The following were used to evaluate Li's skills in physical education to determine if he qualifies for adapted physical education: evaluation of Li's skills compared with the Albemarle County Middle School physical education curriculum, feedback from Li's GPE teacher, and feedback from Li. Martin Block, PhD, CAPE, associate professor at the University of Virginia, along with Kristy McClain, graduate student at the University of Virginia in the area of adapted physical education, conducted the testing. All testing was conducted at East Middle School in Li's GPE class on February 13, 2003, during Li's normal health and physical education time.Li was very cooperative during all testing, and he seemed to try his best in all testing situations. Therefore, these test results are a fair representation of Li's skills in physical education.

Albemarle County Middle School Curriculum

The Albemarle County Middle School physical education curriculum is a criterion-referenced curriculum that focuses on sports skills. Each skill has been broken down into 3 to 5 components. Skills are analyzed to determine if the component is present (1) or not present (0). Results are then tallied across two trials. The curriculum also includes cognitive tests for each sport that were not given to Li at this time. Li was given a demonstration of each skill before he was asked to perform it. According to conversations with Ms. Luck, Li refused to participate in physical education during a soccer unit in the fall, and he has not yet had the chance to participate in any of the other sports skills units that are represented in this testing. Nevertheless, Li was able to demonstrate most of the components of most of the skills tested after a demonstration by the evaluator. This is rather remarkable given that Li has not had formal instruction in physical education for the past 2 years and has chosen not to participate in physical education so far in sixth grade.

Li's strengths were in volleyball and soccer skills. He also did well in softball and basketball skills, but there were components in these skills that Li had yet to master (e.g., shooting was a little stiff, and he used two hands rather than perform a one-hand shot; dribbling forward was a little stiff, although he controlled the ball going forward with his right hand first and then his left hand). Results suggest that Li is not delayed in sports skill development as compared with what is expected of middle school children in sixth grade (see table D.1). In fact, many of the skills that Li already mastered will not be presented and taught to Li until seventh and eighth grades.

Physical Fitness

Physical fitness is another important part of the Albemarle County Middle School physical education curriculum. Fitness includes upper-body and abdominal strength, cardiorespiratory endurance, and flexibility. Results were collected by Ms. Luck during physical fitness testing of Li's class. However, we reevaluated Li's flexibility during our testing.

Results show that Li is significantly behind his peers in physical fitness, especially in cardiorespiratory fitness (mile run). However, Ms. Luck noted that Li walked during testing and did not try. In addition, Li has asthma, which may have affected his cardiorespiratory endurance. In fact, during our testing Li asked to go to the nurse's office for his inhaler. He seems to be a little overweight, but not so much that he stands out compared with his peers. Based on discussions with Ms. Luck, it is difficult to determine whether Li has significant fitness delays as reflected in this testing or whether these results reflect Li's lack of effort during testing.

Results of Physical Fitness Testing

Mile run	24.02 minutes (below average for sixth-grade boys)
Sit-and-reach	14 (below average for sixth-grade boys)
Pull-ups	0 (below average for sixth-grade boys)
Curl-ups	9 (below average for sixth-grade boys)

Conversation With Li

After testing I had a brief conversation with Li regarding his feelings toward physical education. When asked to rate his enjoyment of physical education on

Table D.1   **Results from Albemarle County Middle School Physical Education Curriculum**

Volleyball skills		Trial		
		1	2	Score
Underhand serve	1. Preparatory position: faces net, feet shoulder-width apart; 45° forward trunk lean; holds ball in nondominant hand, with arm extended across body at waist height in front of serving arm	1	1	2
	2. Holds serving arm straight, pendular swing back at least 45° to initiate serve; then brings serving arm forward with pendular arm motion	1	1	2
	3. Strides forward with opposite foot in concert with forward motion of striking arm	1	1	2
	4. Heel of striking hand strikes center of ball held at or below waist height in line with back foot and in front of serving foot	1	1	2
Overhead pass	1. Preparatory position: faces oncoming ball, feet (set) staggered shoulder-width apart; knees slightly bent, arms and hands hanging by knees; eyes are on ball	1	0	1
	2. Moves to get under ball, with head tilted back; legs flexed; hands move up just above forehead	1	1	2
	3. Hand position: palms out, fingers apart and slightly bent	0	1	1
	4. Upon contact, head remains in tilted position, eyes focused on ball, wrists hyperextended and fingers flexed to form a diamond or triangle to absorb force of the ball	1	0	1
	5. Extends knees and arms upward on follow-through	1	1	2
	6. Passes ball to above net height	1	1	2
Forearm pass	1. Ready position: faces ball, feet shoulder-width apart; knees slightly bent, arms hanging below waist and extended in front of body, palms facing up	1	1	2
	2. Preparatory hand position: one hand placed in the other hand, with thumb of lower hand placed across fingers of upper hand, forearms together	1	1	2
	3. Eyes are on ball	1	1	2
	4. Moves to meet ball by transferring weight forward, arms together, knees bent	1	1	2
	5. Contacts ball with flat side of forearms	1	1	2
	6. Upon contact, extends knees to raise the arms upward	1	0	1
	7. Completes pass standing straight up, arms parallel to floor; hands stay together throughout entire motion	1	1	2
	8. Passes ball to a height of at least 8 ft (2.5 m) to stationary teammate	1	1	2

(continued)

Softball skills		Trial		
		1	**2**	**Score**
Striking a stationary ball	1. Dominant hand grips bat above nondominant hand	1	1	2
	2. Nonpreferred side of body faces the imaginary tosser with feet parallel	1	1	2
	3. Rotates hips and shoulders during swing	0	0	0
	4. Transfers weight by stepping with front foot	1	0	1
Catch	1. Preparation phase where hands are in front of the body and elbows are flexed	1	1	2
	2. Extends arms while reaching for the ball as it arrives	1	1	2
	3. Catches ball with hands only	1	1	2
Overhand throw	1. Initiates windup with downward movement of hand	1	0	1
	2. Rotates hips and shoulders to a point where the nonthrowing side faces the target	1	1	2
	3. Transfers weight by stepping with the foot opposite the throwing hand	1	1	2
	4. Follow-through beyond ball release, diagonally across body toward nonpreferred side	1	1	2
Basketball skills				
Dribble	1. Contacts ball with one hand at about belt level	1	1	2
	2. Pushes ball with fingertips (not slap)	1	1	2
	3. Ball contacts floor in front of or to the outside of foot on preferred side	0	0	0
	4. Maintains control of ball for 4 consecutive bounces without having to move feet to retrieve ball	1	0	1
	5. Dribbles while walking forward 15 ft (4.5 m) with dominant hand	1	1	2
	6. Dribbles while walking forward 15 ft (4.5 m) with nondominant hand	1	1	2
Shooting	1. Eyes are on basket, feet shoulder-width apart, knees flexed	1	1	2
	2. Marked flexion of knees before shooting	1	1	2
	3. Shooting hand under ball with fingers apart; holds ball slightly off center of forehead, shooting-hand side; elbow is directly under ball, pointed down; nondominant hand is on side of ball	0	0	0
	4. Coordinated extension of knees, hips, and ankles, while flexing wrist and fingers to guide the ball on release	1	0	1
	5. Follow-through with the shooting hand remaining briefly in the release position toward basket	1	0	1

(continued)

Soccer skills		Trial		
		1	2	Score
Kick	1. Rapid, continuous approach to the ball	1	1	2
	2. Elongated stride or leap immediately before ball contact	1	0	1
	3. Places nonkicking foot even or slightly in back of ball	1	1	2
	4. Kicks ball with instep of preferred foot (shoelaces) or toe	0	0	0
Trap	1. Eyes are focused on moving ball	1	1	2
	2. Moves in line with the ball, weight on nontrapping foot	1	1	2
	3. Trapping foot is perpendicular to nontrapping foot	1	0	1
	4. Contacts ball at center with inside surface of foot	1	0	1
	5. Retracts foot to absorb force	1	1	2
Dribble	1. Contacts ball with any part of foot	1	1	2
	2. Ball travels no more than 2 ft (0.6 m) away from foot	0	1	1
	3. Occasionally looks up to see where he or she is going	0	0	0
	4. Maintains jogging pace	1	1	2

a scale of 1 (hates physical education) to 10 (loves physical education), Li rated his enjoyment as a 3. He said that his least favorite activity was running, and he thought doing Tae Bo to the videotapes was stupid. However, he did say that he tried to follow the tapes. He said he liked to play pickle ball but did not think the rules made sense.

Conversation With Ms. Luck

Ms. Luck has been Li's primary physical education specialist since the start of the school year. She noted that she has been unable to determine Li's motor or fitness skills because he usually refuses to participate in physical education activities. Ms. Luck has tried to make some accommodations for Li such as allowing him to walk part of a lap if he runs part of a lap. However, she noted that Li just walks the entire way. She also noted that Li does not dress with the other boys in the locker room. Rather, he gets dressed in his special education classroom, and this usually makes him late for class. When he arrives to class he tells Ms. Luck that he does not have to participate in the warm-up since the class has already started. During activities, Li often refuses to participate, choosing to sit in the corner of the gym. Regarding his interaction with peers, Ms. Luck noted that Li often gets into arguments with his peers and that his peers often tease Li.

Summary and Recommendations

Li is a sixth grader who qualifies as a child with a disability according to the Albemarle County School District. He was referred for adapted physical education by his special education and physical education teachers as well as his mother. Testing showed that Li is not delayed in gross motor development as measured by the Albemarle County Middle School physical education curriculum. He is delayed in physical fitness compared with what is expected of sixth-grade boys. However, these results are somewhat suspect because it is unclear whether Li's low fitness is due to lack of practice (he chooses not to participate in physical education), lack of effort (he did not try his best), his asthma, or actual fitness delays. Li's social skills and behaviors are clearly causing problems for him as well as his physical education teacher in general physical education. Li's problems seem to be more behavioral than motor, and thus he does not qualify for adapted physical education services.

References

Ajzen, I., & Fishbein, M. (1980). *Understanding attitudes and predicting social behavior.* Englewood Cliffs, NJ: Prentice Hall.

Albemarle County Public Schools. (1995). *Middle school physical education project.* Charlottesville, VA: Author.

American Academy of Orthopedic Surgeons. (1975). *Joint motion: Methods of measuring and recovery.* Chicago: American Academy of Orthopedic Surgeons.

American Alliance for Health, Physical Education, Recreation and Dance. (1976). *AAHPERD youth fitness test manual.* Reston, VA: AAHPERD.

American Alliance for Health, Physical Education, Recreation and Dance. (1988). *Physical Best.* Reston, VA: AAHPERD.

American Alliance for Health, Physical Education, Recreation and Dance. (1995). *Physical Best and individuals with disabilities.* Reston, VA: AAHPERD.

American College of Sports Medicine. (2005). *ACSM's health-related physical fitness assessment manual.* Philadelphia: Lippincott, Williams & Wilkins.

American Health and Fitness Foundation. (1986). *FYT program manual.* Austin, TX: American Health and Fitness Foundation.

American Medical Association. (1988). *Instrumentation: Spine, 13,* 50-53.

Aufsesser, P.M. (1991). Mainstreaming and least restrictive environment: How do they differ? *Palaestra, 4,* 31-34.

Aufsesser, P., Horvat, M., & Austin, R. (2003). The reliability of hand-held dynamometers in individuals with spinal cord injury. *Clinical Kinesiology, 57*(4), 71-75.

Aufsesser, P., Horvat, M., & Croce, R. (1996). A critical examination of selected hand-held dynamometers to assess isometric muscle strength. *Adapted Physical Activity Quarterly, 13,* 153-165.

Bailey, D.B., & Wolery, M. (1989). *Assessing infants and preschoolers with handicaps.* Columbus, OH: Merrill.

Bar-Or, O. (1983a). Noncardiopulmonary pediatric exercise tests. In T.W. Rowland (Ed.), *Pediatric laboratory exercise testing: Clinical guidelines* (pp. 165-186). Champaign, IL: Human Kinetics.

Bar-Or, O. (1983b). *Pediatric sports medicine for the practitioner.* New York: Springer-Verlag.

Baumgartner, T.A., & Horvat, M. (1991). Reliability of field-based cardiovascular fitness running. *Adapted Physical Activity Quarterly, 18*(2), 107-114.

Baumgartner, T.A., Jackson, A.S., Mahar, M., & Rowe, D. (2003). *Measurement for evaluation in physical education and exercise science* (7th ed.). Dubuque, IA: McGraw-Hill.

Bayley, N. (1993). *Bayley Scales of Infant Development.* New York: Psychological Corporation.

Berg, K. (1993). *Measuring balance in the elderly: Validation of an instrument.* Unpublished doctoral dissertation, McGill University, Montreal.

Berger, R.D. (1970). Relationship between dynamic strength and dynamic endurance. *Research Quarterly, 4,* 115-116.

Block, M.E. (1995). Development and validation of the Children's Attitudes toward Integrated Physical Education–Revised (CAIPE-R). *Adapted Physical Activity Quarterly, 12,* 60-77.

Block, M.E. (2000). *A teacher's guide to including students with disabilities in general physical education* (2nd ed.). Baltimore: Brookes.

Block, M.E., Lieberman, L.J., & Connor-Kuntz, F. (1998). Authentic assessment in adapted physical education. *JOPERD, 69*(3), 48-56.

Blumenfeld, H. (2001). *Neuroanatomy through clinical cases.* Sutherland, MA: Sinauer Associates.

Bobath, B. (1990). *Adult hemiplegia: Evaluation and treatment* (3rd ed.). London: Butterworth-Heinemann.

Bohannon, R.W. (1988). Make and break tests of elbow flexor muscle strength. *Physical Therapy, 68,* 193-194.

Bohannon, R.W. (1990). *Muscle strength testing: Instrumented and non-instrumented systems.* New York: Churchill Livingstone.

Bricker, D. (2002). *Assessment, Evaluation, and Programming System (AEPS) for infants and children* (2nd ed.). Baltimore: Brookes.

Brigance, A.H. (2004). *Brigance Inventory of Early Development II.* North Billerica, MA: Curriculum Associates.

Brown, F., & Snell, M.E. (2000). Meaningful assessment. In M.E. Snell & F. Brown (Eds.), *Instruction of students with severe disabilities* (5th ed.) (pp. 67-114). Upper Saddle River, NJ: Merrill/Prentice Hall.

Bruininks, R.H., & Bruininks, R.D. (2005). *Bruininks-Oseretsky Test of Motor Proficiency* (2nd ed.). Circle Pines, MN: American Guidance Service.

Bruininks, R.H., Woodcock, R.W., Weatherman, R.F., & Hill, B.K. (1996). *Scales of Independent Behavior–Revised* (SIB-R). Scarborough, ON: Nelson Thomson Learning.

Burton, A.W., & Miller, D.E. (1998). *Motor skill assessment.* Champaign, IL: Human Kinetics.

Capute, A.J., Palmer, B.F., Shapiro, R.C., Wachtel, A.R., & Accardo, P.J. (1984). *Primitive reflex profile.* Baltimore: University Park Press.

Clark, J.E., Smiley-Oyen, A.L., & Whitall, J. (2004, April). *Developmental coordination disorder: Identification, issues, and interventions.* Paper presented at the convention of the American Alliance for Health, Physical Education, Recreation and Dance, New Orleans, LA.

Clark, J.E., & Whitall, J. (1989). Changing patterns of locomotion: From walking to skipping. In M.H. Woollacott & A. Shumway-Cook (Eds.), *Development of posture and gait across the lifespan* (pp. 128-151). Columbia: University of South Carolina Press.

Clarke, H., & Clarke, D.H. (1987). *Application of measurement to physical education.* Englewood Cliffs, NJ: Prentice Hall.

Cooper Institute, The. (2004). *Fitnessgram/Activitygram* (3rd ed.). Champaign, IL: Human Kinetics.

Cooper Institute for Aerobics Research, The. (1992). *Prudential Fitnessgram test administration manual.* Dallas, TX: The Cooper Institute for Aerobics Research.

Corbin, C.B., Lindsey, R., Week, G., & Corbin, W.R. (2002). *Concepts of physical education* (4th ed.). Boston: McGraw-Hill.

Croce, R., & Horvat, M. (1992). Effects of reinforcement-based exercise on fitness and work productivity in adults with mental retardation. *Adapted Physical Activity Quarterly, 9,* 148-178.

Croce, R., Horvat, M., & McCarthy, E. (2001). Reliability and concurrent validity of the Movement Assessment Battery for Children. *Perceptual and Motor Skills, 93,* 275-280.

Donahoe, B., Turner, D., & Worrell, T. (1994). The use of functional reach as a measure of balance in boys and girls without disabilities 5 to 15 years. *Pediatric Physical Therapy, 6,* 189-193.

Duncan, P., Studenski, S., Chandler, J., & Prescott, B. (1990). Functional reach: A new clinical measure of balance. *Journal of Gerontology, 45,* 192-197.

Education for All Handicapped Children Act of 1975, PL 94-142, S.6 20 U.S.C. §§ 1401 (1975, November 29).

Eichstaedt, C.B., & Lavay, B. (1992). *Physical education for individuals with mental retardation.* Champaign, IL: Human Kinetics.

Federal Register. (August 23, 1977). Education for All Handicapped Children Act, PL 94-142.

Fernhall, B., & Tymeson, G.T. (1988). Validation of cardiovascular fitness tests for adults with mental retardation. *Adapted Physical Activity Quarterly, 5,* 49-59.

Fewell, R. (1991). Trends in the assessment of infants and toddlers with disabilities. *Exceptional Children, 58*(2), 166-173.

Fiorentino, M.R. (1981). *Reflex testing methods for evaluating C.N.S. development.* Springfield, IL: Charles C. Thomas.

Fleck, S.J., & Kraemer, W.J. (2004). *Designing resistance training programs.* Champaign, IL: Human Kinetics.

Folio, M.R., & Fewell, R.R. (2000). *Peabody Developmental Motor Scales* (2nd ed.). Austin, TX: Pro-Ed.

Frankenburg, W.K., Dodds, J.B., & Archer, P. (1990). *Denver II technical manual* (2nd ed.). Denver: Denver Developmental Materials.

Frankenburg, W.K., Dodds, J., Archer, P., Shapiro, H., & Bresnick, B. (1992). The Denver II: A major revision and restandardization of the Denver Developmental Screening Test. *Pediatrics, 89*(1), 91-97.

Gabbard, C. (2004). *Lifelong motor development* (4th ed.). New York: Pearson/Cummings.

Gallahue, D.L., & Ozmun, J.C. (2006). *Understanding motor development* (6th ed.). Madison, WI: McGraw-Hill.

Golding, L.A. (2000). *YMCA Fitness testing and assessment manual* (4th ed.). Champaign, IL: Human Kinetics.

Golding, L.A. (2002). *Y's way to physical fitness.* Champaign, IL: Human Kinetics.

Gorn, S. (1996). *The answer book on special education law.* Danvers, MA: LRP.

Hamill, D.V., Pearson, N.A., & Voress, J.K. (1993). *Developmental test of visual perception* (2nd ed.). Austin, TX: Pro-Ed.

Harter, S. (1988). *Manual for the self-perception profile for children.* Denver: Author.

Haywood, K.M., & Getchell, N. (2005). *Life span motor development* (4th ed.). Champaign, IL: Human Kinetics.

Henderson, S.E., & Sugden, D.A. (1992). *Movement Assessment Battery for Children.* Sidcup, UK: Therapy Skill Builders.

Heymsfield, S.B., Lohman, T.G., Wang, Z., & Going, S. (2005). *Human body composition* (2nd ed.). Champaign, IL: Human Kinetics.

Heyward, V.H. (2002). *Advanced fitness assessment and exercise prescription* (4th ed.). Champaign, IL: Human Kinetics.

Heyward, V.H., & Wagner, D.R. (2004). *Applied body composition assessment* (2nd ed.). Champaign, IL: Human Kinetics.

Hoeger, W.K., Hopkins, D.R., Button, S., & Palmer, T.A. (1990). Comparing the sit and reach with the modified sit and reach in measuring flexibility in adolescents. *Pediatric Exercise Science, 2,* 156-162.

Horvat, M., & Croce, R. (1995). Physical rehabilitation of individuals with mental retardation: Physical fitness and information processing. *Critical Reviews in Physical and Rehabilitation Medicine, 7*(3), 233-252.

Horvat, M., Croce, R., & Roswal, G. (1993). Magnitude and reliability of measurement of muscle strength across trials in individuals with mental retardation. *Perceptual and Motor Skills, 77,* 643-649.

Horvat, M., Eichstaedt, C., Kalakian, L., & Croce, R. (2003). *Developmental/adapted physical education: Making ability count* (4th ed.). San Francisco: Cummings.

Horvat, M., & Franklin, C. (2001). The effects of environment on physical activity patterns of children with mental retardation. *Research Quarterly for Exercise and Sport, 72,* 189-195.

Horvat, M., & Kalakian, L. (1996). *Assessment in adapted physical education and therapeutic recreation* (2nd ed.). Dubuque, IA: Brown.

Horvat, M., Malone, D.M., & Deener, T. (1993). Educational play: Preschool children with disabilities. In S. Grosse & D. Thompson (Eds.), *Play and recreation for individuals with disabilities: Practical pointers* (pp. 58-66). Reston, VA: AAHPERD.

Horvat, M., McManis, B.G., & Seagraves, E.E. (1992). Reliability and objectivity of the Nicholas Manual Muscle Tester with children. *Isokinetics and Exercise Science, 2,* 1-8.

Horvat, M., Ray, C., Nocera, J., & Croce, R. (In press). Comparison of isokinetic peak force and work parameters in adults with partial vision and blindness. *Perceptual and Motor Skills.*

Horvat, M., Ray, C., Ramsey, V., Miszko, T., Keeney, R., & Blasch, B. (2003). Compensatory analysis and strategies for balance in individuals with visual impairments. *Journal of Visual Impairment and Blindness, 97*(1), 695-703.

Hubbard, V.S. (1995). Future directions in obesity research. In L.W.Y. Cheung & J.B. Richmond (Eds.), *Child health, nutrition and physical activity* (pp. 205-209). Champaign, IL: Human Kinetics.

Hui, S.C., & Yuen, P.W. (2000). Validity of the modified back saver sit and reach test: A comparison with other protocols. *Medicine and Science in Sports and Exercise, 32,* 1655-1659.

hyperdictionary. (2004, January 31). Definition of *play* from hyperdictionary [Online]. Available: www.hyperdictionary.com.

Individuals with Disabilities Education Act (IDEA), PL 105-17, 20 U.S.C. §§ 1400, et seq. (1997).

Janney, R., & Snell, M.E. (2000). *Behavioral support.* Baltimore: Brookes.

Jette, M., Campbell, J., Mongeon, J., & Routhier, R. (1976). The Canadian Home Fitness Test as a predictor for aerobic capacity. *Canadian Medical Association Journal, 114,* 680-682.

Johnson, B.L., & Nelson, L.K. (1986). *Practical measurements for evaluation in physical education* (4th ed.). Minneapolis: Burgess.

Johnson, R.E., Bulbulian, R., Gruber, J., & Sundheim, R. (1986). Estimating percent body fat of paraplegic athletes. *Palaestra, 3,* 29-33.

Johnson, R.E., & Lavay, B. (1988). *Kansas adapted/special physical education test manual.* Topeka, KS: Kansas State Department of Education.

Katch, F.I., & McArdle, W.D. (1996). *Nutrition, weight control, and exercise* (4th ed.). Philadelphia: Lea & Febiger.

Kazdin, A.E. (2001). *Behavior modification in applied settings* (6th ed.). Belmont, CA: Wadsworth Press.

Kelly, L., & Rimmer, J. (1987). A practical method for estimating percent body fat of adult mentally retarded males. *Adapted Physical Activity Quarterly, 4,* 117-125.

Kelly, L., & Wessel, J. (1990). *I CAN: Primary skills.* Austin, TX: Pro-Ed.

Kelly, L.E., & Melograno, V.J. (2004). *Developing the physical education curriculum: An achievement-based approach.* Champaign, IL: Human Kinetics.

Kelly, L.E., Wessel, J.A., Dummer, G., & Sampson, T. (Forthcoming). *Everyone CAN: The elementary physical education skill development and assessment resource.* Champaign, IL: Human Kinetics.

Kendall, I.P., McCreary, E.K., Provance, P.G., Rogers, M., & Romani, W. (2005). *Muscles: Testing and function* (5th ed.). Baltimore: Williams & Wilkins.

Kline, G.M., Pocari, J.P., Hintermeister, R., Freedson, P.S., Ward, A., McCarron, R.F., Ross, J., & Rippe, J.M. (1987). Estimation of $\dot{V}O_2$max from a one mile track walk, gender, age, and body weight. *Medicine and Science in Sports and Exercise, 19,* 253-259.

Kraemer, W.J., & Fleck, S.J. (1993). *Strength training for young athletes.* Champaign, IL: Human Kinetics.

Lambert, N., Nihira, K., & Leland, H. (1993). *AAMR Adaptive Behavior Scale–School* (2nd ed.). Austin, TX: Pro-Ed.

Lavay, B., Reid, G., & Cressler-Chaviz, M. (1990). Measuring the cardiovascular endurance of persons with mental retardation: A critical review. *Exercise Sport and Sciences Reviews, 18,* 263-290.

Leger, L., & Lambert, J.A. (1982). A maximal multistage 20 m shuttle run test to predict $\dot{V}O_2$max. *European Journal of Applied Physiology, 49,* 1-12.

Leighton, J. (1955). An instrument and technique for the measurement of range of joint motion. *Archives of Physical Medicine, 36,* 57.

Linder, T.W. (1993). *Transdisciplinary play-based assessment* (Rev. ed.). Baltimore: Brookes.

Lohman, T.G. (1982). Measurement of body composition in children. *JOPERD, 53,* 67-70.

Lohman, T.G. (1986). Application of body composition techniques and constants for children and youth. In K.B. Pantolf (Ed.), *Exercise and sport sciences reviews* (pp. 325-357). New York: Macmillan.

Lohman, T.G. (1987). The use of skinfolds to estimate body fatness on children and youth. *JOPERD, 58,* 98-102.

Lohman, T.G. (1989). Assessment of body composition in children. *Pediatric Exercise Science, 1,* 19-30.

Lohman, T.G. (1992). *Advances in body composition measurement.* Champaign, IL: Human Kinetics.

Lorenzi, D., Horvat, M., & Pellegrini, A.D. (2000). Physical activity of children with and without mental retardation in inclusive recess settings. *Education and Training in Mental Retardation and Developmental Disabilities, 35*(2), 160-167.

Los Amigos Research and Education Institute. (2001). *Observational gait analysis handbook.* Downey, CA: LAREI.

Magee, D.J. (2002). *Orthopedic physical assessment* (4th ed.). Philadelphia: Saunders.

Malone, D.M., & Stoneman, Z. (1990). Cognitive play of mentally retarded preschool children: Observation in the home and school. *American Journal of Mental Retardation, 94,* 475-487.

Margaria, R., Aghemo, P., & Rovelli, E. (1966). Measurement of muscular power (anaerobic) in man. *Journal of Applied Physiology, 21,* 1662-1664.

Mathews, D.K. (1978). *Measurement in physical education* (3rd ed.). Philadelphia: Saunders.

McClenaghan, B., & Gallahue, D. (1978). *Fundamental movement.* Philadelphia: Saunders.

McCloy, C.H., & Young, N.D. (1954). *Tests and measurements in health and physical education.* New York: Appleton-Century-Crofts.

McLoughlin, J.A., & Lewis, R.B. (1981). *Assessing special students.* Columbus, OH: Merrill.

Miedaner, J.A. (1990). The effects of sitting positions on trunk extension for children with motor impairment. *Pediatric Physical Therapy, 2,* 11-14.

Milani-Comparetti, A., & Gidoni, E.A. (1967). A pattern analysis of motor development and disorders. *Developmental Medicine and Child Neurology, 11,* 625-630.

Montgomery, D.L., Reid, G., & Koziris, L.P. (1992). Reliability and validity of three fitness tests for adults with mental handicaps. *Canadian Journal of Sports Sciences, 17,* 309-315.

New York State Education Department. (1966). *The New York physical fitness tests: A manual for teachers of physical education.* Albany, NY: Education Department.

Norkin, C. (2001). Gait analysis. In S.B. O'Sullivan & T.J. Schmitz (Eds.), *Physical rehabilitation: Assessment and treatment* (4th ed.) (pp. 257-308). Philadelphia: Davis.

Norkin, C.C., & White, D.J. (2003). *Measurement of joint motion: A guide to goniometry* (3rd ed.). Philadelphia: Davis.

O'Loughllin, J. (1993). Incidence of risk factors for falls and injurious falls among the community-dwelling elderly. *American Journal of Epidemiology, 137,* 342-354.

O'Sullivan, S.B., & Schmitz, T.J. (2001). *Physical rehabilitation: Assessment and treatment* (4th ed.). Philadelphia: Davis.

Palmer, M.L., & Epler, M. (1990). *Clinical assessment procedures in physical therapy.* Philadelphia: Lippincott.

Pate, R.R., & Shepherd, R.J. (1989). Characteristics of physical fitness in youth. In C.V. Gisolfi & D.R Lamb (Eds.), *Perspectives in exercise and sports medicine* (Vol. 2) (pp. 1-43). Indianapolis: Benchmark.

Payne, V.G., & Isaacs, L.D. (2005). *Human motor development: A lifespan approach* (6th ed.). Boston: McGraw-Hill.

Pitetti, K., Rimmer, J.H., & Fernhall, B. (1993). Physical fitness and adults with mental retardation: An overview of current research and future directions. *Sports Medicine, 16,* 23-56.

Pitetti, K., & Tan, D.M. (1990). Cardiorespiratory responses of mentally retarded adults to air-brake ergometry and treadmill exercise. *Archives of Physical Medicine and Rehabilitation, 71,* 319-321.

Pitetti, K.H., & Fernhall, B. (2005). Mental retardation. In J.S. Skinner (Ed.), *Exercise testing and exercise prescription for special cases* (3rd ed.) (pp. 392-403). Baltimore: Lippincott, Williams & Wilkins.

Powers, M.D. (2000). What is autism? In M.D. Powers (Ed.), *Children with autism* (2nd ed.) (pp. 1-44). Bethesda, MD: Woodbine House.

Powers, S.K., & Dodd, S.L. (2003). *Total fitness and wellness* (3rd ed.). Boston: Allyn & Bacon.

Rarick, G.L., & Dobbins, D.A. (1975). Basic components in the motor performance of children six to nine years of age. *Medicine and Science in Sports, 17,* 105-110.

Rehabilitation Act, PL 93-112, 29, U.S.C. §§ 701, et seq. (1973).

Reid, G., Montgomery, D., & Seidl, C. (1985). Performance of mentally retarded adults in the Canadian Standardized Test of Fitness. *Canadian Journal of Public Health, 76,* 187-190.

Reid, G., O'Conner, J., & Lloyd, M. (2003). The autism spectrum disorder: Physical activity instruction, part III. *Palaestra, 19*(2), 20-26, 47-48.

Rikli, R.E., & Jones, C.J. (2001). *Senior fitness test manual.* Champaign, IL: Human Kinetics.

Rintala, P., Dunn, J.M., McCubbin, J.A., & Quinn, C. (1992). Validity of a cardiovascular fitness test for men with mental retardation. *Medicine and Science in Sports and Exercise, 24,* 941-945.

Roach, E.G., & Kephart, N.C. (1966). *The Purdue Perceptual-Motor Survey.* Columbus, OH: Merrill.

Roberton, M.A., & Halverson, L.E. (1984). *Developing children: Their changing movements.* Philadelphia: Lea & Febiger.

Ross, P.M., & Jackson, A.S. (1990). *Understanding exercise: Concepts, calculations, and computers.* Cornell, IN: Benchmark Press.

Sargent, D.A. (1921). Physical test of a man. *American Physical Education Review, 26,* 188-194.

Sattler, J.M. (1989). Vineland Adaptive Behavior Scales. In J.C. Conolly & J.J. Kramer (Eds.), *The tenth mental measurement yearbook* (pp. 879-881). Lincoln: University of Nebraska Press.

Seagraves, F., Horvat, M., Franklin, C., & Jones, K. (2004). The effects of a school-based physical activity program on work productivity and physical functioning in individuals with mental retardation. *Clinical Kinesiology, 58*(2), 18-29.

Seaman, J. (Ed.). (1995). *Physical Best and individuals with disabilities: A handbook for inclusion in fitness programs.* Reston, VA: AAHPERD.

Shepherd, R.J. (1990). *Fitness in special populations.* Champaign, IL: Human Kinetics.

Sherrill, C. (2004). *Adapted physical activity, recreation, and sport* (6th ed.). Madison, WI: McGraw-Hill.

Shumway-Cook, A., & Woollacott, M.H. (2001). *Motor control: Theory and practical applications* (2nd ed.). Baltimore: Lippincott, Williams & Wilkins.

Silverstein, A.B. (1986). Nonstandard scores on the Vineland Adaptive Behavior Scales: A cautionary note. *American Journal of Mental Deficiency, 91,* 1-4.

Siperstein, G., Bak, J., & O'Keefe, P. (1988). Relationship between children's attitudes toward and their social acceptance of mentally retarded peers. *American Journal of Mental Retardation, 93,* 24-27.

Siperstein, G.N. (1980). *Instruments for measuring children's attitudes toward the handicapped.* Unpublished manuscript. Center for Human Services, University of Massachusetts, Boston.

Snell, M.E., & Janney, R. (2000). *Social relationships and peer support.* Baltimore: Brookes.

Soderberg, G.L. (1986). *Kinesiology: Application of pathological motion.* Baltimore: Williams & Wilkins.

Stephens, T.M., Hartman, A.C., & Lucas, V.H. (1982). *Teaching children basic skills: A curriculum handbook* (2nd ed.). Columbus, OH: Bell & Howell.

Sugden, D.A., & Keogh, J. (1990). *Problems in movement skill development.* Columbia: University of South Carolina Press.

Thelen, E., Ulrich, B.D., & Jensen, J.I. (1989). The developmental origin of locomotion. In M.H. Woollacott & A. Shumway-Cook (Eds.), *Development of posture and gait across the lifespan* (pp. 25-47). Columbia: University of South Carolina Press.

Tripp, A., & Sherrill, C. (2004). Inclusion, social competence, and attitude change. In C. Sherrill (Ed.), *Adapted physical activity, recreation, and sport* (6th ed.) (pp. 240-260). Madison, WI: McGraw-Hill.

Ulrich, D.A. (2000). *Test of Gross Motor Development* (2nd ed.). Austin, TX: Pro-Ed.

Ulrich, D.A., & Collier, D.H. (1990). Perceived physical competence in children with mental retardation: Modification of a pictorial scale. *Adapted Physical Activity Quarterly, 7,* 338-354.

Vaughan, C.L., Davis, B.L., & O'Connor, J.C. (1992a). *Dynamics of human gait.* Champaign, IL: Human Kinetics.

Vaughan, C.L., Davis, B.L., & O'Connor, J.C. (1992b). *Gait analysis laboratory: An interactive book and software package.* Champaign, IL: Human Kinetics.

Walker, H.M., Colvin, G., & Ramsey, E. (1995). *Antisocial behavior in school: Strategies and best practices.* Pacific Grove, CA: Brooks/Cole.

Walker, H.M., & McConnell, S.R. (1995). *Walker-McConnell Scale of Social Competence and School Adjustment, Elementary Version: User's manual.* San Diego, CA: Singular Publishing Group.

Walker, H.M., McConnell, S., Homes, D., Todis, B., Walker, J., & Golden, N. (1988). *The Walker social skills curriculum: The ACCEPTS program.* Austin, TX: Pro-Ed.

Werder, J., & Bruininks, R.H. (1988). *A motor development curriculum.* Circle Pines, MN: American Guidance Service.

Wickstrom, R. (1983). *Fundamental motor patterns* (3rd ed.). Philadelphia: Lea & Febiger.

Winnick, J.P., & Short, F.X. (1999). *Brockport Physical Fitness Test (BPFT).* Champaign, IL: Human Kinetics.

Woods, J.A., Pate, R.R., & Burgess, M.L. (1992). Correlates to performance in field tests of muscular strength. *Pediatric Exercise Science, 4,* 302-311.

Wright, P.W.D., & Wright, P.D. (2000). *Wrightslaw: Special education law.* Hartfield, VA: Harbor House Law Press.

Zetts, R., Horvat, M., & Langone, J. (1995). The effects of a community-based progressive resistance training program on the work productivity of adolescents with moderate to severe intellectual disabilities. *Education and Training in Mental Retardation and Developmental Disabilities, 30,* 166-178.

Index

Note: The italicized *f* and *t* following page numbers refer to figures and tables, respectively.

About the Authors

Michael Horvat, EdD, is a professor of adapted physical education and motor behavior at the University of Georgia, where he is also the director of the Movement Studies Laboratory and the Pediatric Exercise and Motor Development Clinic. Dr. Horvat is extensively published, having authored numerous books, monographs, chapters in books, and articles, as well as dozens of refereed journal publications. He is also a highly sought-after speaker, having presented at more than 100 international and domestic conferences.

Dr. Horvat has been elected to many boards and councils and has professional affiliations with a number of organizations, including the International Society of Adapted Physical Activity, the North American Society of Adapted Physical Activity, and the American Alliance for Health, Physical Education, Recreation and Dance. In 2005 he was named to the Honor Society of Phi Kappa Phi, and he received the Hollis Fait Scholarly Contribution Award in 2006.

Martin E. Block, PhD, is an associate professor in the kinesiology program at the University of Virginia. He has been the director of the master's program in adapted physical education (APE) at the University of Virginia since 1993. During that time he has supervised and graduated more than 60 master's students. Dr. Block has served as an APE specialist in Virginia, working with children with severe disabilities and learning and behavioral problems.

Dr. Block has been a consultant to Special Olympics, Inc., helping to create the Motor Activities Training Program, a sports program for athletes with severe disabilities. He has authored or coauthored four books and more than 50 refereed articles, and he has conducted more than 100 international and national presentations on various topics in APE.

Dr. Block has served as chair for the Adapted Physical Activity Council and for the Motor Development Academy. He was named the Virginia College Professor of the Year in 2004.

Luke E. Kelly, PhD, is a certified adapted physical educator, professor of kinesiology, holder of the Virgil S. Ward endowed professorship, director of the graduate programs in adapted physical education, and chief technology officer for the Curry School of Education at the University of Virginia. He has 30 years of experience working with public schools in evaluating and revising their physical education curricula to meet the needs of students with disabilities. Dr. Kelly has written extensively about the achievement-based curriculum model, assessment, and use of technology in physical education. Dr. Kelly has served as the president of the National Consortium for Physical Education and Recreation for Individuals with Disabilities (NCPERID) and directed the NCPERID adapted physical education national standards project from 1992 to 1999. Dr. Kelly is a fellow in the American Academy of Kinesiology and Physical Education. He has also received the G. Lawrence Rarick Research Award and the William H. Hillman Distinguished Service Award from NCPERID.